AUTHORS:
Leslie Willcocks : Christopher Sauer
David Feeny : Kunal Basu
Karl Moore : Keith Ruddle
Jonathan Reynolds : Graham Costello
Marc Thompson : Robert Plant

RANDOM HOUSE
BUSINESS BOOKS

First published in 2000 by Random House Business Books,
Random House, 20 Vauxhall Bridge Road, London SW1V 2SA

Extract from Turn of the Century copyright © 1999 by
Kurt Andersen. Published by Headline in the UK and
Random House in the US.

Random House Australia (Pty) Limited
20 Alfred Street, Milsons Point
Sydney, New South Wales 2061, Australia

Random House New Zealand Limited
18 Poland Road, Glenfield
Auckland 10, New Zealand

Random House (Pty) Limited
Endulini, 5a Jubilee Road, Parktown 2193, South Africa

The Random House Group Limited Reg. No. 954009

Papers used by Random House are natural, recyclable products
made from wood grown in sustainable forests. The manufacturing
processes conform to the environmental regulations of the country
of origin.

ISBN 0 7126 6983 3

Companies, institutions and other organisations wishing to
make bulk purchases of any business books published by
Random House should contact their local bookstore or
Random House direct:
Special Sales Director
Random House, 20 Vauxhall Bridge Road,
London SW1V 2SA
Tel 020 7840 8470   Fax 020 7828 6681

www.randomhouse.co.uk
businessbooks@randomhouse.co.uk

Printed and bound in Great Britain by Biddles Ltd, Guildford and King's Lynn

Contents

FOREWORD

Ten years hence it will be obvious. Of course we should have known; all the indications were there; how ridiculous it was to have taken any other direction.

It is always like that: blindingly obvious looking backwards, impossibly difficult going forwards. E-business is no different.

Yet some do get it right and we prosper as a result. The important thing is to learn quickly.

This book does not pretend to provide all the answers, but it does surely pose very many of the right questions. And in the models and frameworks each chapter provides it offers managers pointers to help them find the answers that will suit their companies.

Templeton College, Oxford University's focus for executive development, is home to a diverse community of practically minded researchers whose instinct is always to be at the forefront of business change. It was natural, therefore, that their interests would converge on e-business. The result is an admirable guide to the present and a substantial foundation for formulating the right questions about the future.

Sir David Rowland
President
Templeton College
Oxford University

Moving to E-Business: An Introduction

Leslie P. Willcocks and Christopher Sauer

What are you doing about e-business? the board demands. Wrong question, you silently observe. You know the right question. You've asked it of yourself already. What *should* I be doing about e-business? And then, what wins can I achieve and how should I approach the challenge?

In one sense, of course, the board is right. E-business is such a wide-ranging phenomenon that there is something in it for everybody. The trouble is that it is not always obvious what's right for which company.

At its most basic, e-business is an opportunity based on developments in technology. Principal among these has been the Internet allied to web technology. The Internet permits a vastly greater level of connectivity among people and organisations than ever before. Web technology, including web sites and browsers, permits a far richer set of communication possibilities than merely one-to-one communication. Companies can make their products and services directly available to enormous markets. Add to the basic technology some further developments in software such as enterprise systems, customer relationship management and data mining, spice the mix with a touch of creativity, and an array of new business opportunities comes into view. The prospect of pervasive computing (Internet connection from wireless devices such as mobile phones, vehicles and commercial equipment) becoming a reality within two years presents yet further opportunity for growth.

The size of the total opportunity explains the board's desire to have a piece of the action. The statistics are not precisely accurate, being arrived at by processes about as reliable as consulting chicken entrails, but even on 'conservative best guesses' the Internet economy was worth US$301 billion in 1999, rising to an estimated US$1800 billion for 2003.[1]

The e-business opportunity for the individual firm is typically seen as dividing into Internets, extranets and intranets. These cover business-to-consumer (B-to-C), business-to-business (B-to-B) and internal uses of web technology respectively. On some figures B-to-C will be worth US$184 billion in 2003, and B-to-B US$1300 billion. We are also seeing the rise of C-to-B and C-to-C applications of web-based technologies.[2] These ways of viewing e-business reflect companies' initial understanding of e-business as being about direct connection with customers and business partners. Today, there is greater recognition of the opportunities for integration of web-based and allied technologies into the core business processes. The next step, E-to-E (everywhere-to-everywhere) connectivity, is a further hurdle to be contemplated.

But then, to haunt you in the pre-dawn hours, there is a darker side to the question, what should I be doing? Your market may be somebody else's e-business opportunity. If you operate as an intermediary, say as a car distributor, will the manufacturer bypass you en route to your customer? Alternatively, will new competition emerge from left field? For example, stock exchanges worldwide have been carefully tracking technology firms, for fear they might build new exchanges to operate at lower cost and with better performance than the established institutions.

The problem in all of this for CEOs, strategists, e-business leaders and technology managers is that in the world of e-business there are almost no fixed reference points. A venture capital bonanza, allied with the sweated equity of young entrepreneurs, has funded diverse dot.com experiments. A profusion of unproven ideas has been resourced. If they work, then their owners will have first-mover advantage. But will they? If the jury is out and likely to remain out for a year or more, the challenges are how to make sense of the possibilities and how to proceed.

This book confronts these challenges. It offers a rare brand of realism amid the uncertainties and hype. While putting 'e' before the company name, or '.com' after it, may have offered short-term benefits in terms of market perceptions and valuations, our concern is for substantial economic value rather than speculative gain. We reject simplistic rules, principles and 'laws' of the 'one-size-fits-all' variety. Rather, based on their latest research combined with extensive business experience and deep expertise, the authors stimulate understanding by asking incisive questions. Underlying them all is the persistent query: why should we think the old rules, practices and business models no longer apply? The key questions addressed are:

- How have the early leaders progressed towards sustainable profitability from e-business? (Chapter 1)
- Which opportunities make sense for which companies? (Chapter 2)
- Does e-business erode or reinforce global branding? (Chapter 3)
- How should companies structure and what does it take to transform themselves for e-business? (Chapter 4)
- Are the conditions for intermediary businesses changing? (Chapter 5)
- What are the real opportunities in the business-to-business sector? (Chapter 6)
- What are the critical roles of senior managers and top teams? (Chapter 7)
- How can companies secure and retain the right people? (Chapter 8)
- How should the technological underbelly be designed and developed? (Chapter 9)
- What are the rules for sourcing e-business capabilities from business partners? (Chapter 10)

Any manager who can answer these questions for their company will be well positioned to make informed decisions. To assist in this, each chapter aims to communicate its author's findings and to provide frameworks and tools that will help managers see more clearly what they should do about e-business.

What we offer here is a blend of thought, analysis and navigational tools that make deep sense of what is happening, and that help to plot ways forward in terms of direction, timing, focus and implementation. To start off this process of mapping, the remainder of this Introduction provides three frameworks.

These will:

- help position your company as to where it is and where it should be in its approach to e-business;
- clarify the stages the company must pass through on the path to mature e-business.

Navigating E-Domains:
From Hype to Strategic Anticipation

In an earlier book from Templeton College, *Managing IT as a Strategic Resource*, David Feeny presented a model of IT domains.[3] A developed form of this framework can be applied directly to the e-business world and is shown in Figure 1. The e-business jackpot will be won by the companies that reposition themselves to secure a sustainable advantage. Achieving this requires the ability to navigate through five domains. Let us look at these, using a range of examples which draw upon our original research.

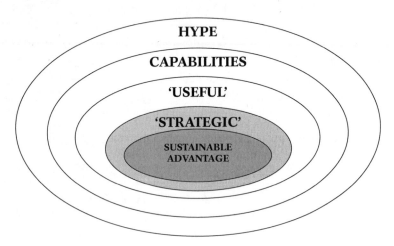

Figure 1 – Navigating Five Domains in E-Business (adapted from Feeny, 1997)

HYPE

To adapt a well-known phrase to the e-business context, suppliers, the media, consulting companies and commercial

research organisations can be said to have 'never knowingly undersold' the potential of e-business. They project a positive image of e-business potential, a view that the Internet is a 'must do' for which there is no alternative and that technology is the critical lever in success. Hype has already encouraged suspension of disbelief among the managers of share and venture capital, supporting high stock valuations.[4] Two examples will suffice. In the UK Dixon's Freeserve had a £2.4 billion valuation on £9 million predicted revenues. Within a few months there were another forty such services available. In May 1999 the on-line discount airline ticket agency Priceline.com had a market capitalisation of US$19.8 billion – bigger than the three major US airlines put together – while facing an ongoing loss into 2000.

Hype has also promoted two probably unsustainable strategies disguised as workable business models: 'hype and hope' and 'hype, build and sell'. In November 1999 Webvan, in the historically low-value online grocery business – with annual sales of $11.9 million, 21,000 customers and predicted losses of $73.8 million – was valued at $8.76 billion on its share debut. It remains to be seen whether it constitutes a workable business model. Post-IPO share price falls for companies such as the much hyped retailer Lastminute.com in the UK suggests that the markets now share these doubts. Actual business failures such as sports fashion retailer Boo.com in Europe in May 2000, after thirty months and US$135 million, are salutary reminders that there has to be a solid business model and sound management for any new idea to succeed. Hype has sustained a number of firms who have pursued growth without profit. At the time of writing, a number – such as CD Now, Value America and Peapod – were in danger of running out of money.[5] Those who have profited from the hype are those smart enough to have sold some or part of their business at a premium. When the Prudential started its IPO process for Egg, the estimated valuation was some four times the eventual valuation based on a trading price. Had Prudential secured sale at the predicted price, it would have benefited significantly from the hype. But as is apparent from its experience and from Dixons' failure to sell FreeServe in June 2000, the opportunity for profit from hype is evaporating fast.

CAPABILITY

This domain is traditionally inhabited by the owners of technical solutions in search of business problems. Technologists and technical specialists tend to set the agenda. The management

challenge, but also the opportunity, lies in the wide variety of possible applications for web-based technologies and the capability required to take advantage. The risk for inhabitants of this domain is that because the technologists have recognised the technology innovation, they will have developed a capability ahead of the business's understanding of its potential. The balance of knowledge then favours pursuit of e-business opportunities driven by technology capability rather than strategic value.

The crucial learning opportunity in this domain is for the company to recognise the extent of its capability and the risks it could face if it pursues opportunity without capability. Many companies have failed to recognise early enough the constraints they may face in relation to security, scalability, bandwidth, technical robustness, functionality, ease of use and speed. High global connectivity can also be a significant problem. Thus 2000 saw a series of damaging virus attacks, raising security alarms.

The cost of not learning the limits of your capability can be high. e-Bay experienced an outage of twenty-two hours on 12 June 1999, causing a $5 million revenue loss and a twenty-five per cent decline in its stock price. When AT&T experienced a two to six hour outage in April 1999 it cost $40 million in rebates.

While it is necessary for firms to acquire capability for e-business, the crucial lesson is to avoid being driven by the imperative to use all and only the capability you have. The best preventative for this is to concentrate on the potential business uses of the technology.

USEFUL E-BUSINESS

Internet analyst Mary Meeker has predicted that 'there will be thousands of winners on the Internet, but there will be very few really big winners'. In late 1999 W.H. Smith announced the piloting of customer Internet access – e-mail, travel information and books on-line – at its book and stationery outlets in one UK railway station and three US airports. Initial positive results led to an extension of the trials to interactive kiosks in twenty further stores.

In February 2000 P&O Stena Line, operating a passenger and cargo service across the English Channel, announced it was importing cheap new cars from mainland Europe (posl.com). Offering new cars at up to eighteen per cent savings, the company received 500 calls and twenty firm orders on the first two days, and expected to sell 10,000 cars in the first year.[6]

However, the order and fulfilment process was arduous and largely off-line. It was expected that most vehicles would be delivered within three to five months. Moreover, there was already growing on-line competition, from niche specialists, for example Oneswoop.com, Direct Line and Carbusters.com.

In both these examples the companies are looking to be among the thousands of winners. Both saw useful ways to apply web technology. But in both cases the initiative appears to be of quite limited value for the main business. What is needed to be a big winner is to move from the domain of useful to strategic applications of e-business.

STRATEGIC E-BUSINESS

While almost anyone can identify useful applications of e-business, it takes deep understanding of your business and its competitive environment to identify strategic e-business opportunities for your company. It involves identifying ways of leveraging at least one of Porter's five forces – customer power, supplier power, substitute products/services, new entrants, competitive rivalry – decisively in favour of the organisation. The insightful strategist recognises that in today's dynamic environment the elements of Porter's model must be reviewed regularly to take account of radical changes such as sectoral intrusions and co-opetition.[7] Sectoral intrusion occurs when, for example, a company like UK insurer Direct Line moves into new areas of business such as on-line car sales and auctions as it did in 2000. Co-opetition occurs when collaboration helps a company generate substantial new value, as Cisco Systems has through its policies of partnering.

Strategic uses of web-based technologies are founded invariably on a strong value proposition and strong business benefits. Thus, through disintermediation, direct computer company Dell Corporation achieved breakthroughs in unit cost and superior customer service. Likewise electrical parts distributor RS Components brought down its costs from £60 to £10 per order, while customers also achieved large cost savings. Many companies achieve service-based differentiation on the web, either as a multi-channel strategy as in the case of distributor UPS and car rental hire company Alamo by sharing information with customers, or using the web as a dominant transaction channel, like Charles Schwab. US-based pension planning company Fidelity Investments has over five million accounts on-line, with daily access exceeding 80,000. It spends over $35

million a year on just developing the retirement account function. It offers superior value by allowing clients to move funds on-line, plan pensions, to come up with the best personal deals, and offers personalised information and cross-selling. Such initiatives are strategic by virtue of affecting the core of the business in ways that involve major investment and offer the chance to be a big winner.

Companies in the strategic domain have asked themselves most of the right questions. Their final remaining step is into the domain of sustainable advantage.

SUSTAINABLE ADVANTAGE

The final domain involves sustaining any competitive advantage achieved through being Internet-based. This issue is dealt with in detail in Chapter 2, where David Feeny proposes a highly useful sustainability model. Scale– gaining a dominant position in a broad or a niche market, brand and business alliances are significant factors for high-profile Internet exponents such as Dell, Amazon, Cisco Systems, Yahoo! and AOL. They can also be seen to follow Feeny's model closely, taking advantage of generic lead time and, more importantly, building asymmetry and pre-emption barriers.

Consider the case of a smaller company, Virtual Vineyards (V-V, subsequently wine.com). The company was established in California in January 1995 to market and sell Californian wine from small producers shut out from large US retail outlets. The target segment consisted of people who appreciated good wine, were interested to learn more about it, were willing to pay a premium for a bottle of fine wine, were not connoisseurs and could therefore benefit from the knowledge of an expert. Along with a wide selection of unusual wines from small producers, V-V offered information about wine and its history, ratings and descriptions of all wines sold, and personalised answers to individual requests. The Internet initiative was a lasting success and subsequently the company offered other products, including food. In this case generic lead time gave little substantial advantage, nor did the technology and its applications. Rather, the key lay in developing asymmetry and pre-emption barriers in the form of non-replicable resources such as partnerships with suppliers and distributors, reputation and brand, its unique customer and wine databases, the provision of expertise and the locking-in of customers by offering personalised service in conjunction with customised information.[8]

Consider also the example of an established company. By mid-2000 MeritaNordbanken, the Swedish-Finnish bank, was probably the biggest Internet bank in the world, with over 1.1 million customers and 3 million log-ons per month. It continually kept ahead of its European rivals in terms of the scale of its on-line activities and the breadth of services on offer. In launching its on-line service in 1996, it first took advantage of the unusually high mobile-phone and Internet penetration rates in Finland. By March 2001 it aimed to increase customers to 2 million and monthly log-ons to over 5 million, and to expand outside the Nordic region. Apart from driving on market share and more frequent customer interaction, the bank also boosted revenue through electronic shopping and services such as electronic signatures and salary statements. By mid-2000 it had over 350 merchants active on its shopping mall. For consumers the advantage of using the mall lay in avoiding the need for credit and debit cards, with money being directly debited from the customer's account.

The bank was also an early, informed mover into banking via mobile phone via Wireless Application Protocol. By mid-2000 the WAP service allowed customers to pay bills and shop, access prices and trade shares, view portfolios and be notified that a salary had arrived in the bank account.

The lesson of Virtual Vineyards and MeritaNordbanken is that sustainability is not achieved through any one thing. It requires the combination of a range of resources and services that together are hard to imitate. Thus we have found that despite having been the route to market share for companies like Amazon, low-price commodity strategies are not defensible. Indeed, it is very noticeable that Amazon is now by no means the cheapest supplier of books and CDs but rather promotes its superior service and enjoyable experience, both far harder characteristics to imitate than price.

Moving to E-Business: A Four-Stage Model

Understanding the five domains helps any organisation to position its thinking in relation to e-business. While such self-

knowledge can help you think more clearly about what to do, further frameworks are needed to see the way ahead. How will a company's e-business strategy evolve? That is the question for this section. In the next section we look at what the company needs to undertake e-business transformation.

Based on our combined research into 'bricks and mortar', 'bricks and clicks' and 'pure play' companies, we have found organisations at many different points in their moves to e-business, and achieving widely different levels of success. From their experiences and plans, we offer a four-stage model of how moves to e-business take place. Some organisations have already reached Stage Four, while others, on our estimates, may well be, at best, some three years away from being fully operationalised e-businesses.

Our evolutionary model is shown in Figure 2. As Chapters 1 and 4 will show, even in 2000 we have found many organisations that have still not surmounted the 'anxiety gap', let alone the 'organisational capabilities gap'. What are the principal anxieties of companies at this point? One is the faddishness of the web and involves questioning whether a move to the web is, in fact, a good idea. A related concern is whether the technical developments actually affect 'our sector' and the basis of competition in it. Other typical concerns include security and payment issues, and the robustness of the technology. In some cases, faced with a history of IT disappointment in their organisations, managers are sceptical about the leverage possible from the new technologies.

By 2000 most organisations were somewhere in Stage Two, with quite a pile-up at the 'organisational capabilities' gap. These organisations have reorientated their thinking and mindsets about the web. The role of the top team, the CEO and CIO are critical in making progress, as Chapter 7 will underline. Furthermore, defining e-business and e-marketing strategy becomes a much higher agenda item at this stage (see Chapters 2 and 3). Companies at this point have often started to develop a different skills base and are proactively attempting to build web-based technologies into their business operations and direction. Many are running some business-to-business and internal applications, and transacting e-commerce on the web. As Chapter 10 describes, many at this stage are utilising external allies and suppliers to speed up their moves to the web. However, they have typically not yet broached the major reorganisation, process re-engineering and technology infrastructural build

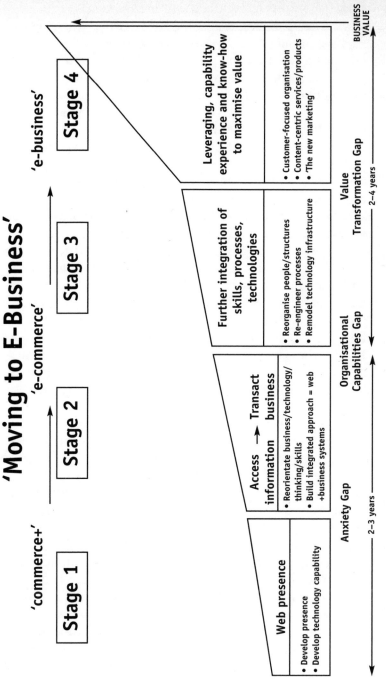

Figure 2 – Moving To E-Business: A Four-Stage Model

described in Chapter 9, and so necessary for remodelling themselves as e-businesses. The result in some cases was what might be called the 'Wizard of Oz' syndrome. It will be remembered that everyone was afraid of the Wizard until it was discovered that he was a frail old man, hiding behind a curtain and shouting through a megaphone. At this stage the attempt to do business over the web is not backed up by the right systems, skills and processes. It is in this stage that companies are likely to experience the kind of costly outages we have mentioned earlier.

Stage Three of our model implies what has been called 're-engineering on steroids'. We have seen some large players bite the bullet at this point, for example MeritaNordbanken and DeutscheBank in banking, Chevron in petroleum, Enron in gas and electricity, and Ford and General Motors in car manufacture. Here the opportunities and models described in Chapters 5, 8 and 9, and the processes of transformation detailed in Chapter 4, have proved particularly pertinent. However, building capabilities and integrating skills, processes and technologies are still not tantamount to leveraging them in a sustained manner. During the latter part of Stage Three, then, organisations frequently experience what we call a 'value transformation gap'. By late 2000, relatively few organisations had actually surmounted this barrier. In our estimation, the transformation implied by surmounting the 'organisational capabilities' gap and moving through Stage Three well into Stage Four could take a large corporation anything between two and four years. However, we did find a number of organisations that had not fully become e-businesses but were leveraging considerable value out of the capability so far built in Stage Three. In 2000 such companies included UPS, FedEx, Alamo and Office Depot (see Chapter 1).

In later chapters we describe several of the organisations that by the end of 2000 were already operating in Stage Four. These include Dell Computer Corporation (see Chapters 8 and 10), Cisco Systems (see Chapter 10), Charles Schwab (see below), Fidelity Investments (see above). In other words not only were web-based technologies integrated fully into the core business, but the organisations in question were exploiting these technologies, and making disproportionate profits and achieving rapid market growth from their deployment. It can be taken as read that these organisations were all very good indeed at business and marketing Internet strategy. That they had robust and flexible organisational, technical and human resource capabilities (see Chapters 4, 8 and 9) and effective sourcing and alliance strategies (see Chapter 10). [8] Exploitation thereafter depended fundamentally on being not just highly customer-focused, but on developing long-term relationships with customers. This involved recognising the importance of content and information in adding value, using adaptive profiling of customers, getting branding right (Chapter 3), and the adoption of mass customisation and one-to-one marketing techniques (see Chapters 1 and 2). [8]

Moving to E-Business: Targeting Change

Our E-Domains model helps to identify and focus effort on strategic applications for e-business. The Four-Stages model enables a business to locate its position in, and map an evolutionary route through, four phases and three sets of barriers in its moves to e-business. But what components in the organisation have to change? Keith Ruddle, co-author of Chapter 4, has carried out a major study of transformational journeys by over twenty-five large businesses including Citibank, IBM, Siemens Thames Water and SmithKline Beecham. [9] He developed a framework for capturing specific issues in understanding transformations, interconnectivities and change processes. A version is shown in Figure 3. Moves to e-business can be accurately seen as transformations and so the framework is particularly useful for decomposing the challenge of e-transformation into its interconnected components.

At the top of the framework are stakeholders, whose changing expectations and requirements need to be monitored in the light of the outcomes from the organisation's business (e- and non-e) activities (note: 'complementors are synergistic business allies, and receive detailed treatment in Chapter 10). The expected result of a move to e-business should be an improved performance **outcome** for stakeholders. The firm is then viewed as having a **strategic intent**, including a competitive strategy and related customer value propositions. Specific **organisational capabilities** and **enabling infrastructure** are required to deliver

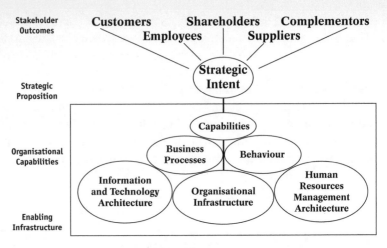

Figure 3 – A Framework for Targeting Change (adapted from Ruddle, 2000)

on this strategic intent. Thus a strategic view of transformation can be described as the alignment over time between strategic intent and organisational capabilities, grounded in competitive advantage and responding to particular external forces, to achieve a superior outcome for stakeholders.

In this framework, capabilities are delivered through the execution of **business processes** by people adopting distinctive culturally determined **behaviours**, the latter built on certain values and beliefs. This delivery is enabled by various interrelated elements of architectural infrastructure. These are: **information and technology infrastructure** (management information systems, IT systems, information strategy); **organisation infrastructure** (structures, management control systems, communication and co-ordination mechanisms); and **human resource management architecture** (skills, people development processes, reward and motivation systems). What enables this journey of transformation is described in detail in Chapter 4. For the moment it is useful to illustrate the changes in the components of the framework by reference to the successful transformation of Charles Schwab into an e-business.

A CASE IN POINT

US-based broker Charles Schwab had no exposure on the Internet before 1996. By mid-2000 the company had about 7 million customers (Active On-line accounted for 3.7 million) and US$800 billion worth of funds under management. It was then the largest single Internet-based broker, handling over 1.7

million trades a week, accounting for $25 billion in transactions. Over seventy per cent of trades were being made on-line on its schwab.com site.

Charles Schwab's move to the web was driven from the top, though the company also had a history of technical innovation.[10] In October 1995, its stand-alone e.Schwab web site was launched to provide investors with account and research information. In March 1996 it was the first major brokerage firm to offer discount and limited service trading via the Internet. In 1998 electronic brokerage was integrated into the main body of the company, and pricing and availability were reorganised so that every Schwab customer could deal with Schwab through any channel, and experience consistency in Internet pricing and service. This move cost the company some $125 million, but paid off in terms of subsequent revenues. According to co-CEO David Pottruck, this was a customer-driven innovation: 'They did not want electronic trading or branch trading. They wanted both.' By the end of 1998 fifty-eight per cent of transactions were on-line, representing $4 billion worth of trades each week. The site offered trading of stocks, mutual funds, US treasuries, listed corporate bonds and options. It also supplied a range of tools to give access to an investor's account holding and to information providers. Available, too, were interactive investment guides, calculators for retirement and college planning, and real-time quotes.

Internet trading has allowed reductions in commission throughout the industry. In 1999 Schwab charged $29.95 for an Internet trade; the equivalent via phone was $80. However, the company's growth is not explained by being the cheapest. For example, at that time e-Trade was charging $15 per trade. Rather for CEO, Charles Schwab: 'The transforming event is the ability to deliver personalised information to the customer, at virtually no cost . . . this is possible because the Net is totally imbedded in the centre of our business.' As one Barclays stockbroker observed perceptively in 1998: 'Execution-only commodity broking will become a technology-driven business, built on sand.'

By 2000 Charles Schwab offered an array of financial services and products, investment guidance and trading and brokerage services through a network of over 300 branches, offices, telephone service centres, automated phone services and the Internet. For Schwab, technology and customer service would seem to be two sides of the same coin. According to its CIO:

'Technology allows us to deliver on a twin commitment: offering customers convenient access to a wealth of services, and delivering exceptional service at reasonable prices.' Throughout 2000 it continued to expand its services on-line, for example, in April establishing an alliance with E-LOAN to offer customers a complete mortgage solution, including the ability to research, compare and apply for a mortgage loan on-line. In March 2000 Schwab.com was averaging 40 million hits a day. Customers could screen thousands of mutual funds, track investment performance, get real-time stock quotes, enter trade orders, view asset allocation models, participate in on-line forums with investment experts and conduct research. Additionally, using MySchwab.com – a free link with Internet portal Excite – customers could create customised investment information like Watch lists of stocks, and receive current news and content.

Here one can see a process of migration over a five-year period. Schwab started with a reputation and strong brand in retail stockbroking and investing. Innovation was valued by top management and the nature of the **strategic intent** was heavily determined by learning about what customers valued and used, and by realisation that the Internet needed to be integrated into the core of the business. As a result, Schwab developed on the web a range of differentiated services, as well as offering competitive pricing. New **behaviours** were developed based on customer orientation, new services and experimentation. Within three years **business processes** were reassembled to fit with the web-based business. On the information and technology front, the website 'front office' was developed with high functionality and easy-to-use facilities. It also featured such aspects as personalised pages for research and account management, and customised services and information. Meanwhile the **information and technology infrastructure** eventually included effective use of database management, XML and related technologies, management information systems and effective collection, analysis and use of information. Schwab became very certain in the 1990s of the opportunity to differentiate itself by the use of leading-edge technology and by 2000 had done so.

On **organisation infrastructure** Schwab greatly restructured itself for the virtual world in terms of roles and responsibilities, and by moving from budgets to dynamic management measurement tools. It had already decentralised the company into 'customer enterprises' in 1994. It further flattened its structure in the late 1990s when it reinvented itself into what it called the 'new model for full-service investing'. On **human resources management architecture** Schwab established strong values through the co-CEOs' style of leadership. It also looked to provide individual incentives for risk and growth, moved to 360-degree appraisals and separated out personal development from any fixation with quantified performance measures. It also sought to cultivate commitment through gender parity and diversity.

Such a case reveals that there can be no quick technology, or any other, fix when moving to e-business. It is indeed a long haul, even for those moving quickly, but especially for large 'bricks and mortar' companies. The relevance of the framework, then, is also demonstrated. It allows the organisation moving to e-business to isolate the many factors that need to be focused on, thereby permitting allocation of change roles. It also stresses that it is the **integration** of supporting infrastructure with processes, behaviours and strategic intent that will serve to determine ultimately the degrees of success experienced.

Conclusion

For companies to move to e-business it is necessary to position themselves appropriately and transform themselves over a number of years through a series of stages. We cannot give a detailed answer to the question, what should you do about e-business?, but we can help prepare you to answer it in a way that will satisfy you and your board.

In this introduction we have presented three frameworks that can help make sense of the journey to come, the time it will take and the demands it will make on the travellers. The frameworks presented in subsequent chapters enrich the overall picture by providing specialist insight into specific aspects of e-business. We wish you success in moving to e-business.

NOTES

1 A bewildering number and range of estimates are regularly published. Here we select from the most conservative, including those from the Centre for Research into Economic Commerce at University of Texas, Austin, and Forrester Research Group. At the upper end are estimates of 2003 B-to-C revenues of US$700

billion for USA, US$220 billion for Japan, and US$100 billion for Europe. B-to-B gross revenues for 2003 have also been estimated as high as US$1700 billion for USA, US$1200 billion for Europe and US$500 billion for Japan. IDC have suggested that the web will handle nine per cent of all business transactions by that date. The figures we quote cover on-line sales of industrial and consumer goods and services, and the software and equipment needed to support e-business.

2 C-to-B is exemplified by companies such as Priceline.com that enables consumers to set a price and ask suppliers to meet it. C-to-C companies act as intermediaries for buying and selling among consumers. Auction sites such as E-bay in the US and QXL in the UK and Europe are typical examples.

3 Feeny, D. 'Information Management: Lasting Ideas within Turbulent Technology' in Willcocks, L., Feeny, D. and Islei, G. (eds), *Managing IT as a Strategic Resource*, McGraw Hill, Maidenhead, 1997.

4 A refreshing, well-researched antidote is provided by Shiller, R., *Irrational Exuberance*, Princeton University Press, New Jersey, 2000.

5 PricewaterhouseCoopers' report in *Sunday Business*, 21 May 2000, p. 22.

6 'Car buyers in rush for ferry firm's discounts', *Daily Telegraph*, 1 February 2000, p. 12.

7 Evans, P. and Wurster, T., *Blown to Bits: How the New Economics of Information Transforms Strategy*, Harvard Business School Press, Boston, 2000.

8 A full analysis appears in Graeser, V., Willcocks, L. and Pisanias, N., 'Assessing the Business Value of Internet-based Electronic Commerce', Chapter 9 in *Developing the IT Scorecard*, Business Intelligence, London, 1998.

9 Ruddle, K., 'Understanding Journeys of Transformation', unpublished D. Phil. thesis, Templeton College, Oxford, 2000. See also Ruddle, K. and Feeny, D., 'Benchmarking Organisational Transformation and Performance', Executive Research Briefing, Templeton College, Oxford, 1998.

10 Charles Schwab's move to the Internet is a particularly intriguing story of organisational transformation. The cultural and leadership dimensions and management disciplines involved are also engagingly described in Pottruck, D. and Pearce, T., *Clicks and Mortar: Passion-Driven Growth in an Internet-Driven World*, Jossey Bass, San Francisco, 2000.

Business Internet Strategy: Moving to the Net

Leslie P. Willcocks and Robert Plant

S peaking at the 2000 Outsourcing Summit in Florida, Jack Kemp, a former US presidential candidate, commented: 'E-commerce, e-money, e-bay, e-trade . . . it's e-topia!' By mid-2000 the shine had been taken off the euphoria he was, in part, parodying. In the 1996–2000 period, for most existing and start-up businesses, the adoption of web-based technologies had passed through an initial technology trigger period into a period of significant commercial optimism. This was buoyed by dramatic stock valuations and the related wide availability of investment capital. The shakedown that followed as we entered the new millennium hit business-to-consumer, business-to-business, then technology stocks in general. The message is clear – the initial learning and speculation period is over. For 2000–2, financial and business realism are to be the order of the day. As the chairman of the New York Stock Exchange commented in May 2000: 'E can stand for electric or electronic, but at some point it will also have to stand for earnings.'

The potential for companies to achieve revenues through e-business is unarguable. On the more conservative estimates

available, on-line business-to-consumer (B-to-C) transactions in the dominant marketplace of the USA were worth US$20 billion in 1999 and will rise to $184 billion in 2004. Retail sales on the web in Europe were $3.6 billion in 1999. They will rise to $9 billion in 2000, with accelerating rises in subsequent years. Similar rises can be expected in Asia, where estimated sales will reach $6 billion in 2000.

The potential of e-business is not equally distributed across every sector. In the USA in 1999 over seventy per cent of trans-actions were concentrated in relatively few sectors, mostly computer goods, travel, financial brokerages and collectables, with other revenues spread thinly across a diverse range of services including mainly books, videos, music, clothes, sporting equipment, flowers/cards/gifts, department stores, event tickets and consumer electronics.[1]

The potential for profitability is a different matter again. IDC has estimated e-sales worldwide in 1998 at $32 billion on $17 billion costs, excluding product costs. While the gap between sales and costs will narrow as the volume of transactions climbs to the levels estimated for 2004, we must conclude that for the time being there are many companies on the web, but few businesses.

Against this background, companies face two crucial chal-lenges. They must identify where e-business profitability lies for them. And they must discover how to get there. The purpose of this chapter is to shed light on these challenges through reporting on the experience of a number of companies we have studied around the world. We focus here mainly on B-to-C, and on existing 'bricks and mortar' businesses, though the study included, for comparative purposes, a small number of Internet start-ups and organisations that had moved most of their business to the Internet.[2] We were particularly concerned to look at how strategies evolve over time, to study a cross-section of sectors, and also to identify the leading and lagging practices exhibited. The chapter starts by describing generic characteristics of leading e-business organisations. An e-business strategic grid is presented to help map the leading and lagging strategic prac-tices of organisations in their moves to B-to-C e-business.[3] These are discussed in detail, and the chapter concludes by drawing together the lessons learned.

Four E-Strategic Directions

How well, in practice, have organisations navigated the domains spelt out in the Introduction? Throughout 1999-2000 we studied fifty-eight mainly major, established corporations in the USA, Europe and Australasia that were concerned with developing their business-to-consumer initiatives.[4] We found some wide differences in state of preparedness, ability to operate strategically, degree of progress between organisations in different sectors, but also between some organisations operating in ostensibly similar lines of business. However, several generic characteristics marked out the leaders. Let us look at these before moving on to mapping and discussing the four main areas of strategic focus uncovered by the study.

TOWARDS LEADERSHIP: GENERIC ISSUES

Several generic, distinctive attributes that marked off the leaders can be pointed out immediately:

- B-to-C leaders regard *the Internet as a foundation stone for a network-centric business era*. In many ways they have been following the advice of Carver Mead, a pioneer of the microprocessor: 'Listen to the technology. Find out what it is telling you.' We found leaders such as John Chambers of Cisco Systems, Michael Dell of Dell Computers and Charles Schwab listening to the technology in relation to their businesses and including technology into their strategy as first-order thinking (see also Chapter 7 for elaboration of this point).
- E-business leaders are astute at *distinguishing the contributions of information and of technology, and considering them separately*. Enduring advantage comes not from the technology but from how information is collected, stored, analysed and applied. As the director of corporate communications at an American biotechnology company put it: 'We really need to manage this from an information perspective.'
- Leaders recognised that not just technologies, but *competition, opportunities and customer expectations are all evolving very fast*. Time-based competition has become critical. Leaders we spoke with talked, to the point of cliché,

about the need to develop a strategy in Internet time. There emerged five imperatives for working in Internet time. Businesses must:

† become 24-hour, 365-days-a-year, real-time operations in their interactions with customers;

† constantly update information and their web sites. As one Northern Telecom manager put it: 'We are six months from obsolescence';

† navigate quickly through their own version of the five e-domains described in the Introduction;

† anticipate very rapid changes in customer and supplier expectations and needs;

† apply the same thinking to the likelihood of unexpected and changing competitor activity, especially in the threat of new entrants, of new products or service-based differentiation.

• Leading organisations *learn quickly and have the capacity to shift focus* – no easy matter in established corporations, as Chapter 4 illustrates. B-to-C leaders were intent on building an integrated technology, information and marketing platform, which enabled them to deepen their understanding of technological capabilities in order to convert them over time into revenue and profitability streams.

• Leaders found two routes to business innovation via the web. A 'top-down' business-led approach saw the *top team focused on business plans and goals, and the integration of web-based applications into business initiatives*. The process was marked by high awareness of e-business, of related technologies, and of opportunities and threats (see also Chapter 7). Prudential, Coles Myer, Charles Schwab, Fidelity Investments and Direct Line exemplified this leadership characteristic. The 'outside-in' approach is reminiscent of the application of 'skunk works' (see Chapter 10) in earlier rounds of technology.[5] In the 'outside-in' approach *managers working at the periphery of the organisation, close to customers, suppliers and the competitive action, identified new applications for web-based technologies*. Where powerful management champions were brought to bear, the initiative became quickly and widely adopted. We saw such developments in the B-to-C and the B-to-B areas in Motorola, Lufthansa, Cisco and Millipore.

• A critical element in the leaders is *the quality of business thinking that informed their e-business processes*. They

challenge themselves to ask whether the company has the intellectual capital and execution capability to imagine and apply a business model that makes sense in an e-enabled world. We found considerable disparities even in similar lines of business. Thus in the direct grocery business Tesco Direct and e.ColesMyer seemed good long-term prospects, founded on a multi-channel strategy and building on established brands and the pre-existing strengths of 'bricks and mortar' companies. By contrast, among grocery start-ups consider the different fates of Peapod, Netgrocer and our study company Streamline in the USA. In 1999 Peapod had 1000 delivery vans, a 100,000 household customer base, annual revenues of $100 million and was making a $45 million loss over four years. The business model was to collect groceries from partners, and charge a subscription and delivery charge. Peapod moved to a warehouse model in 1999 but by mid-2000 four investors were refusing to provide additional capital and the CEO had resigned. Netgrocer, founded in 1996, operated from a New Jersey warehouse, shipped only non-perishable goods via FedEx, incurring low shipping charges. Its IPO had to be withdrawn in late 1998 and the company subsequently had to relaunch with an expanded offering of drugs and gift items. Streamline, however, operated in neighbourhoods and added a range of services to that of grocery deliveries. Throughout 1998 and 1999 it attracted considerable investment, made profits and in 2000 continued to expand 150 warehouses in twenty neighbourhoods (for further details see below). The message: web-based technologies enable, but the superiority or otherwise of the business model, and of its execution, are decisive.

- Leaders invariably see B-to-C as *part of a larger strategic investment in e-business*. We found the leading B-to-C companies had made, or were making, even heavier investments in intranet, extranet and supply chain applications. Examples included Ford, Motorola, Coles Myer, Tesco, Dell, Cisco and Federal Express.

While it is helpful to know what characteristics distinguish leaders in e-business, it is important also to understand where their advanced thinking has led them. The remainder of the chapter explains this.

Mapping Evolution: The Business-to-Consumer Strategic Grid

Not all companies have started their e-business journey at the same time. For many of the firms we studied – for example, American Express, Dow Jones, Motorola, Citicorp, Alamo, Royal Caribbean, Charles Schwab – the technology trigger point began around 1995–6. Others responded much later. In our research we examined the evolution of B-to-C initiatives to see if there were any common paths and practices. To do this we needed to identify crucial strategic locations which might form part of the path. Figure 1 provides a map of these locations. In practice, laggard organisations did not get past first base. They typically got stuck in debates about the relevance of the technology, believed that the technology itself provided the way forward, or assumed that the technology was a fad, or believed that the technology was not relevant in their specific case.

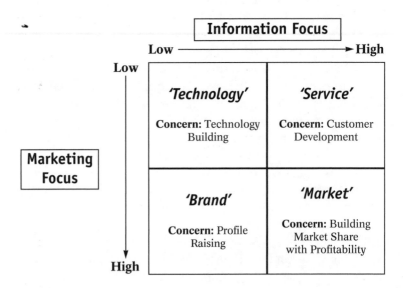

Figure 1 – Moving to E-Business: The Business-to-Consumer Strategic Grid

Leading and medium-performing organisations quite quickly moved beyond their starting point. They migrated to either the 'brand' strategy, with a primary focus on marketing, or to the 'service' strategy, with a primary focus on information and customer service. Very few migrated directly into the 'market' strategy, with a primary focus on building profitable market share. Rather, the most recurring patterns were evolution through Technology–Brand–Service–Market or through Technology–Service–Market. By late 2000 we found many more of the study organisations operating a more integrated approach to information, marketing and customer service, and combining these to operate in the 'Market' quadrant. For the large majority, including those 'bricks and mortar' companies with multi-channel strategies, disproportionate market share was proving elusive, as was profitability. High margins seemed an impossible dream. In most cases, though, this was both expected and accepted. Many of our respondents talked, for example, of 'being in the game for the long haul'; of the need to 'sort out channel conflicts'; of 'the complexity of integrating web sites with legacy systems and business processes'; and of the need 'to include the whole management team and employees in the transformation process'.

As we shall see, there emerged both more and less progressive ways of operating in each quadrant (Technology, Brand, Service, Market). In what follows we look in more detail at these differing approaches and how organisations have been progressing their B-to-C operations.

TECHNOLOGY LEADERSHIP

We found in all sectors e-initiatives that focused primarily on the technology. Some eighteen companies we studied – including, in addition to the ones cited above, Citicorp, BMW, Pratt and Whitney, WR Grace, Genentech – began in this quadrant in the mid-1990s. Others followed on in the 1997–2000 period. But developing technology just to be in the race rarely pays off. Those familiar with the adoption of previous generations of information and communications technologies will know two lessons that in our study were found to be highly pertinent to web-based B-to-C applications. First, *being first technology mover is not always successful*, even if applied to a viable business model. As long ago as 1986 Michael Vitale pointed to what he termed 'the growing risks of information systems success'.[6] One might add that in classic 'prime mover' examples like the SABRE airline

reservation system, invariably it was the management of information that explained success. As the American Airlines CIO commented in 1990: 'We don't much worry if the competition has access to the technology; we think we can be smarter in how we use it.'[7] Second, the organisational and managerial context in which the technology is deployed is critical. Where the technology is treated as an asset with a role in the transformation of the business, there is much greater likelihood of technology leadership and eventual business pay-off.

Technology laggards are those whose web-based initiatives stay stuck in the 'technology' quadrant, often rationalised as 'pilot' or 'learning' vehicles, or underachieve when attempts are made to move them to one of the other quadrants. In our study they shared five characteristics:

- The IT department was seen as largely responsible for e-business developments.
- Limited budgets led to underfunding and subsequent disappointment.
- Senior business managers were disengaged, and tended to see a limited role for IT and e-commerce within the business.
- IT and web-based technologies were seen as 'support', 'cost', 'liability' with little history of demonstrable business value.
- The CIO was positioned as a specialist functional manager.

What, then, characterised the 'technology leaders'? We found companies like Lufthansa, Motorola, Citicorp and Royal Caribbean Cruises *making judicious moves into the web-based technologies with a view to harnessing these for leadership in business terms*. Their concern was for appropriate technology that could match business strategy and customer requirements. Several respondents remarked on their plans to build excess capacity ahead of need, while others characterised this in terms of the constraints that would operate if they failed to build such technological capacity. All were building technology platforms to support Internet, intranet and extranet applications, with a view to utilising their strength in web technology to reinforce, improve or change the core business value propositions. Most were also ensuring that appropriate technology capability was either internally in place or available through partnering (see Chapter 10). In these terms technology leadership amounted to early adoption of web-based technologies to achieve a pre-emptive position in their application for competitive advantage. In

practical terms this meant learning the technology in the context of developing an information or marketing strategy, enabling a shift in focus fairly rapidly to one of the other quadrants.

Technology leaders did not always see their path from the start as clearly as our retrospective analysis implies. Lufthansa is just such a case. In 1995 the German airline had already embraced the TOnline system (an electronic data service) and CDRoms as part of its developing on-line passenger booking system: 'Given our involvement in emerging technologies, there was a strong feeling we should get involved in the Internet at this time, just to see how it develops.' However, web-based applications were subsequently developed in the light of the following statement from its sales executive: 'We recognised that our competitive advantage would move on from being the company with the best network, to one which knows its customers best.' By 2000 Lufthansa had migrated through all four quadrants and had built a viable on-line business.

Technology leader companies share in common the ability to see the business opportunity the technology presents, to shift focus and move into another quadrant. Consider the US power utility industry, which uses the Internet to buy and sell natural gas and pipeline capacity. This is mandated by the Federal Energy Regulatory Commission through a system called OASIS (Open Access Same-time Information System). The two utilities we studied see their mandated technology leadership as an opportunity to increase and lock-in market share for both residential and corporate consumers. While their mandate is to reduce their customer's power consumption, they balance this with a strategy of increasing their market share, which is made possible at dramatically lower cost by the Internet. Internet technology has boosted the utilities' ability to monitor customers' usage (even individual appliances can be monitored) and to make suggestions on energy saving. The strategic focus, therefore, has moved from 'technology' to 'market'. Competition in the industry is no longer based on the cheapest solution per kilowatt, but on the use of technology to add value. The ultimate aim, via the Internet, is to get closer to customers, and to create wider market coverage.

To position your business in the Technology quadrant is strategic in the sense that it is an investment in the future. But to remain in this quadrant is to become a laggard, because the business value lies in moving focus to brand, service or market.

BRAND AS STRATEGY

According to Lou Gerstner, chief executive of IBM: 'Branding in a network world will dominate business thinking for a decade or more.' Certainly, we found all our leading organisations coming to be highly concerned with how their brands translated into the Internet B-to-C context. A detailed exposition of branding strategy is provided by Kunal Basu in Chapter 3. Here we concentrate on mapping and analysing the brand approaches uncovered by the study. It should be noted throughout that what we have defined as leading organisations took 'brand' as a route stop, not the final resting place.

One of the first routes out of the Technology quadrant was to seek *brand reinforcement* via the Internet (Figure 2). Established companies not wanting to develop a new sales channel immediately, instead pursue a 'brand' focus, reinforcing the customer's awareness of, and regard for, the brand. BMW in 1998 was a good example of this. In fact, the company moved astutely from a 'technology' to a 'brand' strategy, bridging both; its mission, it said, was to make its site 'drive and feel like a BMW'. Into 2000, it allowed customers to build their own dream cars and even to hear the sound of its M-series engine in the Z3 Roadster. BMW has tended to prefer potential new owners to visit a traditional dealer, not because it has lacked the technology to sell via the Internet, but because it felt that the relationship between customer and company is best served by face-to-face interaction and bonding. The dilemma of how far to move over to direct Internet car selling was also faced by Land Rover and Ford in our sample. Restricted by regulation in its ability to sell over the Internet, biotechnology company Genentech used a 'brand' strategy 'basically to let people know about Genentech, by providing information on products to doctors and educationalists'.

The notion of brand reinforcement is brought home by an American Express executive: 'The Internet is where the home run is – when you leverage what you are good at and you use on-line in a way that cannot be duplicated. It reinforces what your products and service are, makes them better, and reinforces your brand and what it means.' American Express subsequently took on 'service' elements and moved into the 'market' quadrant.

In the UK from 1998 to 2000, Tesco has been an example of brand reinforcement moving over into some brand repositioning. In 1998 the supermarket chain trialled six sites selling 20,000 products on-line and making a £5 charge per delivery.

Brand Creation	**Brand Reinforcement**
'Creating New Internet Brand'	'Amplifying Existing Marketing Messages'
e.g. Amazon.com	e.g. BMW, AMEX
e-Trade	Genentech, Royal Caribbean
e-Toys	Office Depot, Lennar
Brand Follower	**Brand Repositioning**
'Replicating Early Movers'	'Repositioning Against Cyber-Competition'
e.g. New virtual	e.g. Alamo
bookshops/winesellers	Dow Jones, Citicorp
RS Components	Lufthansa, FedEx/UPS
Land Rover	

Figure 2 – Brand Strategies on the Internet

Throughout, Tesco Direct has used existing stores for supply, even after being separated off as Tesco.com. In 1999 the on-line business had 500,000 users and made a £11.2 million loss on £125 million sales, but it expects a profit by 2001. It expects to have made a £56 million investment in its on-line retail business, with almost all 600 stores on-line by the end of 2000, and 7000 dedicated staff. Throughout 2000 it moved into other goods and services, intending to make them about half of total sales. The power of the existing brand and of relationships with shoppers were also helping to reposition Tesco through its TescoPersonal Finance on-line joint banking venture with the Royal Bank of Scotland. Clearly, both Internet businesses were throughout 2000 intending to move much further into the 'market' quadrant.

However, we found the power of existing brands no guarantee of subsequent Internet market success. Levi Strauss launched its own on-line stores levi.com and dockers.com. It prohibited key retail partners from selling Levi Strauss merchandise over the web. This created channel conflict between the manufacturer and its selected retailers. Retailers turned their attention to private brand offerings while Levi Strauss proved inexperienced at on-line sales. Sales floundered against increasing on-line costs (estimated at $10–100 million). By 2000 on-line sales of clothing and accessories were being moved to retailer web sites such as Macy's and J. C. Penney. However, part of the problem had been lack of appeal of its e-operations to the teenage market. As one example, its on-line interactive advertising overlooked the limitations of bandwidth and the painfully slow on-line audio and video streams that resulted. Clearly,

overlooking the limitations of bandwidth and the nature of the customer for the sake of branding can be a costly error.

Several organisations took the opportunity to achieve *brand repositioning*. Thus Federal Express and UPS sought to stress they were not just courier companies but information providers. Alamo used the Internet to reposition itself more widely as a booking agency, while, against major on-line threats, Dow Jones used its move to the web to underline its global vision and bundling of services. Through its InfoFlyway service, Lufthansa sought to reposition itself as much more than an airline but also as highly customer-focused, a travel agency and an information provider.

Another approach has been *brand creation*. This has been most evident in the case of Internet start-ups including, among those we studied, Buy.com and Streamline.com. More pertinent for present purposes is where a 'bricks and mortar' company like Prudential Assurance moves into Internet banking under, in this case, the Egg brand. Launched in October 1998, Egg quickly achieved high brand recognition and also over 600,000 customers (50,000 on-line) and £5 billion of deposits in its first twelve months. By mid-2000 it had 940,000 customers, including 250,000 credit card customers, had taken £7.6 billion in deposits and lent £679 million, and was being part floated as a separate entity on the stock market. It was offering on-line savings accounts, credit cards, loans and a shopping mall.

This brand success was partly founded on its ownership by a well-known insurance company. Success came at a cost, with Egg spending £75 million on advertising in its first year and an expected loss of £377 million before breaking even in 2001. While Egg branding succeeded in attracting customers, it has achieved this through its savings account paying well above base rate – a strategy described by rivals as 'handing out £20 notes in exchange for £10 ones'. In our terminology, Egg has attempted to move into the 'market' quadrant, but its customer focus has sometimes been dogged by a series of failures on its web site, long waits in telephone services overwhelmed by new customers, lack of integration between credit card and savings account systems, and delays in the launch of its cut-price unit trust sales. Profits are expected to derive from cross-selling new products and services to its savings account customers.

The fourth category in the brand quadrant are the *brand followers*. Essentially these have consciously copied the early on-line movers in their approach to branding. Parts supplier RS

Components, for example, looked at Dell, while bookseller Amazon has taken legal steps to protect its technologies and business model from competitive threats such as that posed by Barnes and Noble. RS Components has subsequently moved on in its on-line marketing and customer initiatives, and Barnes and Noble have attempted to create their own on-line identity. In practice, we found brand followers needing to reposition quickly. However, this did not always happen – those established organisations that had no real Internet-based branding strategy often merely reflected their wider reluctance to build on the opportunities the Internet presented.

What lessons from all this? On the plus side, the Internet allows low-cost global branding and wider market reach. On the minus side, delivering on the brand – your promise to the customer as it has been called – can be expensive and difficult. As the Levi Strauss example shows, marketing, in the form of high presence, means little if it is not connected to knowing customers very well and delivering the service they require. And, as Egg reveals, even that and market growth may take a considerable time to translate into profitability. There is also something about what the brand represents. Thus Levi Strauss was no longer appealing to the vital teenage market.

The points come together when one reconsiders Peapod, Netgrocer and Streamline. The brand value propositions differ. Peapod focused on Fresh Food plus, Netgrocer on Technology plus, while Streamline focused on problem resolution. According to its CEO: 'Time is the commodity we should be selling. We should be creating a brand that simplifies people's lives.' In other words the brand is based on an analysis of what customers want and don't like doing. Thus, where Peapod offered customers a three-hour delivery window and Netgrocer shipped within two–three days by FedEx, Streamline asks customers to leave a refrigerator in the garage to be stocked without ringing the doorbell. Streamline also creates a regular custom shopping list for the on-line account, tracks what the customers use and provides a 'don't run out' function. It also adds a number of other delivery services, for example, returning rented videos, running errands. The brand supports a much wider value proposition than on-line groceries and as a result the business is eminently more expandable. As a result, Streamline has managed to move much more clearly into the 'market' quadrant than either Peapod or Netgrocer.

TOWARDS THE SERVICE PAY-OFF

It has been said that in many companies before the Internet, customer ignorance has been a profit centre. When dealing with customers on the Internet, however, the converse is probably true: ignorance of customers by a company can fatally damage its B-to-C strategy. The businesses that have faltered on the Net have usually talked the language of customer focus but have failed to organise accordingly – for example, many banks continue to be geographically or product structured, in comparison with Dell, that is structured by customer segment.

Leaders passing into the 'service' quadrant all possessed an obsessive focus on the customer and on information. They quickly learned to take advantage of the Internet's service strength to add information provision to the customer, on the customer's terms. Information about the customer was also seen as key. 'Service' leaders were to be found variously adopting adaptive profiling, mass customisation and one-to-one marketing concepts.[8] They applied customer resource life-cycle-type analysis (see Chapter 2) and focused heavily on customer retention. Moreover, seamless service was found to be the outcome of integration. As an Office Depot executive commented: 'The integration of systems is key; customer support and service through this is something we put a lot of emphasis on.' Increasingly effective operationalisation of such concepts and practices facilitated these companies crossing into the 'market' quadrant.

Leading service-focused organisations also develop service variations for specific contexts. Value-adding practices we observed include:

- **Personalisation** – According to a UPS executive we interviewed: 'One of the things we can show is "yes" we are this huge company, but we can come down to the level of detail of each customer.' Dow Jones has successfully offered on-line the Interactive Journal, which allows considerable customisation of information at the point of customer interaction, depending on customer preferences. On-line mass customisation is possible in this and other examples through personalising product attributes (e.g. colour of car, type of upholstery) and/or how the product is presented to the customer (e.g use of customer's name).

Allowing the customer to select the standard and level of service – An illustrative example here is Dell's on-line

information policy. Dell has four main categories of customer – 'all customers', 'registered customers', 'contracted' and 'platinum' customers. Anyone who comes to the web site is automatically in the first class. The services available include product information, order and lead-time information, PC ordering, configuration and pricing, together with support and forms, investor relations and employment adverts. Successive classes experience more in-depth relationships. Thus registered customers indicate which pieces of information they want to track and receive e-mail notification of its availability. On-line newsletters, customised by account, provide the on-line information. Contracted customers also receive discount pricing, order history details and custom links and offers. Finally, platinum customers receive customisation of all these services, their own home pages, replication of their web site, and are encouraged to have on-line discussions with designers to ensure new offerings reflect the requirements of key customers.

- **Collecting information on and enhancing the customer's total experience** – e.g. Alamo, Office Depot, RS Components, Dell (see also Chapter 2). Cisco, Dell, UPS, FedEx were the more well-known examples in our sample of organistions that (a) collected data around the customer resource life cycle and (b) used the data to support customers' preferences, and track purchases through to delivery and after-sales service.

- **Making it easy for the customer to do business with you and to do their jobs . . . then making it even easier** – e.g FedEx, Alamo, Direct Line. Again, Dell has made a point of making it exceedingly easy for all types of customer to achieve their required levels of access and satisfaction. Thus Dell developed customised intranet sites for over 200 of its largest global customers. These Premier Pages are protected by customer firewalls, and give on-line access to permit purchasing staff to view and select all products in the configurations authorised by the client company.

- **Finding and responding to what customers do not like doing, or do badly** – Direct Line was founded on the recognition that motor insurance was a necessary chore for car owners. One-stop insurance by telephone achieved a competitive advantage over traditional insurance channels in terms of cheapness and speed. Direct Line also operates through an Internet site integrated into its core insurance business, expanded into other insurance areas

such as household and travel. It has also set up a Jamjar.com site targeted at motorists and offering them information, advice, and the ability to buy vehicles and import cars at keen prices. MeritaNordbanken discovered that customers do not like paying bills and do this badly. Therefore it focused attention in early 2000 on developing an Internet bill payment application.

Providing one-stop shopping for enquiry, information, sales and problem resolution – Here Pratt and Whitney and Northern Telecom provided examples with their development of virtual call centres. Again, Direct Line in insurance and Lufthansa in ticketing on-line have also streamlined on-line services to reduce delays and reduce the number of parties involved in any transaction.

Delivering on the right levels of self-service – American Express has moved from being a credit card company to also being an on-line bank, permitting on-line share deals and providing tools for on-line financial portfolio management. Getting the balance right in self-service and support is not easy. Handing over as much of the task as possible to the customer may well be the cheap option, but it may not enhance the customer's experience or desire to return. Fidelity Investments in pension planning, and W. W. Grainger with its three web sites operating in the hard good supplies market, are just two examples of companies that do this well.

Competing on knowing the customer best – With detailed knowledge of their customers ('we could even monitor the refrigerator') Entergy and Florida, Power and Light group provide on-line analysis of customer bills and usage to suggest how customers can achieve greater efficiencies and lower costs. Lufthansa explicitly positions superior knowledge of its customers as a competitive goal. In 1998 its InfoFlyway service had developed 400,000 registered users who had made 41,000 electronic bookings producing £17.6 million in revenues. By 2000 it was offering home pages in over thirty-five languages, providing an award-winning web site in terms of the categories listed below and was tracking customer tastes closely. It provides individual e-mail, allows frequent-flyer and other accounts to be accessed via the web, provides monthly auctions, an on-line booking system for 700 airlines, hotel links, travel guides and baggage tracing.

- Voss usefully captures many of the critical service criteria we observed. He points to three building blocks for service on the web:[9]

1. *The foundation of service: 'What is expected'* – site responsiveness (including time, quality, ease of navigation); site effectiveness (e.g. time taken by customer to perform task, subjective satisfaction, quality of outcome); fulfilment and delivery (Charles Schwab and Direct Line were strong examples).

2. *Customer-centred: 'What differentiates'* – trust, for example on privacy and security of data and financial transactions; configurisation and customisation (Dell and Cisco are obvious exemplars here – both allow configuration of products on-line); information and status (in package delivery UPS and FedEx have competed vigorously on this dimension).

3. *Value-added: 'What excites'* – proactive service (e.g. Amazon provides suggested reading), value-added service (for example, single-contact point of service, hot links to allied services).

IN SEARCH OF (PROFITABLE) MARKET GROWTH

Let us now bring together a mapping of the optimal paths leaders have been pursuing through the e-strategic grid. These are shown in Figure 3.

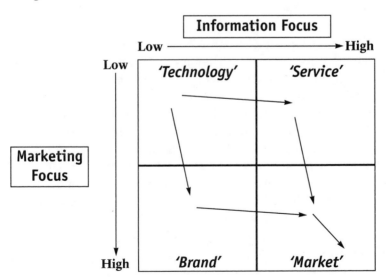

Figure 3 – Leadership Paths on the E-Strategic Grid

Businesses operating in the bottom right of the 'market' quadrant of Figure 3 stood out in their ability to combine marketing, service and information capabilities in order to achieve disproportionate web-based B-to-C market growth and profitability. The most notable among these were Fidelity Investments, Cisco Systems, Charles Schwab, Office Depot and Dell Corporation. By 2000 a number of other companies had moved to different degrees into the 'market' quadrant, some just edging in, but generally their marketing–service–information integration was less, as was the intensity and focus with which they deployed the relevant capabilities. All were driving hard on B-to-C market share but, by 2000, only some were making profits. Examples include Grainger, MeritaNordbanken, Direct Line, AMEX, Lufthansa, Alamo, Royal Caribbean Cruises, UPS, Federal Express and Tesco.

Let us look at three cases, in order to illustrate the evolution process. Also worth noting is the 'clicks and mortar' strategy in each case, the customer and service orientation throughout, and the focus on keying the use of the Internet into core concerns of the business.

- **Car Rental** – By late 2000 Alamo Rent-a-Car was serving more than 15 million travellers a year through 550 locations in America and Europe. It is a division of ANC Rental Corporation, which had combined annual revenues of US$ 3.5 billion. In 1995 Alamo was the first car-hire company to offer on-line, web-based reservations. From that time Alamo has seen the Internet as just another, if cheaper and more efficient, way to transact: 'There are a lot of ways to get a customer in our door and we make sure we get all those' (marketing manager). The aim in 1995 was to be first to market – being first in front of the customer was competitively important. In practice, Alamo moved very quickly from a 'technology' to a 'service' focus. Alamo has found that customers tend to be loyal to a specific channel. The need for speed meant a lot of the initial technical work was outsourced and for several years travel agents were not web-connected but had to use the legacy reservation system. As the importance of the web channel grew, Alamo brought its further development in-house (see Chapter 10 for details), coinciding with a further move into the 'service' quadrant.

In July 1999 Alamo relaunched Alamo.com with a stream-lined, single-screen, four-step reservation process, and a comparison shopping feature for cost and vehicle data. The 'service'

imperative had required a revisiting of the technology base. Easily clicked information became available on rentals, travel, destination attractions, contacts, special deals and arrangements for corporate clients. Alamo also provides e-mail access and notification, a help-line and call-back feature, and has sought to replace call centres with the more efficient Internet option: 'Through the web we can now automate some of the relationships, which it was not previously cost-effective to do.' The redesign was based on detailed research into customer preferences. For example, many did not know what a 'Buick LeSabre or similar car' looked like or how many passengers and pieces of luggage it could carry. According to the Alamo president, Karen Beard: 'Our innovations were prompted by what our customers told us they wanted – a faster, simpler process with less guesswork and more comparison shopping features.'

In February 2000 Alamo finally introduced a web site designed expressly for travel agents. It contains up-to-date information on Alamo programmes, services, special offers, commissions and special rates available only to travel agents. A range of tools enables agents to describe vehicles more accurately, provide rental agreements in different languages, make and revise reservations, offer safety tips to clients, join incentive programmes and order Alamo supplies.

These developments strengthened its position in the 'market' quadrant. In fact, Alamo experienced rapid Internet business growth from 1995. It has proved a highly profitable channel, experiencing disproportionate growth in some countries outside the USA. For example, in Japan it has produced many times the revenue over that of traditional channels, and also a steadier flow of business, with fewer peaks and troughs.

Distribution – By late 2000 United Parcel Services (UPS) had 2500 centres, over 330,000 employees and 500 airplanes, was delivering 12.4 million packages a day around the world and handling fifty-five per cent of all e-commerce shipments. This compared with Federal Express's 10 per cent. UPS has also planned to move its role from pure package deliverer to information delivery company and problem solver, helping companies manage inventories, reshape distribution networks and simplify accounting procedures. The Internet's networking, information and interactive capabilities have been brought to bear on achieving these strategic moves. As its president, Jim Kelly, pointed out: 'UPS does business where the virtual and

physical worlds meet, where "tire and wires" converge'. Such web-based technologies have become an integrated part of the technical infrastructure, and provide the key to fundamental services that UPS offers and develops.

UPS moved into web-based technologies in the mid-1990s but for a time FedEx, with its package tracking system, led in its use for customer service. By 1998 UPS was catching up in building its 'technology' infrastructure (in 2000 UPS was spending US$1 billion on IT) and developing its information capability for its customers down to the package level of detail. From 1998 it introduced a series of 'service' innovations on the Internet, including secure document exchange and customised logistics, for example, organising shipping of units from different country locations to arrive at the right place and time for assembly. In its B-to-C web-site design and internet use UPS would seem to have been driven by four marketing principles more widely applied in the company: listening to customers to determine their needs; creating a portfolio of services based on those needs; leveraging technology to forge tighter customer connections; and staying committed to international expansion.

For the vice-president for marketing: 'We have shifted through the economic noise to providing customers with infor- mation, and ways of doing business, over the Internet.' In practice, by 2000 UPS offered an interactive facility for precise ordering, paying for and tracking document/package delivery. It offered a range of services to businesses on their logistics, including a range of free on-line tools to help businesses add web-site functionality, reduce costs and improve customer service. These tools developed the relationship and lock-in with business customers, thus securing repeat business for UPS. By 2000 on-line consumers could find UPS shipping links built into more than 100,000 business web sites. By this date over half of UPS's business came from customers connected to the company electronically. Additionally, customers using UPS On-line Tools tended to increase their shipping volume by up to twenty per cent and to utilise UPS over several years.

Office Supplies – In late 2000 Office Depot was the world's largest seller of office products, dealing with over 300,000 orders a day, operating in nineteen countries and with 868 stores throughout the USA, Canada, France and Japan. Its 1999 revenues were US$ 10.3 billion. In the USA it also operated a business-to-business delivery network. Moving to the web in

early 1998 was a natural extension of its brand, business and processes. The technology infrastructure already in place supported the move (common processing, warehouse management and inventory systems); it had an existing catalogue sales operation with the service, delivery and after-sales infrastructure to support a web-based operation; and by that date the web itself had reached critical mass in the USA, representing a great opportunity for new revenue. The web also gave greatly expanded market coverage into areas without Office Depot supply depots, that could be supplied by distributors like UPS.

In January 1998 www.officedepot.com offered a twenty-four-hour, seven-day-a-week store, targeted at the fastest-growing market of small and home-based businesses. It offered the same benefits as its stores, plus navigability, ease of shopping, on-line order tracking in real time, payment facilities and guaranteed next-day delivery in ninety-five per cent of the USA, at no charge for orders over $50. Based on customers' specifications, the site and service continued to be developed over the next three years. The company also provides added value to its 55,000 plus contract customers by offering customised entry points and information, orders by authorised personnel, and special dis-counts for certain purchases and for buying on-line (see also the Dell example above). For all its retail activity Office Depot keeps detailed information, not just to ensure the right products and services are available, but also to provide the right level of information customers require. According to one executive: 'We have a sophisticated metrics tracking system, we know the specific margins for specific products, what customers are buying and I can either promote products with a higher margin, or ones that need a higher volume of sales that we have a lot of. It ties back to the integrated infrastructure we had before we went on to the web. It allows us to do a lot of that tracking, reporting and analysis.' Subsequently, Office Depot has moved even further into database and one-to-one marketing.

Between 1998 and 2000 the company's B-to-C web use be-came progressively more customised and interactive. The web has operated as an adjunct not a replacement to the existing stores and catalogue service, offering customers choices in how they pur-chase. Indeed some mix channels, for example using the web site for information, then physically buying and collecting the goods from the nearest store. Office Depot has also regularly developed strategic alliances to enable extensions of its advertising and business into other geographical locations and web sites.

LESSONS FROM LEADING PRACTICES

After experiencing an early but indifferent technology start, Alamo quickly moved into the 'service' quadrant and redeveloped its Internet offering in the light of customer preferences and the realisation that the Internet plugged straight into the heart of what it was doing as a business. It managed the problem of channel conflict with travel agents by subsequently developing a special web site tailored to their needs. It realised that counter rather than on-line payment continued to be a better option for both customers and the company, and did not develop this function.

For UPS, web-based technologies came to be integrated into the business model, and greatly extended the power of the model and the number and speed of services offered. Likewise for Office Depot, which also had the further advantage of prior robust, integrated technology infrastructure, systems and processes. Here the Internet could so easily have been used merely as an information catalogue, rather than a fundamental means of transacting business. Charles Schwab also built on a history of technical innovation, but it would be easy to underrate its transformation in five years to an Internet-based 'bricks and mortar' company[10] (see also Introduction).

All such companies making it deep into our 'market' quadrant do integrate web-based technologies into their core business, do use information gathered in the virtual value chain as a product, to gain insight into the customer and to augment service, and do have an intensive focus on customers and marketing. They all have identified ways of utilising web-based technologies 'strategically' and all are actively seeking ways to sustain their advantage – through, for example, brand, size, customer relationships and differentiation.

The practice of differentiation emerges as key to success. Our findings suggest that in most sectors commodity-based, price-sensitive competition on the web will not be an ultimately sustainable business model. Mathur and Kenyon's work is particularly pertinent here, and its prescriptions have been observable in many of the leading B-to-C companies found in our research. What competes in the marketplace is what a customer sees as alternatives or close substitutes – in other words what the customer can choose instead.[11] A business enters the competitive arena with a customer offering – the inseparable bundle of product, service, information and relationship. The challenge over time is continually to differentiate, and make less price-sensitive, this offering in ways that remain attractive to the targeted market segment. The options are captured in simplified form in Figure 4.

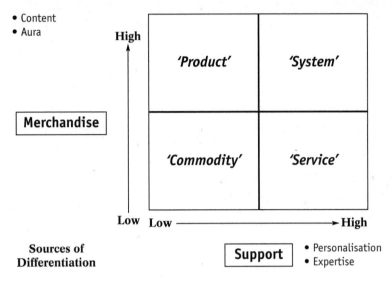

Figure 4 – Sustaining the E-Advantage through Differentiation
(adapted from Mathur and Kenyon, 1997)

The support dimension of an offering represents those differentiating features which customers perceive in the way the seller helps them in choosing, obtaining, then using the offering. All other differentiating features belong to what is called the merchandise dimension. The merchandise features of a car sold over the web would include its colour, shape, size, performance characteristics and in-car entertainment. Its support features would include availability of information, ease of purchase, the test-drive, promptness of delivery, service arrangements. The merchandise component can be further differentiated by augmenting **content** – what the offering will do for the customer – or **aura** – what the offering will say about the customer. Amazon can make available a wider range of books and products while MeritaNordbanken can provide WAP phone access to a customer's account; both companies' brands will augment the aura of the offering. The support dimension can be augmented by **personalisation** – the personal attention and distinctive familiarity offered to each customer's needs – and **expertise** – the superiority displayed by the seller in the brainpower, skill or experience in delivering and implementing the offering. Federal Express facilitates personal Internet tracking of your parcel;

Virtual Vineyards offered on-line access to information on wine and to the expertise of a sommelier. As we have seen, leading organisations in our study have striven to leverage both collective sources of differentiation, not least through leveraging information bases, to get closer to, and 'lock in', customers.

What matters is achieving differentiation in a particular changing competitive context, so that the dynamic customer value proposition – simplified in Figure 4 as commodity, product, service or systems alternatives – is invariably superior to what else is available to the customer. This may sound simple but it is deceptive. It requires a knowledge of and relationship with customers, and a speed and flexibility of anticipation and response that many organisations have found difficult to develop, let alone sustain. Moreover, as many commentators observe, it has to be achieved in specific Internet environments where power has moved further, often decisively in favour of the customer.[12]

Finally, the 'bricks and mortar' companies in the 'market' quadrant have also all found routes through the dilemmas posed by moving to a 'clicks and mortar' strategy. Gulati and Garino[13] have provided some useful advice on this, suggesting that integrating – as in our three cases – makes sense only in specific circumstances. These are where: (a) the brand extends naturally to the Internet; (b) current executives have the skills and experience needed to pursue the Internet channel; (c) executives are willing to judge the initiative by different performance criteria; and (d) distribution and information systems translate well into the Internet and provide a significant competitive superiority. For Gulati and Garino, separation is a more viable alternative where: (e) a different customer segment or product mix is being offered; (f) pricing needs to be different to stay competitive; (g) there are major channel conflict and threats to the current business model; (h) outside capital is needed; (j) there are problems retaining or attracting the right talent; and (k) a specific partner is key to the venture's success. This issue – of separation or integration – is such a fundamental one that Karl Moore and Keith Ruddle pursue the analysis further in Chapter 4.

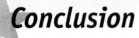
Conclusion

Faced with the many uncertainties associated with e-business, many executives have felt the need for advice and guidance based upon solid experience. This chapter has reported key lessons from an extensive study of companies with e-business experience. It offers two frameworks that managers can use to help understand the landscape of e-business and the routes through it. The first framework was the E-Business Strategic Grid (Figure 1). This identifies four strategic positions, any one of which a company may choose to emphasise in its application of web technology. The second framework is represented by the paths companies take through the Strategic Grid (Figure 3). Together, the main lessons they provide are that 'technology' focus is only a starting point. It is a foundation on which to build business advantage. 'Brand' still counts for a lot, so most companies should move from a 'technology foundation to consider the 'brand' implications of their move to the Net. The bottom-line benefits start to emerge when companies adopt a 'market' focus. Some can proceed straight to this point from 'brand' whereas others, particularly where they lack a 'service' focus, must explore the 'service' possibilities of their Internet strategy.

In addition, this chapter has provided a variety of useful lessons from leading companies. These can be summarised for established companies as saying that e-business has to be understood as part of the company's total vision, and must be managed with the same commitment and management skill as any other strategic initiative. Relegation of e-business to lower executive levels or its banishment to some forgotten corner of the business empire will inevitably result in disappointment.

In statistical analysis of business unit data Nievelt (1999) and Nievelt and Willcocks (1997) provided strong evidence for a significant, often positive, multifaceted IT effect on business productivity. This impact is invariably not in isolation but as a result of interaction with other factors, for example, organisational structure, percentage of knowledge workers, relative competitive position. The context, timing and focus of IT investment emerged as all important. In separate studies, including the one described in this chapter, we are already finding similar results for web-technology investments in e-business.[14] In other words,

the journey through the e-business strategic grid in order to achieve business Internet exploitation has to be guided by certain perennial, as well as new, management thinking, principles and practices. This theme is taken further into the marketing arena by the next chapter.

NOTES

1 See Sauer, C. and Willcocks, L. *Building the E-Business Infrastructure,* Business Intelligence, London, 2000. Also Forrester Research and Boston Consulting Group research quoted in 'Shopping Around the Web: E-Commerce Survey', *The Economist,* 26 February 2000.

2 The study was carried out in USA, Europe and Australia throughout 1999–2000. Interviews with over 130 executives lasting from forty-five minutes to two hours were carried out, and internal and published support documents collected. The study covered car manufacturers and retailers, technology suppliers, biotechnology companies, financial services including credit card, stock broking, insurance and banking firms, airlines, information providers, pharmaceutical companies, energy utilities, a range of retailers and service operations, for example, Coles Myer, Levi Strauss, Dixons, UPS, Alamo, Ryder, Lennar, and manufacturers, for example, Lockheed, RS Components. The objective was to examine a variety of sectors to identify generic and sector-specific practices characteristic of organisations that lead, lag or otherwise in their use of web-based technologies. The study was much broader than just B-to-C, and also looked at B-to-B and development/sourcing practices, the latter findings feeding into Chapter 10. Note also that B-to-C is used throughout as shorthand and refers also to the potential for C-to-B, for example, Priceline, Accompany, and C-to-C, for example, E-Bay, though these companies were not in our sample.

3 An earlier version, based on a smaller number of case studies tracked provisionally to February 1999, appeared in synopsis form as Plant, R. and Willcocks, L., 'Moving to the Net: Leadership Strategies', *Financial Times* Mastering Information Management Supplement, 15 March 1999, pp.11–12.

4 Criteria included degree to which web site applied across the customer resource life cycle, degree to which B-to-C was achieving disproportionate market growth/profitability or moving to profitability; extent to which customers were being attracted and retained; size of spend and expected returns on

marketing and e-development; B-and-C position in sector and against competition. We gained some quantified measures of these in each case, but more often subjective judgements by respondents. It should be remembered that the sample was opportunistic and deliberately spread across sectors and across what we prejudged as differently performing organisations, and deliberate over-representation of what we thought to be leaders. With these criteria and qualifications, we found some fifteen 'leaders', twenty-five 'laggards' and sixteen medium-performing organisations.

5 See Ciborra, C., *Markets, Teams and Systems*, Cambridge University Press, Cambridge, 1993. Ciborra refers to incremental development of strategic systems through learning characterised by 'bricolage' rather than top-down-determined systems. Also Earl, M., *Management Strategies for IT*, Prentice Hall, London, 1989, Earl proposed a multiple methodology for the development of a portfolio of strategic applications.

6 Vitale, M., 'The Growing Risks of Information Systems Success', *Management Information Systems Quarterly*, December, 1986. The article points to systems that change the basis of competition to a company's disadvantage; that lower entry barriers; that bring litigation or regulation; that increase customers' or suppliers' power to the detriment of the innovator; that turn out to be indefensible and may even induce disadvantage; that are badly timed; that transfer power and are resisted by other market players; and that may work in one market niche but not in another. All this implies an over-reliance on the technology and inadequate analysis of the competitive context to which it is applied.

7 On this point see also Davenport, T., 'Putting the I in IT', in Davenport, T. and Marchand, D. (eds), *Mastering Information Management*, FT-Prentice Hall, London, 1999.

8 See Pine, J., *Mass Customisation: The New Frontier in Business Competition*, Harvard Business School Press, Boston, 1993. Though written before the Internet took off as a business tool, Pine's work is highly applicable to Internet applications.

9 Voss, C., 'Developing an E-Service Strategy', *Business Strategy Review*, 11, 1, 2000, pp.21–33.

10 Charles Schwab's move to the Internet is a particularly intriguing story of organisational transformation. The cultural and leadership dimensions and management disciplines involved are engagingly described in Pottruck, D. and Pearce T., *Clicks and Mortar: Passion-Driven Growth in an Internet-Driven World*, Jossey Bass, San Francisco, 2000.

11 See Mathur, S. and Kenyon, A., *Creating Value: Shaping Tomorrow's Business*, Butterworth – Heinemann, London, 1997, particularly Chapter 5. The importance of customer perceptions and relative customer satisfaction in sustaining competitiveness also emerges from Nievelt's research – see below, note 14.

12 See, for example, Seybold, P. with Marshak, R., *Customer.com: How to Create a Profitable Business Strategy for the Internet and Beyond*, Random House, New York, 1998; Vandermerwe, S., *Customer Capitalism*, Nicholas Brearley Publishing, London, 1999; Newell, F., *Loyalty.com: Customer Relationship Management in the New Era of Marketing*, McGraw Hill, New York, 2000.

13 Gulati, R. and Garino, J., 'Get the Right Mix of Bricks and Clicks', *Harvard Business Review*, May–June 2000, pp.107–114.

14 See Nievelt, A. M. van, 'Benchmarking Organisational and IT Performance,' in Willcocks, L. and Lester, S. (eds), *Beyond the IT Productivity Paradox*, Wiley, Chichester, 1999. Also Nievelt, A. M. van and Willcocks, L., 'Benchmarking Organisational and IT Performance', Executive Research Briefing, Templeton College, Oxford, 1997. In 1999 the study was extended into the use of web-based technologies in insurance, with corroborative results. See also Sauer, C. and Willcocks, L., *Building the E-Business Infrastructure*, Business Intelligence, London, 2000. Also Corbitt, B. and Willcocks, L. (eds) *Strategic E-Business*, Wiley, Australia (forthcoming).

'E' Opportunity – The Strategic Marketing Perspective

David Feeny

A NEW ERA OF STRATEGIC OPPORTUNITY

'The power of technology as a competitive variable lies in its ability to alter competition through changing industry structure'.[1] So wrote Harvard Professor Michael Porter in 1980, in the book (*Competitive Strategy*) which brought him to international prominence. Twenty years later, as we enter the new millennium, his words are worth remembering. Today 'e-business' (with its many 'e' variants) is established as the topic of the moment – among business leaders, the investment community and, above all, within the media. The common wisdom is apparently that the Internet and associated technology change everything. There is a 'new economy' replacing the 'old economy'; every business must become an 'e-business' or perish; leaders of even the most profitable companies of today are being urged to 'cannibalise your products', 'destroy your value chain', 'hire the children' and so on.[2]

In the midst of all this rhetoric, the underlying truth is too easily forgotten. New technology is a potential lever for strategy,

not a substitute for it. As more recent writings have begun to suggest,[3] the task is not simply to be part of the 'e' action, it is to refocus – in the light of available technology – on competitive advantage and on strategies to achieve it. In the concluding words of an *Economist* supplement on the topic:[4] 'e-business is far more about strategy than about technology.'

This perspective on e-business does not deny the importance of recent technological change, nor its scale and pervasive impact. Web-based technology introduces the prospect of universal connectivity, at astonishingly low levels of cost, with a simple and inherently standardised user interface. It represents the most profound and far-reaching discontinuity in the already dramatic history of information technology, a genuinely new era as identified in Figure 1.[5] It is the phenomenon of *discontinuity* which is crucial to the strategist. In contrast to periods of technological evolution, revolutionary and discontinuous change brings the potential for new forms of competition, for major shifts in industry structure and market share. When the combination of PCs, minicomputers and data networks introduced the 'Distributed Era' – the previous discontinuity charted in Figure 1 – Porter and Millar, in 1985, described 'How Information Gives You Competitive Advantage'.[6] Other leading academics in strategy and information management, in a series of high-profile articles, agreed that IT now represented a competitive weapon, and companies such as American Airlines, American Hospital Supply and Merrill Lynch were identified as the 1980s precursors of Amazon, Dell and E-Bay. In retrospect, we can see that the distributed era did indeed herald widespread changes in the way businesses organised and interacted with each other along the supply chain. However, the economics of the distributed era meant these changes were mainly confined to large- and medium-scale business contexts. Given the characteristics and economics of the web-based era, the scope for change and strategic advantage is dramatically greater. The small business as competitor, customer, or supplier; the individual employee rather than the department; the individual consumer; all become potential participants in a new strategic landscape.

Having recognised that a new era of technology brings the potential for new strategic business initiatives, the strategist now faces three additional and critical questions:

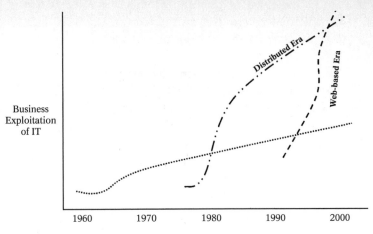

Figure 1 – Major Eras in Information Technology

- Of all the many business initiatives the technology now enables, which will generate significant value for the business? The answers will, of course, be a function of the specific context of the business. The stories of Amazon, Dell, E-Bay and others may serve as an effective wake-up call to the strategist. But if my business sells chemicals, helicopters, or credit card services, it is highly probable that my strategic opportunity will take an altogether different form. What form might that be?
- Is it clear that any initiative I propose to undertake provides sufficient benefits to the customer as well as to my business? For example, providing customer service across the Internet rather than through a call centre may create business value through significant improvement to my cost structure. But will the customer see the new service as an improvement, which rewards his/her investment in learning the new procedures required? Or does it represent to him/her a tedious route to a service that is already familiar through a more simple and friendly process? Unless new value is created for the customer, we cannot expect customer adoption of the new approach and the hoped-for business value is an illusion.
- Finally, if we have hit upon a winning idea and the business is beginning to experience the benefits, what will protect our competitive advantage? The idea is now plain to see, the technology is available to competitors large and small, implementations are increasingly rapid. In what circumstances can the prime mover expect to sustain his advantage? In a particular

competitive context, is it worth incurring the learning costs of
an innovator, or better to position as a fast follower?

The traditional issues of strategy need to be interpreted into
the new era of enabling technology. Recent publications collectively convey a sense of massive scope for new strategic
opportunity, but in general each focuses on developing insight
into one strand of that opportunity – and in the process introduces yet more new terminology into an already overcrowded
field. For the strategist, it is rather like being asked to complete a
jigsaw without the benefit of an overall key – while believing that
the pieces probably come from several different jigsaws and
sensing that lots of pieces are currently missing.

Against this background, my objective here is to develop at
least one version of the overall key to the jigsaw or jigsaws, a set
of blueprints that can provide some sense of shape and structure
to the executive team. I want particularly to address the executive
teams of the established businesses which form the bulk of the
existing economy and will therefore try to use, wherever possible,
a language that is at least broadly familiar to them. The intention
is to create a structured mapping of the 'e' opportunity; with
frameworks that facilitate the high-level understanding and
diagnosis of each dimension of that opportunity, as a function of
industry and business context.

 # Towards an E-Opportunity Framework

So how many jigsaw puzzles are we trying to piece together? I
suggest there are three, which each contains a distinctive set of
strategic ideas. We can describe them as the 'E-Operations', 'E-
Marketing' and 'E-Vision' opportunities:

- The **'E-Operations'** opportunity refers to those uses of web
  technology that are directed at strategic change in the way a
  business manages itself and its supply chain, culminating in
  the production of its core product or service. BP Amoco's
  knowledge-sharing initiatives provide one prominent
  example. The GE Corporation's move to electronic

procurement represents a very different concept within the same overall category.

- The '**E-Marketing**' opportunity covers web-based initiatives, which are designed to achieve strategic change in the 'downstream' activity, either through direct interaction with the customer or via a distribution channel. In e-marketing, as I am defining it, a traditional product remains the focus of the business and its revenue generation; but the way the product is delivered and (potentially) the scope of service provided around it are changed. The provider may be a traditional one, or a new entrant – a Barnes and Noble or an Amazon.com, a Toys'R'Us or an E-Toys. The financial services sector illustrates the many options for change, with established companies and new competitors linking to established intermediary channels, to new ones such as supermarkets and to the customer directly; but the focus remains on the delivery of traditional financial services products – of savings accounts, of credit cards, of mortgages etc.

- In contrast to those web-based e-marketing initiatives that disrupt competition through enhanced marketing of a traditional product, I classify as '**E-Vision**' opportunities the new business ideas which provide transformational responses to customer needs. They are transformational in the sense that the new business is defined as addressing an identified set of needs, whereas the old provided a portfolio of products; and also transformational in that the customer service provided has – in most cases – no close parallel in the 'old economy'. A further characteristic is that an e-vision business typically derives its revenue from fees for the services provided rather than from the production and sale of the products consumed. Most of the current examples are from 'new economy' businesses – Chemdex, the information intermediary business in the bio-sciences sector; Adauction.com, which provides buyers and sellers of advertising space with a radically new set of services; 'Shopping Robot' businesses like MySimon.com – but 'old economy' businesses such as Ford[7] are increasingly moving towards an e-vision.

While any business should be considering its strategic opportunities across the spectrum of e-operations, e-marketing and e-vision, the separation of these categories is not just a basic exercise in mapping – it is critically important in two further respects. First, the potential significance of each category will

vary widely from sector to sector and each business needs to establish its priorities across them. Second, the concepts and frameworks which are helpful to the strategist are quite different in each category. Assessing the 'e' opportunity requires a three-pronged approach, with examination of the key ideas and the appropriate approaches for each category, before consolidation of initiatives into an overall 'e'-opportunity strategy. While it is tempting to begin with the excitement of e-vision, the logic I will follow is that e-operations and e-marketing provide the most urgent attention and the most certain rewards. As so many dot.com businesses have demonstrated, if you have e-vision but a one-club (advertising) approach to marketing, and a poor fulfilment capability, you don't really have a business.

The Shape of the E-Operations Opportunity

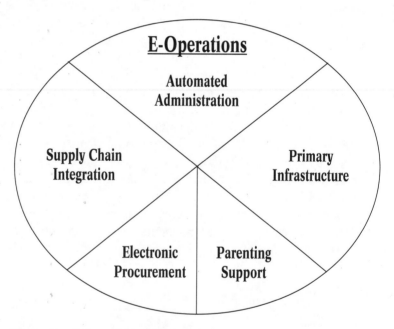

Figure 2 – E-Operations Components

While the initial e-operations applications of most organisations involved electronic versions of policy documents and newsletters mounted on an intranet, Figure 2 suggests that the real e-operations opportunity should be thought of as having five potential components:

- The first and most straightforward is the opportunity for 'automated administration'. Businesses are increasingly using their intranet infrastructure as the vehicle for low-cost administration of what we might call 'necessary evil' processes – everything from the enrolment and training of new employees to the claiming of travel expenses, the buying of pencils, the registration of vacation dates etc. The improvements in cost efficiency, the savings in management time from improvements to such an individual process are, of course, small; even in aggregate these initiatives are unlikely to make a fundamental difference to cost structure. But – as Cisco[8] and Schlumberger[9] have demonstrated – these applications create a more IT-literate workforce and a more 'nimble' business culture and posture, which is certainly of interest to the strategist.

- More fundamentally, the new technology triggers an opportunity to review the 'primary infrastructure' – the core processes of the business, and the technology and software base which supports them. To what extent is web technology the enabler of a new round of re-engineering of this infrastructure, leading to faster turnaround of customer orders and service requests, to improvements in the product's unit cost structure, to shorter time to market for new products? For example, it was suggested by a Booz Allen and Hamilton study in 1996 that the expense ratios of banking businesses may be reduced by a factor of 2 to 3.

- The third component I have labelled 'parenting support', the opportunity to gain advantage by leveraging important corporate characteristics across the operational units of the group. In these initiatives the intranet and related technology are enabling the achievement of some of the parenting advantages identified by Campbell, Goold and Alexander[10] – particularly the leveraging of corporate scale in purchasing and/or 'back office' operations; and the application of group-wide learning and knowledge to local problem solving. In the first of two contrasting examples, the fast-growing serviced-office company Regus is using its intranet as a means of achieving 'best practice' process standards in each of the new offices it is opening every week around the world. Meanwhile the long-established giant BP Amoco claimed an astonishing

$700 million saving through knowledge management in 1998.[11]

- The fourth component of e-operations is the sort of electronic procurement initiative pioneered by the General Electric Corporation. Here an extranet web site is used by buyers to post their requirement specifications and tendering conditions. All suppliers who have been 'qualified' by the company can access the web site and submit bids to it. The benefits are seen to extend beyond lower administrative costs to the achievement of more competitive prices and shorter fulfilment cycles. When General Motors, Ford and Daimler Chrysler announced their collaboration to introduce such an electronic procurement capability, analysts calculated that it could result in costs savings equivalent to $1065 per vehicle manufactured – a potential $18 billions per year saving across the North American automotive industry.[12]

- The final component of e-operations also concerns interactions with suppliers, but underpins quite a different approach through support for supply chain integration. In this model of procurement strategy the business seeks long-term relationships with what are effectively single-source suppliers. The role of technology is to make information transparent throughout the supply chain so that it can operate with the advantages of a vertically integrated business – albeit a virtual one – while at the same time realising the benefits of focus and speed of response at each point in the chain. Dell provides a famous example. CEO Michael Dell is quoted as believing that he would have the 'drag effect' of five times as many employees if his company were vertically rather than virtually integrated (see also Chapter 10). Any business which operates a build-to-order strategy will need to embrace supply chain integration concepts in order to deliver it. And as in the case of Land Rover's Freelander, the best-selling vehicle in the European small sports utility vehicle market, customers' individual specifications can be delivered despite remarkably low levels of inventory.[13]

Expressed in these terms, the e-operations opportunity looks to be largely familiar and evolutionary. Businesses are long accustomed to evaluating the benefits of updating their infrastructure as technology changes. Supply chain integration represents the logical and economical extension to all suppliers of the EDI links which were laboriously established with large

suppliers in the previous decade. Even the parenting ideas pursued by a Regus can be compared with the 1980s example of Mrs Fields Cookies.[14] Only the electronic procurement and the (smaller) automated administration opportunities look to represent radical advance. In my research I have indeed found most executive teams to be relatively comfortable with discussion of the e-operations opportunity, in contrast to their fascination but discomfort with the more revolutionary ideas described in articles about 'e-commerce'. But for some businesses, some industry sectors, the highest priority should be investment in e-operations. The question is: which ones?

DIAGNOSING THE E-OPERATIONS OPPORTUNITY

When the onset of the distributed era (Figure 1) brought IT to prominence as a competitive weapon, Porter and Millar (1985) introduced an 'Information Intensity' matrix to diagnose the relative significance of the strategic opportunity across different industry sectors.[15] Businesses might have high information intensity within their value chain in the sense that extensive or complex information was required for successful performance of operational activity; and/or there might be high information content in the product. Thus for banks or newspapers (high on both dimensions) technology was critical to strategy. Whereas for cement companies (low on both dimensions) it was not. While I have found this framework to have a number of shortcomings, its basic ingredients can still be helpful in diagnosing the importance of today's e-operations opportunity. Together with the 'configuration' concept of another Porter framework,[16] the information intensity constructs form part of the E-Operations Opportunity Model of Figure 3.

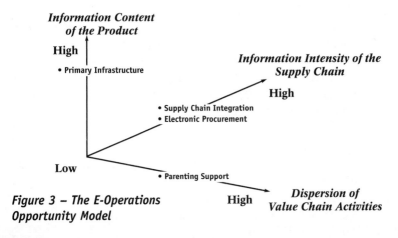

Figure 3 – The E-Operations Opportunity Model

- **High** product information content signals the importance of the 'Primary Infrastructure' component. Of course an 'adequate' infrastructure is a necessity for every company, a qualifier for being able to do business. But if the product is information intensive, adequacy is no longer the goal: the new technology is likely to enable radical change in the infrastructure, which can lead directly to competitive advantage. In any publishing firm the absolute imperative is to identify and implement the infrastructure that takes best advantage of web technology. For a banking business attention to infrastructure should take priority over the launch of an Internet banking service; the long-term success of the bank will depend fundamentally on the infrastructure for its cost structure and responsiveness, its Internet offering will be one of a number of services that thrive or wither on the back of it. In a research-based pharmaceutical firm, which has a tangible product but high information content in its associated development process, the infrastructure that supports the set of discovery, trials, regulatory submission, product advice activities will be the priority for attention.

- **High** information intensity in the supply chain (the end-to-end value chain of the industry) points to the importance of the electronic procurement and/or supply chain integration components of e-operations. Examples include automotive and aerospace firms, whose final products are built from tens – even hundreds – of thousands of component parts; the availability, quality and cost structure of the product are dependent on the way the supply chain is managed. Electronic procurement schemes extend the logic that cost structures dominated by bought-in content can be minimised by the most competitive possible tendering. However, exponents of the build-to-order philosophy – the 'mass customisers' – have demonstrated that they can deliver the customer's specification at high-quality and competitive-price levels. The choice ultimately will depend on the package of options, delivery and price which the business seeks to deliver to the target market.

- The parenting support opportunity is greatest when there is a *high* 'dispersion' configuration of some value chain activities – in other words when the same activity is performed at many different geographical locations. Thus BP Amoco's knowledge management benefits have resulted from the sharing of learning across its many business units within exploration and production. Like Mrs Fields before it, Regus seeks to embed the operational thinking of its founder and CEO into the management processes of its hundreds of (mostly small and young) locations around the world. The higher the dispersion, the greater will be the potential benefits from leveraging the overall business's knowledge and scale to support the dispersed activity.

- The 'automated administration' opportunity is missing from Figure 3. It seems to offer, in any business context, quite a different sort of benefit – the creation of a culture in which the workforce collectively is comfortable with and welcoming of the new technology. Investment in automated administration does not bring substantial economic benefit, but it may represent a vital step in readying the organisation for the other initiatives of e-strategy.

The framework of Figure 3 demonstrates that businesses will differ widely in the extent and nature of their e-operations opportunity. Diagnosing this opportunity (or the lack of it) is the first essential task for the strategist, since action in this dimension will shape the basic competitive capabilities of the business, and its subsequent readiness to grasp e-marketing and e-vision opportunities. Even the 'low information intensity' cement company can be seen to have an e-operations opportunity if it operates numerous sites and falls into the 'high dispersion' category. Certainly, as the case of the Mexican group Cemex illustrates,[17] low-information intensity is not a predictor of e-marketing opportunity.

The Shape of the E-Marketing Opportunity

E-marketing strategy capitalises on the potential of new technology to enable more effective ways of achieving the sale of the business's product to existing or new customers. As Downes and Mui[18] note, its theoretical underpinnings come from the Internet's potentially dramatic impact on the transaction costs of market exchange. While I have preferred to use language more familiar to the marketing practitioner, the interested reader will be able to relate each of the ideas discussed to its effect on one or

more of the transaction costs identified back in 1934 by economist Ronald Coase – search costs, information costs for buyers and sellers, bargaining costs, decision costs, policing and enforcement costs.

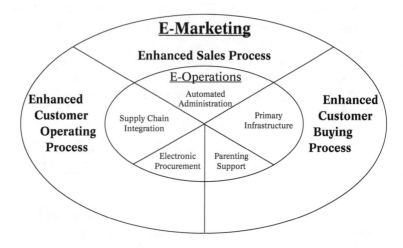

Figure 4 – E-Marketing Components

Since the opportunity mapping is rather more complex in this area, let us start (Figure 4) by identifying three broad categories of e-marketing opportunity:

- Enhancing the sales process – making the sales effort more effective through better product/market targeting, and/or more successful expression of the characteristics and benefits of the product.
- Enhancing for the customer the process of buying from the business – providing a set of services around the product which make the product easier to buy and/or better fitted to the customer's needs.
- Enhancing the customer's operating process – providing a set of services which result in the customer achieving additional benefits while the product is in use.

While the full scope of these components is probably bounded only by marketing creativity, I have found some ideas within each category to be regular features of marketing initiatives in both the 'distributed' and 'web-based' eras. These are listed and defined in Table 1, together with one of the many potential examples that exist to illustrate each idea.

Category	Marketing Idea	Concept	Example
Enhanced **Sales** **Process**	**Development Feedback**	We can improve our products by interacting with our customers during development.	Ford has put its design studio 'on-line' to obtain the feedback of selected customers.
	Customer Tracking	By understanding the status of our customer, we can approach them at the relevant time/with the relevant product.	Amazon notifies customers of new book-buying options based on their profile of previous purchases.
	Niche Aggregation	We have a new ability economically to reach and serve a dispersed customer segment.	e-Hobbies uses the Internet as a channel to reach model train enthusiasts around the world.
	Benefit Selling	We can improve the way we illustrate to the customer the benefits our product provides.	The instrument company TRUE Technology provides a downloadable simulation of how its products will benefit the customer's production process.
	Performance Tracking	We can improve customer loyalty by showing our track record of meeting commitments to them.	1-800-FLOWERS provides corporate customers with a full record of their service history.
Enhanced **Customer** **Buying** **Process**	**Fastest Source**	We represent your best chance of getting what you need with minimum hassle.	The core of Amazon's proposition to buyers of books.
	Retail Alliances	We are collaborating with partners to provide a one-stop shop for all your needs.	Through links to complementary sites such as stamps.com and TelePost.com, Office Depot increases its coverage of overall customer needs.
	Customer Guidance	We will help you understand how your needs can be addressed by available products.	Home Depot provides customers with details of everything they will need to carry out a DIY project.
	Product Elaboration	We provide a service to help you understand which product specification is right for you.	Lands End allows the customer to create a 'personal model' on which they can test the fit/look of swimwear.
	System Specification	We provide a design facility which helps you create the system in which our product is a component.	Herman Miller provides a room-planning program, which allows the customer to evaluate how new furniture will fit in with existing.
	Tailored Product	We rapidly deliver exactly the product specification you want.	Chipshot.com allows the expert golfer to configure clubs to their own preferred specification.
Enhanced **Customer** **Operating** **Process**	**Added Service**	As well as providing you with product, we will help improve troublesome aspects of your operational activity.	Guidebook company Lonely Planet provides travellers with an on-line 'travel vault' in which to deposit all their critical information.
	Tailored Support	We will provide our products to you in a way that reflects your special needs and practices.	As well as offering 'tailored product', Dell sets up for its large customers a 'Premier Page', which reflects the agreed tailored support.

Table 1 – A Portfolio of Marketing Ideas

- Apart from the specifics of Table 1, its general form highlights several important points about the e-marketing opportunity. First, the 'marketing ideas' listed are not new, they are familiar from before the days of technology – for example, the hugely successful retail chains of the 1980s and 1990s succeeded

through implementation of the 'fastest source' idea; the IBM of the 1960s and 1970s won the loyalty of large corporates through account managers who provided 'tailored support'. E-marketing does not reinvent the *theory* of marketing, it succeeds by reinventing within particular contexts the *practice* of marketing – implementing established ideas that previously have not been viable. Second, each idea – each 'enhancement' – targets one piece of an overall marketing approach and seeks to improve it with the help of web technology. While a few companies, such as Amazon and Office Depot (see Chapter 1), can each be seen to embrace several of the ideas listed, this is not the general case. The objective is not to implement as many ideas as web technology allows, but to identify and pursue the few that will bring competitive advantage. Finally, it should be clear that the ideas are not sector specific, nor do they come with stickers marked 'for B-to-C use only'. For each of the ideas there may be examples for both business and consumer customers. For instance, when the Air Products web site helps customers to determine whether to opt for deliveries of liquid nitrogen or for an on-site production facility, it is implementing a form of 'product elaboration'. It is very different in shape from the Lands End swimwear example of product elaboration, but it is fundamentally the same marketing idea. The real question is whether either Air Products or Lands End have identified contexts in which customers will reward them for implementing what is now a viable idea.

DIAGNOSING THE E-MARKETING OPPORTUNITY

Given that web technology makes so many new marketing initiatives technologically and economically viable, the strategic task is to identify which initiatives will succeed in the marketplace. A framework to support diagnosis of e-marketing opportunity will point to the business and customer contexts in which the ideas of Table 1 are most likely to bring value to the customer and reward to the business. After many years of seeking to articulate the technology/marketing connection – to explain success and failure in the technology-enabled marketing initiatives of both 'distributed' and 'web-based' technology eras – I have found that the two constructs below have consistently been the most powerful determinants of business and customer context:

Perceived product differentiation captures the strategic marketing stance of the business. In a stance of high

differentiation, the marketer will want to emphasise the 'enhanced sales process' ideas – those which promote the creation of distinctive products, the targeting of distribution to customers who will appreciate the distinctiveness, the successful articulation pre- and post-sale of the benefits of the product to those customers. By contrast, a stance of low differentiation (of the core product) is supported by initiatives from the 'enhanced customer buying process' and 'enhanced customer operation process' categories – leading to the potential support differentiation of a total offering which surrounds an undifferentiated core product. The logic of these broad prescriptions is that the buyers of differentiated products will want carefully to evaluate alternative providers before making a choice; whereas the buyer of a product which has low differentiation (including the price dimension) will be less inclined to 'shop around' and more likely to settle quickly for an offer that matches expectations. Of course, if a particular customer does not share the provider's view of the level of differentiation provided, this logic breaks down. 'Perceived product differentiation' is therefore the key and it may point to new patterns of customer segmentation.

Frequency of purchase is the other dominant determinant of behaviour in the buying process – customers who are regularly in the market for a particular product have different requirements from those who are not. The lower the frequency of purchase, the more likely it is that the customer will have information needs in the buying process and will respond favourably to the provider whose marketing initiatives help them navigate the unfamiliar territory to identify exactly the product they require. However, customers with high frequency of purchase will have already assimilated the necessary learning and are more likely to respond to initiatives which minimise their overall transaction costs. In this dimension it is even more apparent that both 'high' and 'low' conditions can exist simultaneously, leading to the requirement for segmentation: the customer who buys books to read every week is attracted by a different proposition from the customer who buys them once a year as Christmas presents.

Once again the constructs can be defended and explained by reference to transaction cost theory: high differentiation situations are characterised by high information and decision costs, low ones by high search and bargaining costs; high frequency purchasing contexts exhibit high bargaining/policing/enforcement costs, whereas low frequency purchasing involves high

search and buyer information costs. The cost categories to be addressed by new initiatives vary as a function of positioning on the two dimensions.

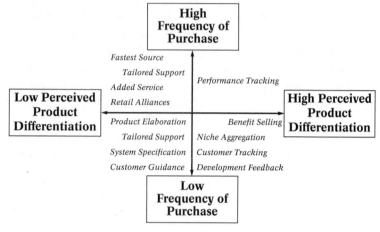

Figure 5 – E-Marketing Opportunity Model

Combining the constructs now gives us the matrix of Figure 5, the E-Marketing Opportunity Model. Displayed in each quadrant are the marketing ideas which most directly respond to the business context implied:

- The *High Frequency of Purchase/Low Perceived Product Differentiation* quadrant contains four ideas. While two are from the 'enhanced customer buying process' category, and two from 'enhanced customer operating process', all four contribute to making it as easy and efficient as possible for the regular customer to purchase items which he/she perceives will be no better/no worse than those available from other providers. The relevant ideas represent the 'reduction of hassle'. Many of the high-profile dot.com companies are operating in this quadrant, using the new technology's ability to extend product reach and service range.

- The *Low Frequency of Purchase/Low Perceived Product Differentiation* quadrant also displays four ideas, all from the 'enhanced customer buying process' category. These are the ideas that support the 'refining of choice' for the inexperienced buyer. The public web sites of most 'old economy' businesses demonstrate the first steps towards these ideas, in the phenomenon often referred to dismissively as brochure-ware. Certainly the implementation is often weak, particularly

in the 'customer guidance' area. But examples such as Dell demonstrate the potential and the importance of these ideas will grow as businesses more deliberately integrate them into an overall 'clicks and mortar' marketing strategy. According to *The Economist*[19], as many as forty per cent of US buyers of new cars may have used the Internet as part of their buying process in 1999 – but only 2.7 per cent of sales were concluded in that way.

- In the *Low Frequency of Purchase/High Perceived Product Differentiation* quadrant, we find four of the five ideas in the 'enhanced sales process' category. Their purpose is to increase the 'richness of targeting' in a context where customers' irregular forays into the market must be captured and the benefits of distinctive products appreciated. At present there is relatively little activity in this quadrant. But as broadband access becomes the norm, the use of video material will greatly increase the potential power of 'development feedback' and 'benefit selling' implementations; and the increasing availability of customer activity information will support new ways of 'customer tracking'.

- The *High Frequency of Purchase/High Perceived Product Differentiation* quadrant contains just one outlier idea – 'performance tracking'. The positioning here reflects the danger of a regular buyer (or user) of a distinctive product beginning to take for granted the benefits being achieved. The quadrant requires a 'reinforcement of choice'. 'Performance tracking' can capture the track record information, which is the basis for repeat purchase – or for a reference sell to a potential new customer.

Superficially it may seem that the model of Figure 5 is narrowly prescriptive, a mechanistic approach to a marketing strategy. Used in that way, the model will not work. It needs to be seen as a structure to facilitate a debate within the business executive team. Their first task is to agree the business context, the quadrant which represents their product/market environment. If it is difficult to get agreement on this, what is the cause? Do team members have contrasting views on the level of perceived differentiation? Are they basing their thinking on different sorts of customers? What information will help to resolve the different opinions, to arrive at a rich and shared picture of the context for e-marketing?

There are a number of reasons why the business quite properly may conclude that it is operating in more than one

quadrant. The business may have customers in both high- and low-purchase-frequency categories, and/or customers who have contrasting views of the level of differentiation in the marketplace. More subtly, a single customer might be operating in more than one quadrant. For example, the typical customer of a popular music retailer might be a high-frequency purchaser of CDs, a medium-frequency purchaser of CDs recorded by their favourite artist, a low-frequency purchaser of a particular recording. Allternatively, corporate buyer of an industrial good may 'purchase' infrequently in the sense that they sign an annual enabling contract; but the weekly or daily call-offs against that contract effectively place them also in the high-purchase-frequency category. In each case the framework correctly suggests that ideas in more than one quadrant will be of relevance.

Having decided in which quadrant or quadrants the business is operating, the team can debate the potential form and effectiveness of each of the relevant ideas and decide on their priorities. The highest-priority candidates will be those where it is clear that new technology can implement the relevant idea in a way that is substantially superior to its present incarnation. It is pointless to offer, as one US manufacturer does, an ability for the consumer to buy chewing gum across the Internet. They may have diagnosed correctly that the typical customer is a high-frequency purchaser of a low-differentiation product; but the 'fastest source' for that customer will surely be the nearest corner store or filling station.

Even in information-orientated industry sectors, the best e-marketing initiative may represent an incremental enhancement within an integrated 'clicks and mortar' marketing approach. Personally I find the best solution to my banking needs includes Internet access to the status of my accounts, ATMs for cash withdrawals, traditional branch facilities for financial planning discussions. e-marketing analysis identifies pragmatic and incremental steps forward, just as e-operations analysis does. The longer-term future – and the imagination – may be captured by consideration of what I refer to as the e-vision opportunity.

The Shape of the E-Vision Opportunity

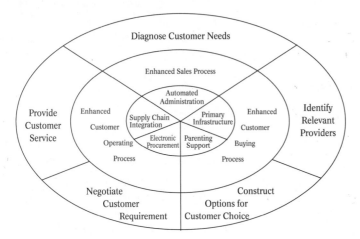

Figure 6 – E-Vision Components

E-vision (as I have called it) represents the ultimate aspiration of the information age, the electronic orchestration of a set of services, which span both the breadth and lifespan of the customer's needs within a chosen and defined market area. Vandermerwe refers to this as the target 'market space'.[20] Examples might be 'the always available service for the vacation traveller', or 'the lifetime information provider for the medical professional'. While there is no single business that has visibly implemented a total e-vision yet, this is the active space for what might be called the second wave of dot.com businesses, following the e-tailers; and an increasing number of 'old economy' corporates can be seen moving towards the opportunity. There is certainly enough progress to illuminate what each component part of the E-Vision Opportunity Map (Figure 6) may contain.

- E-vision starts with the diagnosis of customer needs. This is not a repeat of the 'customer guidance' initiative of e-marketing. First, its objective is to draw out a complete set of requirements for goods and services, rather than point to which parts of a producer's product range are relevant. The second difference is that the e-vision service partner business holds the customer histories, and uses them to focus and prompt the diagnosis. A current example of this second feature is the Easi-Order

initiative of UK grocery chain Safeway.[21] Based on the individual customer profile generated from its five years of on-line data, Safeway downloads a potential grocery list, which includes that customer's familiar items, together with highlights of those current special offers and new products that the profile suggests may be of interest to the customer.

- In the next component, having 'agreed' the total customer requirement, the e-vision service partner (in real time) identifies all relevant providers and assembles the possible options. Chemdex provides this ability within its chosen arena of the bio-sciences.

- The service partner (still in real time) now presents to the customer the most promising options. Again, it is using customer knowledge to determine what 'promising' means. Software developed by Frictionless.com provides an embryo example of how this component may work: it enables all options for purchase to be pre-evaluated against the customer's preferred criteria (size, service provided, ease of use etc.) and weighting factors.

- With confirmation of the customer's preferred option, the service partner now negotiates electronically the closure of the deal, including its price. Priceline and Mercata in their different ways are currently demonstrating the scope for innovation in this component.

- The service partner is not yet finished with this cycle. Knowing the full plan, it stands ready to make alterations if the need arises. If I decide that the vacation it has arranged for me must be cancelled due to family illness, a single alert will lead it to cancel all arrangements and, of course, to submit my claim to the insurance it included in my package. If the building project I have undertaken experiences an unexpected problem, the service partner is at hand to help troubleshoot, and reschedule all future materials and services in line with the revised plan that results.

This vision of the perfect agent, knowing my mind and acting in real time on my changing needs, may sound too good to be true – and presently it is. But the e-vision serves an immediate purpose in guiding the development of target capabilities, and will have an impact on the priorities for the more accessible e-operations and e-marketing strategies. CEO Jac Nasser's vision that Ford will transform into 'the world's leading consumer company for automotive service'[22] may take many years to deliver

and the vision may change in some ways along the road. But it has already influenced the company's acquisition policy and its drive to make the whole workforce more IT-literate.[23] The e-vision opportunity cannot be ignored or its diagnosis deferred to some far-off future date.

Diagnosing the E-Vision Opportunity

In diagnosing the e-vision, the first decision is clearly about the focus and boundaries of the potential vision – the choice and definition of the target 'market space'. For an already established business, the obvious start point is consideration of the existing customer set, and particularly the brand image and values that have been established with them. An e-vision for Ford is clearly going to be something to do with personal transportation, for Lonely Planet it will be about personal travel. Some businesses may have a wider choice: for example, the brand name of the UK's Virgin Group is associated more generally with a certain style and approach to life; it can potentially establish an e-vision in a number of different fields. A second issue at this stage is whether the e-vision is defined around the customer's needs over time (e.g. 'lifetime needs for financial services'); or the needs of a periodic 'event' in the customer's life (e.g. an 'everything for getting married' service, or a 'corporate roadshow' service). The dominant criterion for choice will be credibility of the vision in the eyes of the customer.

Because consideration of and insight into the customer context is the only route into selection and implementation of an e-vision, the appropriate framework for diagnosis is the Customer Service Life Cycle (Figure 7). Originally an IBM-generated planning tool, it represents a simple intuitive structure for orchestrating a discussion about the experience a customer undergoes at each of thirteen stages associated with any purchase. It was first popularised during the 'distributed era' of technology by Ives and Learmonth as the Customer Resource Life Cycle[24] and was used to consider the customer events surrounding the 'resource' (i.e. product) which the business provided. In the diagnosis of e-vision, the focus is on the 'service' (e.g. 'getting married') rather than any one 'resource' (e.g. wedding dress).

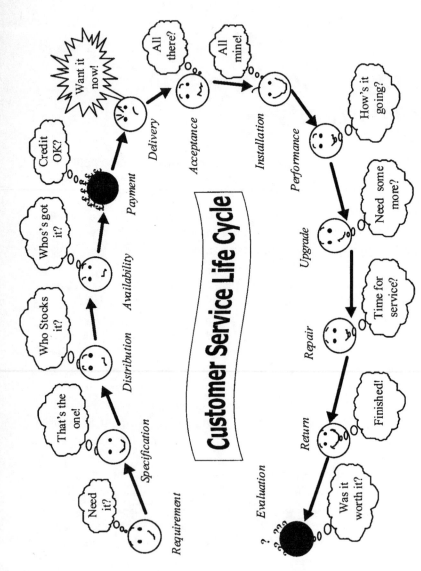

Figure 7 – E-Vision Opportunity Model

I present the framework here (Figure 7) in my own cartoon-style version in order to stress, through the customer face icons, the importance of understanding the customer's psychological state. Unless the customer is seriously unhappy at some point of the cycle in its present form, it is unlikely that the opportunity for an e-vision service exists. However, if there is at least one stage where the existing cycle is significantly defective, that signals the e-vision opportunity and its entry point. Thus Chemdex enters at the 'distribution' and 'availability' stages because up-to-date market information is problematic in the fast-changing world of the bio-sciences; having solved a customer problem, it can extend its service into the later stages of the cycle. By contrast, Kodak with its Photonet initiative identified that 'performance' – the success or otherwise of the customer in sharing their images with friends and relatives – is the stage that could be most improved. For John Deere, with its DeereTrax initiative, the target is the 'repair' stage – helping farmers to ensure that equipment usage is monitored so that timely maintenance avoids costly unscheduled downtime. In each of these cases successful targeting of a first problematic stage brings two vital benefits: the customer information to assist extension of the overall e-vision; and the customer trust, which comes from the benefits achieved by the first initiative.

The DeereTrax initiative – which covers monitoring of all the farmers' equipment, not just that from John Deere – illustrates one of the principal challenges established companies will generally face in moving to an e-vision: the value of the service provided, will probably depend on becoming provider-neutral, unmistakably 'affiliated'[25] with the customer rather than a single provider however large. This is a challenge for the AOL/Time Warner plan. It will also be an issue for Ford if the Nasser vision becomes a true e-vision in which the customer does not buy cars, but is provided each day of the week with whatever personal transportation is most appropriate.

The final headline issue of e-vision strategy is: who needs one? The generic threat to all sectors is that if the opportunity exists and it is seized by another company (new or old), that company will own the customer relationship and will profit accordingly, while traditional providers are reduced to commodity players. That is why it is so important for the executive team to spend time diagnosing what the opportunity might be. More specifically, for the business whose product is 'information intensive' (see e-operations section) the emergence of e-vision

service providers seems inevitable. For a Lonely Planet, the issue is not *whether* their traditional book product is replaced by on-line information from a service provider; the issues are *when* will it happen and *what will it take* to be the successful provider?

★ *Diagnosing the Sustainability of E-Strategy*

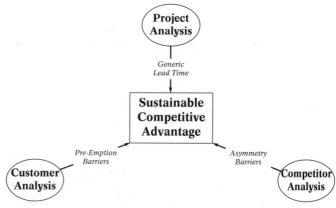

Figure 8 – The Sustainability Model

The fourth diagnosis of e-strategy is to understand the potential for sustaining the competitive advantage gained by e-operations, e-marketing and e-vision initiatives. The model (Figure 8) is based on that first published by Feeny and Ives.[26] It points to three potential sources of sustainability:

- The first and most obvious guide to sustainability – **generic lead time** – comes from analysis of the technological and business change components of the project required to implement the strategic initiative. How long will it take for them to be replicated by any competitor? Because applications of web technology may be rolled out in a matter of weeks – or sourced from a specialist software supplier – there is a tendency to assume that this contribution to sustainability is no longer significant in the modern era. But this may not always be correct – particularly for e-operations initiatives. The upgrading of IT infrastructure in a business which has an information-intensive product may take a couple of years

rather than months, especially if a new generation of integrated ERP systems is required as the backbone of the new infrastructure. And while the supply-chain-orientated initiatives may have short lead-time technological components, they may well involve lengthy negotiations with a large number of supply organisations.

- The second element of the model calls for analysis of the characteristics of competitors, particularly their business models and structures. If a competitor copies the planned initiative, will they have directly cancelled out any competitive advantage? Or are there **asymmetry barriers**, which mean that initiative copying is not enough? Arch rival Compaq could obviously see the success of Dell's direct selling of customer-tailored PCs from the Internet, but they were starting from a different place. They had not designed their products for mass customisation and their supply chain structures, relationships and processes were quite different from those of Dell. Market scope – the breadth of product line and/or geographic coverage – is another important dimension to consider. The scale and scope of Office Depot allows it to negotiate for their customers attractive 'retail alliance' initiatives which are beyond the reach of smaller more locally focused competitors.

- The third analysis considers whether the customer context allows the creation of **pre-emption barriers**, of first-mover advantage. The critical question is whether a *'natural monopoly'* position exists for the product or service being supplied. For example, if as a customer I perceive that an electronic bookstore provides access to all books, then I only need one of them. If I have already enrolled with Amazon, I shall consistently use Amazon: I know my way around their system, they hold information about me, which they use to make my buying of books as efficient as possible. Replication of this mutual learning represents switching costs, which discourage my move to an alternative provider. In these contexts competitive parity is not enough to cancel out competitive advantage. The customer will stay with the first-mover business unless a competitor produces a substantially *better* offering, which compensates for the switching costs involved in moving. More commonly the first mover retains the business unless the customer becomes seriously dissatisfied – the Bezos obsession with customer service demonstrates that Amazon understands this. Pre-emption barriers are

particularly important in e-vision initiatives, since an insightful e-vision will almost always involve the creation of a natural monopoly service, and the capture and use of customer information.

As we entered the web-based era in the mid-1990s the consensus thinking was that sustainable competitive advantage was based almost entirely on the existence of asymmetry barriers, favouring asset-rich companies. When companies like Amazon and E-Bay grew rapidly from effectively zero-asset bases, it was increasingly suggested that assets were liabilities and first-mover advantage was all. In practice, attention to all three sources of sustainability remains important. If Barnes and Noble is to prise away loyal customers from Amazon, its best chance is surely to find an integrated approach, which uses the existence of their physical bookstores (their asymmetry) to offer on-line customers some advantages that Amazon cannot provide. What has changed in sustainability analysis is that some significant levers have become much more available.

Asymmetry barriers can be increased by the protection of the intellectual property which is often created in e-strategy initiatives; and by the negotiation of exclusivity with the partner organisations (database owners, niche product providers) whose products are integral to the proposition being offered. Preemption barriers can be raised by initiatives that orchestrate customers into a community, which adds value through mutual exchange – in 1990, Feeny and Ives could find few examples of this idea, but authors such as Armstrong and Hagel[27] argue that the opportunity is widespread in the web-based era. Attention to sources of sustainability – and a proactive approach to increasing them – remains a critical part of e-strategy development.

Conclusions

Through Figures 2, 4 and 6 I have illustrated the very wide range of opportunities which the new technology may enable. In many business situations it will be possible to identify that all of these opportunities are technically feasible and represent potential investments. The purpose of the diagnostic frameworks – Figures 3, 5 and 7 – is to help clarify which investments are likely to bring

benefits as well as incur costs: a business whose product is already distinctive and well accepted by customers does not need to invest in 'added services'; an 'electronic procurement' initiative is not a strategic priority for a software house. The diagnostic frameworks are not intended to be tightly prescriptive, but they serve to direct the focus of the strategist's attention.

For 'old economy' companies, components of e-operations and e-marketing are likely to represent immediate opportunities with real economic benefits. The e-vision opportunity will usually be much longer-term in its realisation, but will signal the strategic intent[28] (see also Introduction) which influences the evolution of e-operations and e-marketing strategy. Equally, it is likely that experience gained in these latter two dimensions will add insight to the content of the vision – the three are inevitably interrelated within an overall approach to e-strategy.

Earlier I used the analogy of the jigsaw to introduce the context for e-strategy development. An alternative might be the idea of a primeval jungle. Few believe that collectively we have yet penetrated more than a few per cent of the territory before us. In these circumstances, as my colleague Robert Davies is fond of saying, the right metaphor for strategy may not be a map, but a compass. There is no reliable map at a level that enables the strategist to identify and select the precise route to the hoped-for destination. But decisions must be made, directions must be chosen, priorities assigned – and then revised in the light of experience. When the strategic tool is a compass, the business needs to pinpoint its current position and set out to stay as close as the new territory will allow to a bearing that leads towards the other side of the jungle. The frameworks I have described are intended to support and facilitate those high-level decisions on strategic direction – the understanding of what opportunities are available and how choices between them may vary, depending on the starting point of the business. The strategist may then find at least some detailed support from those who have pioneered and described some of the territory that will be encountered along the way.

NOTES

1 Porter, M. C., *Competitive Strategy*, Free Press, New York, 1980.
2 See, for example, Hamel G. and Sampler, J., 'The E-Corporation', *Fortune*, 7 December 1998; also Downes, L. and Mui, C., *Unleashing the Killer App*, Harvard Business School Press, Boston, 1998.

3 Evans, P. and Wurster, T. S., 'Getting Real about Virtual Commerce', *Harvard Business Review*, November–December 1999.

4 *The Economist*, 'Survey of Business and the Internet', 26 June 1999.

5 The Figure is taken from Ross, J. and Feeny, D., 'The Evolving Role of the CIO', in Zmud, R. (ed.), *Framing the Domains of IT Management*, Pinnaflex Educational Resources, Cincinnati, 2000.

6 Porter, M. E. and Millar, V. E., 'How Information Gives You Competitive Advantage', *Harvard Business Review*, July–August 1985.

7 Melymuka, K., 'Ford's Driving Force', *Computerworld*, 30 August 1999.

8 Nolan, R. L. and Porter, K., 'Cisco Systems Inc', HBS Case Library, 3–98–127, Harvard Business School, Boston, 2000.

9 Diamant-Burger, A.-M. and Ovans, A., 'E-Procurement at Schlumberger', *Harvard Business Review*, May–June 2000.

10 Campbell, A., Goold, M. and Alexander, M., 'Corporate Strategy: The Quest for Parenting Advantage', *Harvard Business Review*, March–April 1995.

11 Stewart, T.A., 'Telling Tales at BP Amoco', *Fortune*, 7 June 1999.

12 The figure is quoted in the *Financial Times*, 26–7 February 2000. See also Chapter 10 on this subject.

13 Feeny, D., Plant, R. and Mughal, H., 'Land Rover Vehicles: the CB40 Project', European Case Clearing House, Case Study 600–001–1, ECCH, Cranfield, 2000.

14 Cash, J. I. and Ostrofsky, K., 'Mrs Fields Cookies', HBS Case Library, 1–89–056, Harvard Business School, Boston, 1989.

15 Porter, M.E. and Millar, V. E., op. cit.

16 The configuration/co-ordination matrix. This appears in Porter, M. E., 'Competition in Global Industries: a Conceptual Framework', in Porter, M. E. (ed.), *Competitive Strategy in Global Industries*, Harvard Business School Press, Boston, 1986.

17 Dolan, K. A., 'Cyber-cement', *Forbes*, 15 June 1998.

18 Downes, L. and Mui, C., op. cit.

19 *The Economist*, 'Survey of E-Commerce', 26 February 2000.

20 Vandermerwe, S., *Customer Capitalism*, Nicholas Brearley Publishing, London, 1999.

21 Anthes, G. H., 'Safeway Gives Away the PDA, Cements Customer Loyalty', *Computerworld*, 20 March 2000.

22 Melymuka, K., op. cit.

23 Copeland, L., 'Ford Drives Employees to the Web to Help Connect with On-line Customers', *Computerworld*, 3 February 2000.

24 Ives, B. and Learmonth, G. P., 'The Information System as a Competitive Weapon', Communications of the ACM, 27, 12, December 1984. See also Ives, B., Rane, P. R. and Sainani, S. S.,'The Customer Service Life Cycle', URL: http://isds.bus.lsu.edu/cvoc/projects/cslc, 1999, who update the framework as the Customer Service Life Cycle, while Vandermerwe , op. cit. above, further enriches it under the label Customer Activity Cycle.

25 Evans, P. and Wurster, T. S., op. cit..

26 Feeny, D. and Ives, B., 'In Search of Sustainability', *Journal of Management Information Systems*, 7, 1, Summer 1990.

27 Armstrong, A. and Hagel, J., 'The Real Value of On-Line Communities', *Harvard Business Review*, May–June 1996.

28 Hamel, G. and Prahalad, C. K., 'Strategic Intent', *Harvard Business Review*, May–June 1989.

E-Branding Or Re-Branding?

Kunal Basu

D ifferent futures have been predicted for brands in the world of e-business. According to some, conventional branding, as we know it, needs to be thoroughly over-hauled if brands are to survive the inevitable commoditisation ushered in by the WorldWideWeb. In its most extreme form, advocates of this view foresee the Net becoming the ultimate brand – the vehicle as well as the guarantor of customer needs. According to others, brands will become even stronger as customers, faced with the bewildering market of the web, retreat to the security of names they know. These two opposing perspectives are agreed on one point – that e-business has the capacity to revolutionise marketplace transactions and usher in a breakthrough in business thinking. Drawing frequent parallels with the Industrial Revolution, they share assumptions about change which constitute the 'Transformation View', that is to say they anticipate radical shifts in fundamental business conditions – supply, demand, value creation and, most particularly, the thinking and behaviour of customers. Either way, on the 'transformation view', branding must be reinvented not simply adjusted; it's an open game calling for creativity and risk, rather than the cold calculation of business as usual.

By contrast, some commentators have taken a 'tools view'. They see e-technologies as offering a plethora of tools to enhance

efficiencies and improve the effectiveness of the marketer–customer relationship. Guiding images are those of a 'new medium' more powerful in communicating than conventional media; or that of a 'data mine' capable of amassing intellectual capital hitherto unavailable; or that of a 'hot channel' delivering faster and better than even direct mail. In the 'tools view' of e-business, branding requires a healthy dose of integration – between the old and the new – capitalising on synergies and using the Net as support for a firm's marketing plans.

Of course, examples abound for both. Amazon and Dell, credited with anticipating latent customer needs and creating innovative brands (with industry-wide ripple effects), are examples of the 'transformation view'. American Airlines and travel firms like Travelocity and, in the UK, Travelodge, in successfully replacing conventional brand communication tools such as printed brochures with interactive web sites, are examples of the 'tools view'.

Experience suggests that neither view is 'right'. Just as the marketplace exhibits great variety, so the impact of e-business is likely to be variable. The key for a manager is to be able to act appropriately in whatever conditions arise. It is critical to know of opportunities and threats in advance. It is necessary to know when to undertake transformation and when to use the tools of e-business to enhance the brand. If the firm's branding strategy requires a total overhaul, tinkering with web sites won't help. Likewise, launching a new brand where an Internet channel offers a consistent reinforcement of the existing brand is an unnecessary overreaction. This chapter identifies the potential effects of e-business on branding and defines the conditions under which managers should take action to develop the effects they desire.

In the wider landscape of marketing as a whole, branding is an excellent lens through which to view and predict the impact of e-business. Why? Because it is critically located at the intersection of marketing strategy, and implementation. On the one hand it conveys the long-term thrust – taking into account a firm's goals in a market (segmentation and targeting) and its intended differentiation from competitors (positioning). Radical shifts, as implied in the 'transformation view', would then most certainly warrant re-examination of a firm's branding. On the other hand a firm's branding strategy is intimately connected to a number of decisions that have to do with communication, delivery and research – domains in which e-business impacts have also been

predicted (i.e. the 'tools view'). Thus, regardless of the type of impact, branding appears located at a convenient level, crystallising marketing thought and action, capable of quickly alerting a manager to opportunities or threats posed by e-business.

The purpose of distinguishing the 'transformation view' from the 'tools view' is to provide a starting point for mapping e-business impacts, and prioritising managerial action. Simply put, the 'transformation view' is associated with re-branding, viz. the creation of new brands or radical revision of an existing brand, while the 'tools view' is associated with e-branding, viz. the adoption of e-technologies to supplement or develop an established brand. It is important to recognise that this distinction is a simplification. The two are not mutually exclusive. For example, a profound change in the business model could usher in the adoption of e-tools in the form of new ways of communicating (e.g. e-mails, WorldWideWeb), delivery (e.g. direct sales), or research (e.g. neural networks). Equally, systematic and concerted changes in tools could ultimately bring about a radical transformation in ways the firm addresses its customers.

The chapter starts with an overview of branding, followed by a description of first- and second-order impacts that could result from e-business practices. Finally, the 'Four Cs Model' is defined to assist managers to identify four conditions on which to base appropriate branding responses: should we be **E-Branding** or **Re-Branding**?

Branding: A Framework

As a result of extensive research we know a great deal about the essentials of branding. By selectively distilling this knowledge, we can see brands as resting on two pillars: Expectation and Experience (Figure 1). Expectation represents the psychological contract that binds a customer to an offering. It could be one that is deeply held, supported by information (s)he considers valid, such as the political commitment that sees a consumer prefer one established newspaper's Internet channel to that of another; or it could be a fleeting wish aroused at a particular moment, for example, the impulse that has seen many Net surfers buy products just to try out a new site. Either way, our expectations towards a brand are influenced by communications. These,

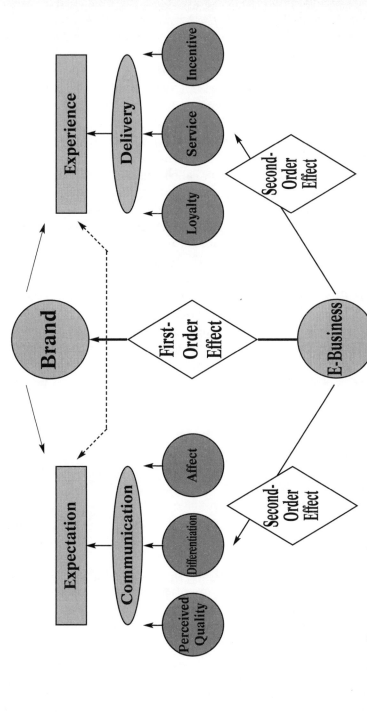

Figure 1 – Branding: A Framework

either formal and marketer-initiated (such as media advertising, or a salesperson's pitch), or informal (word-of-mouth), help to create a perception of quality with regard to the brand, a sense of similarity/dissimilarity with other brands and an emotional response – either positive or negative. If carefully designed, expectations help to locate a brand strategically, that is, to specify who should expect what from it, and to what extent the benefits offered by the brand are likely to be different or similar to other brands. Amazon.com has created expectations that in markets such as books and CDs the customer needs no other supplier (what Feeny in Chapter 2 has called a natural monopoly).

Experience is the other pillar that locates a brand viscerally – in a customer's senses. The nature of delivery is critical in creating such sensations – of satisfaction or dissatisfaction with the brand. Other equally critical influences are the customer's loyalty status with respect to the brand, that is her/his previous encounters with it, the various elements of service provided (e.g. speed, reliability) and the incentives that are offered in order to precipitate the purchase (e.g. price discounts).

Expectation and experience, then, together hold a brand in its strategic space. Consistent, they reinforce the brand's value for a customer. Inconsistent, confusion and dissatisfaction result. The two-pillars model affords insights to managers in examining both the precise (or desired) location of a brand, as well as the systems and processes in place that support aspects of communication and delivery. It provides a diagnostic tool and also suggests alternative paths for change. Crucially, it allows a systematic mapping of the impact of any emerging trend – such as e-business – on branding.

E-business – in terms of emerging technologies and associated marketplace expectations – could impact on a firm's branding in one of two ways:

- First-order effects that demand rethinking of a brand's strategic location in terms of segmentation, targeting and positioning.
- Second-order effects on expectation and experience.

Responses to the first *I* term 're-branding' and to the second 'e-branding'. As the names imply, re-branding involves rethinking the value proposition offered by a firm to existing or even new segments of customers and ways of differentiating the brand from competing alternatives. It follows recognition of substantial

changes (or impending changes) in customer perceptions, preferences and behaviours, involving a range of strategic decisions such as portfolio management and brand extension. Re-branding fits well with the 'transformation view', and although expectations and experiences may need to be realigned, given the new branding strategy, managerial priority must centre around the choice of long-term and appropriate brand location, rather than adaptations within elements of the two existing pillars. Lufthansa has successfully re-launched its travel reservation service brand – emphasising 'access' and 'choice' – recognising emerging needs among customers with regard to direct booking and purchase (bypassing travel agents) and flexibility in choice across several different airlines (see also Chapter 1).

E-branding, on the other hand, presumes no strategic shift in branding strategy, but appropriate changes in managing expectation and experience. These leverage new ways of communicating with customers, delivering value and researching the marketplace that are afforded by emerging e-technologies. E-branding goes well with the 'tools view', calling essentially for a careful evaluation of all systems and processes, rendering them more efficient and effective from a customer's viewpoint. Thus, the strategic location of the brand remains the same as before, with facilitation by e-business. Managing the mix of e-channels with conventional channels, combining e-mails with media advertising and incorporating web-based measures of promotional effect with traditional redemption rates fall within e-branding. There is recognition that changes will occur, but that these will not be far-reaching enough to alter the basic rules of the game, i.e. the fundamental marketer–customer contract and ways of competing. Thus, in the UK, ICI Paints has strengthened the 'user-friendly' aspects of its brands by allowing customers to select shades over the web without requiring store visits.

Problems arise when first- and second-order effects are confounded: when re-branding is chosen in place of e-branding and vice versa. Since the price for ignoring e-business impacts on branding is rightly perceived to be high within some firms, re-branding exercises take up valuable time, when attention could deservedly be focused upon adopting new channels for communicating with customers. Alternatively, the 'get a web site fast' mindset tends to rule when firms are in denial regarding the potential impact of e-business, refusing to rethink the whole game even under a radically changed scenario. The late, and

often inadequate, forays made by established UK retail banks into the on-line-banking sector are telling examples.

In the next section we discuss five first-order effects, that is, five ways in which e-business can impact directly on branding. We then proceed to identify six second-order effects, that is, ways by which e-business can influence expectations and experience.

First-Order Effects on Branding

The five sources of first-order effects on branding are:

- industry convergence;
- transformation in the value chain;
- expansion in geographical scope;
- expectation of change and obsolescence;
- change in marketer–customer power.

INDUSTRY CONVERGENCE

Paradoxically, while the web does appear to lower entry barriers in many industries, e-business can also be a driver for convergence within certain industries, leading to higher rather than lower concentration. Powerful trends towards convergence have emerged in those industries such as financial services, media and software with potential for (a) high economies of scale, (b) efficiency gains from restructuring information technologies and (c) rise in profitability from elimination of redundancies in processes and tasks (Figure 2). The climate of deregulation is further likely to help such a fundamental shift.

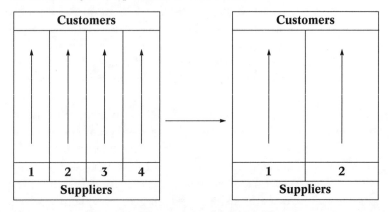

Figure 2 – First-Order Effects: Industry Convergence

The implications for branding are profound. Global alliances among major airlines, such as the Star Alliance and One World, are instructive in relation to the problems for branding. While there are obvious efficiency gains in creating a centralised platform for on-line reservations, ticketing and schedules, with equally strong effectiveness gains in service delivery (e.g. baggage handling), if the alliance were to become the principal brand, its individual members would be obliged to rethink their own positioning. What would the customer value proposition be for such an alliance brand? An amalgam of constituent brands united under an umbrella? How would contradictions within the portfolio be resolved to present a cohesive image to customers? Would certain segments need to be 'vacated' or 'upgraded' in terms of service expectation and delivery? How would one alliance brand differentiate itself from another, as both strive to create technology platforms capable of providing maximum support for long-term distinction?

Lufthansa, a member of the Star Alliance, faces just such issues. The re-branding issues brought forth by e-business involve (1) locating long-term brand values for itself within the alliance brand, given rapidly evolving customer preferences, and (2) managing expectations of domestic customers on domestic routes as well as international ones that share (or are soon likely to share) similar e-infrastructure but somewhat different experiences as a result of different carriers.

TRANSFORMATION IN THE VALUE CHAIN

A key impact of e-technologies has been the increased scrutiny of business processes within a firm, as well as in relation to its links with suppliers and market intermediaries. As advances in information processing transform key functions, entire value chains are being redefined. This has taken one of two forms: industries are vying to extract value from each other on grounds of superior competencies (e.g. vendor-managed inventory), or they are shedding tasks to become more focused and specialised. In the latter case network relationships are replacing vertical integration, a change most evident in the consumer electronics and computer hardware industries. Michael Dell, a premier exponent of this approach, describes this as 'virtual integration'[1] (see also Chapter 10).

If the customer's value proposition remains unaltered, re-structuring value chains with the objective of efficiency or profitability may have few implications in terms of branding.

However, in instances where transforming business processes leads to significant dispacements – in terms of whom the customer sees as providing critical values – strategic location of a brand may have to be redefined (Figure 3). Retail banks with credit card operations (such as Citibank in the US) are increasingly taking over the business of managing retail risk (i.e. with respect to defective or damaged goods purchased with the credit card). This, of course, calls for re-branding, both on the part of the bank in question, as well as retailers, with opportunities for creative collaborations.

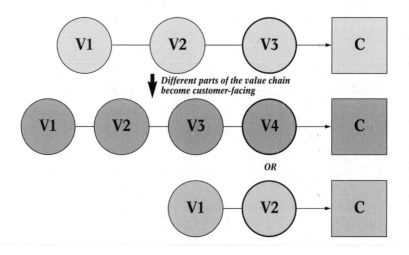

Figure 3 – First-Order Effects: Transformation in the Value Chain

EXPANSION IN GEOGRAPHIC SCOPE

Most commentators agree that the Internet will dramatically expand the geographic scope of a firm's business. Direct communications via the web and direct sales channels will attract hitherto unserved customer segments. For both multinationals, as well as domestic or regional firms, such a potential poses a critical question: should brands be redefined to suit preferences of geographically (and culturally) diverse customer segments? If so, how would one go about the task? Figure 4 shows four potential global branding strategies a firm could adopt.

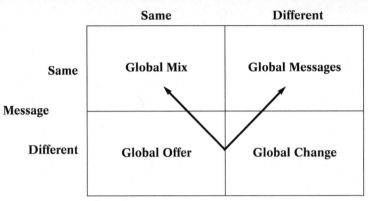

Figure 4 – First-Order Effects: Expansion In Geographic Scope

The Global Change strategy signifies maximum flexibility – both in terms of the message communicating desired expectations to customers, as well as specifics of the product/service. Unilever's diversity in both product formulation and advertising across countries is a good example. Its direct opposite is the global mix, which favours a singular brand location – such as Coca-Cola's – in terms of expectation and experience. There are two intermediate positions: global message and global offer. The global message strategy standardises on message (a generalised set of expectations regarding core brand benefits), while allowing for adaptations in the offer to suit diverse tastes. McDonald's, for example, allows the menu to vary across countries, while holding constant its image of 'American-style fast food'. Finally, the global-offer strategy standardises the offer, but allows messages to be crafted differently. So, car companies such as Volvo position the same vehicle differently in different countries – a 'dependable family sedan' in Sweden becomes a 'luxury item' in Thailand.

Expansion in geographic scope, then, raises several key issues in brand management. Strategically, expansion would mean either rethinking an existing brand's central value proposition in order to adapt and embrace new customers, or searching globally for segments that match current ones, leaving the brand's strategic location unchanged. It is important to note that adopting a specific position within the matrix (Figure 4) also implies ensuring adequate support from the two pillars – Expectation and Experience. If the decision is to shift from a global change to a global message strategy, then expectations of different segments

located around the world would need to be managed sensitively to converge on a common set of brand values.

Does e-business, in addition to opening up the choice of global-branding strategies, prompt firms to adopt specific ones? Given the ubiquitous nature of the WorldWideWeb, it is becoming increasingly problematic to discriminate in terms of information (about a product/service). Information has truly become global, even when physical products and service experiences are not. Thus, a prospective customer of Volkswagen in Germany has access to the same information as someone in the UK. The resultant brand image is one that is global. Unless specific features need to be different across countries (for regulatory purposes), customers are likely to form expectations based on such a global image. Thus, the global-mix strategy may become the preferred alternative, or where non-core brand features are allowed to vary, the global message. The former may be more relevant for geographically mobile customers who desire similar brand benefits at all parts of the globe. Where brands create an aspirational value (e.g. catalogues for designer clothing) but consumption is largely local, the global-message strategy may be more suited, as it allows nuances in expectation and experience to emerge without compromising the brand's overall strategic location.

EXPECTATION OF CHANGE AND OBSOLESCENCE

Revolutionary changes in communication and computer-based technologies have led to an enhanced expectation among customers for similar changes across a broad range of product/service sectors. Whether realistic or not, they imply a significant shift in customer behaviour – in adoption of innovation, loyalty, price sensitivity, and willingness to abandon tried and tested products for those seen as novel and at the 'cutting edge' of technology. There is even a degree of impatience with product/service markets that are seen as slow to change compared with some idealised standard. Firms manufacturing cameras, for example, are increasingly faced with consumer discontent with what is viewed as slow product development (particularly in coming up with better interfaces with other audio-visual devices such as PCs) compared with software, which has an extremely high rate of planned obsolescence.

In terms of life cycles, it is likely that the expectation of rapid obsolescence will lead to quicker transit through brand life cycles (Figure 5). Customers may become more open to trials,

creating a reasonably active introduction phase, leading firms to invest in expansion plans. Rapid communications regarding successful brands (via Internet chat rooms and user-initiated brand communities) may create the momentum for rapid growth. But equally, customers may be far more reluctant than before in remaining brand loyal once maturity sets in. Given the ease of shopping for lower prices over the Net, migration from a previously preferred brand could start easily and precipitate a quick decline.

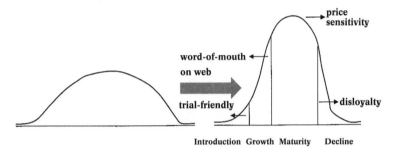

Figure 5 – First-Order Effects: Expectation of Change and Obsolescence

Brands, then, may have a shorter lifespan than before. Strategically, converting customers from a rapidly maturing brand to one that is growing quickly must feature as a critical activity. Cascades of brands aimed at successively occupying a strategic location may then be necessary – a notion that goes well beyond conventional portfolio planning. The proximity of a firm's own brands in time (i.e. the quick sequence of brand introductions) will obviously also run the risk of unintended cannibalisation. We see this with the Waterstone Internet bookshop site, which offers some books more cheaply than its 'bricks and mortar' shops but will deliver them to a bookshop at no delivery charge. The bookshop is obliged to bear some of the order fulfilment cost, while being undercut on price by its Internet cousin.

CHANGE IN MARKETER–CUSTOMER POWER

Perhaps the most far-reaching impact of e-business on branding will derive from a renegotiation of power between marketers and customers, a point made in earlier chapters. Traditionally, the key task of uniting diversely located customers and presenting them with an offer was left to the marketer. It was achieved through

research that allowed marketers to identify which customers to bunch together and which to separate (i.e. segmentation), and through a marketer-led design process that effectively proposed a single product/service as the approximation of benefits desired by many. Branding under such a context was (and still *is*, largely) comprised of 'matching' and 'persuasion' tasks on the part of the marketer.

E-business, however, particularly the propensity of customers to seek out each other's benefit requirements and come up with their own segmentation, is changing the traditional power axis radically (see Figure 6). Now marketers are often asked to bid for customers' attention (Go.To.com allows marketers to bid for 'first show' on customers' search results), as well as on available brand features and price.

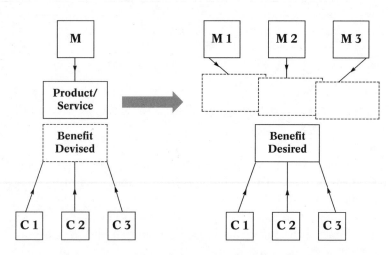

Figure 6 – First-Order Effects: Change in Marketer – Customer Power

As marketers jostle to please empowered customers, brands will need to be seriously rethought. On the one hand it might mean working with maximum flexibility, that is, with a portfolio of brands that could be marshalled depending upon customers' preferences at any point. Of course, boundaries between a firm's brands would need to be sufficiently fuzzy to allow movement in terms of value adjustments. On the other hand, brand differentiation may have to stem more from core competencies and organisational excellence than 'hard and fast' brand values that are designed to last, rather than change.

In exploring first-order effects on branding, we have seen that e-business poses some potentially unprecedented challenges.

MOVING TO
·E-BUSINESS·
MOVING TO

The up side for managers is that first-order effects afford the opportunity of creative first moves. It is important to recognise, though, that e-business will not change whole industries. The firms that win will be those that are able to seize opportunities and use branding not as a tool of continuity but one of transformation.

Before we turn to conditions that might alert a manager to impending first-order effects, it is useful to map at least six critical second-order effects of e-business, three of which are on expectation and three more on experience. They are:

- faster transit through the hierarchy of effects;
- cued access to evoked sets;
- enhanced and effective feedback;
- restructured intermediation;
- incentivised action;
- redefined value package.

Second-Order Effects on Branding

FASTER TRANSIT THROUGH HIERARCHY OF EFFECTS

The classic hierarchy-of-effects (HOE) model (Figure 7) post-ulates six stages that a customer is likely to experience in succession before purchasing a brand. That is, any brand-related communication must be able to take customers through message exposure to attention to comprehension to liking the brand, followed by strong preference towards it and ultimately to purchase. Movement from one stage to the next is not assured, but depends upon crafting of the 'right' message and selection of the 'right' medium. Research, for example, shows that the print media (e.g. brochures, magazine ads) are better than audio-visual media (e.g. TV ads) in fostering comprehension about a brand's benefits (especially if these are complex in nature). Audio-visuals are in turn superior in situations where usage needs to be demonstrated to create liking or preference for the brand.[2]

I. Faster Transit Through the Hierarchy of Effects

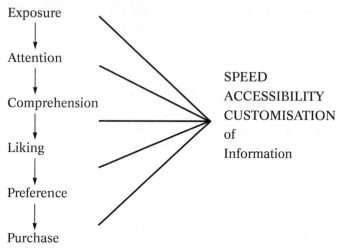

Figure 7– Second-Order Effects on Communication (A)

The capacity of the Internet to tailor information to customers (both in form and content) and appeal to various stages of the HOE is likely to enhance the speed of transit. Unsuccessful brands will fail faster – think of Boo.com in Europe in mid-2000 – just as success will manifest itself more quickly – as with the growth of on-line share trading companies such as Charles Schwab (see Introduction). Overall, the greater speed, accessibility and customisation will allow brands greater flexibility in adopting new messages or even correcting old ones – bringing 'achieved' positioning closer than ever to 'desired' positioning.

CUED ACCESS TO EVOKED SETS

Traditionally, marketing theorists have likened customers' brand choices to a gradual reduction in set size (Figure 8). Customers are generally believed to be equipped with a 'knowledge set', that is, a number of brands belonging in a given product category that they can recall from memory. In choosing a brand, the knowledge set is successively reduced to a consideration set (i.e. brands viewed as acceptable, following some broad criteria), then to a choice set (based potentially on prior experience) and finally to an evoked set – a small number of brands that are called to mind at the precise time of choice.

Branding activity – particularly in communications and point-of-sales display – is centred around provision of appropriate cues

to the customer that would lead to the firm's brand being included within the evoked set. The above view of choice also assumes a 'from the general to the specific' process, that is, the customer first thinks about consuming in a product category, then narrows down her/his choice to a particular brand (e.g. I need fast food . . . I need a McDonald's burger').

The capacity of the Internet to cue brands by anticipating a customer's likely preferences across a broad range of product categories is ushering in new ways of positioning. Thus, a web site for a furniture brand may carry links to a brand of home electronics goods, or an on-line restaurant may display links to a neighbouring theatre. In branding terms it implies that the 'general to the specific' may not be necessary. So rather than establishing brand X by comparing it with its rival brand Y (i.e. comparative positioning), or claiming it to be the 'best of all brands' (i.e. category-based positioning), it can be positioned through direct comparison with another brand from a different product category altogether (complementary positioning) – one which fosters similar consumption values.

II. Cued Access to Evoked Sets

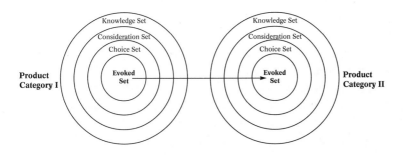

Figure 8 – Second-Order Effects on Communication (B)

ENHANCED AND EFFECTIVE FEEDBACK

A substantial body of opinion has already emerged in support of the view that e-technologies are changing the speed and effectiveness of customer feedback. In the case of on-line purchasing this is more than opinion, it is a firm reality. Today a marketer can assess directly the effectiveness of communication at the point at which the communication seeks to influence a purchaser on the web (Figure 9). This contrasts with the past, when the same

marketer had to go through a time-lagged process, researching purchase behaviour or purchase intent.

In addition, e-technologies often provide means for a customer to recall her/his previous purchase behaviour. This reinforces loyalty and, in a sense, may be more powerful than marketer-initiated approaches, as customers tend to draw greater validation through their own actions vis-à-vis a brand.

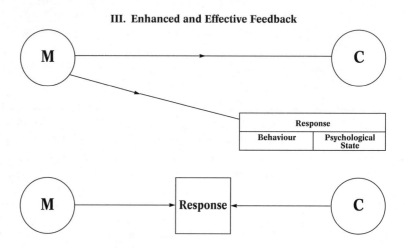

Figure 9 – Second-Order Effects on Communication (C)

From a branding perspective, two distinct ways of enhancing communication effectiveness are made possible: (1) the message–behaviour–feedback loop allows faster adjustments in brand communications to achieve desired positioning; and (2) customer profiles generated over successive contacts allow segments (especially as they pertain to loyalty) to emerge more clearly than through traditional survey-based market research.

RESTRUCTURED INTERMEDIATION

The potential for reaching customers directly has introduced new business concepts such as disintermediation and reintermediation. Applications of the Internet could radically transform the basic value-added/margin equation in sales channels, leading to transformations in value chains discussed earlier. What will such changes do to branding?

It is important to recognise that unless a marketer already sells directly to her/his customers, the brand image is a composite of images drawn from and projected by each member of

the channel. The brand a customer buys in reality embodies collective branding with the dominant member's (typically the primary manufacturer/service provider's) vision rising above others. Thus, issues surrounding brand image/retail image congruence/incongruence have long concerned marketers. Needless to say, there is a lot that can go awry in the delivery process, driving a wedge between expectation and experience.

Restructuring of intermediation can impact branding by reallocating critical elements of delivery among the new channel partners. If the local distributor for a multinational firm is removed in a bid to service customers directly via the web, the brand now must be able to subsume elements of local value, such as trust and instant redress. We see car manufacturers struggling with this dilemma as they seek to sell new vehicles direct without losing the sales and service support value offered by locally known and respected dealers.

I. Restructuring Intermediation

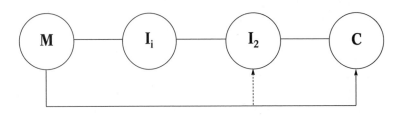

Figure 10 – Second-Order Effects on Delivery (A)

INCENTIVISED ACTION
Traditional branding practices have tended to favour Thinking and Feeling (Cognition and Affect) elements over Doing (Action) (Figure 11). This accounts for a disproportionate interest in pre-purchase customer decision processes, and explains marketers' emphasis on persuasion attempts that aim to change or reinforce how customers think and feel about a brand. In part, the above is due to the assumption that customers have to expend minimum effort to attend to a message in their homes or offices, but require extra motivation to go through with a purchase, often involving store visits or cumbersome ordering procedures. Thinking and feeling 'right' is therefore seen as a prerequisite for that motivation to take hold.

Of course, facilitation in transactions ushered in by e-business is likely to shift the locus to doing or action. In branding terms, superior transaction values ('This one's really easy to buy and install') may then have to feature more significantly within the core benefit package offered by the brand.

II. Incentivising Action

Thinking — Cognition ← Classical Branding

Feeling — Affect ← E-Branding

Doing — Action

Figure 11 – Second-Order Effects on Delivery (B)

REDEFINED VALUE PACKAGE

In an age of 'smart products', that is, products connected to software-managed networks, distinctions between products and services offered by a firm are likely to become blurred. It may no longer be feasible to hold separate-value offers and delivery systems as more and more customers begin to purchase total-value packages. For successful firms, stronger interconnections between products and services offered is likely to strengthen the overall brand proposition, allowing flexibility in replacing weak-performing/obsolete products, or by taking advantage of strong products and relating them to new ones through an overall service interface. Thus, if customers begin to view home electronics as an overall service rather than a collection of discrete products, then a company like Sony may be able to develop a brand proposition that is directed at total satisfaction to the end user while retaining for itself the flexibility of additions and substitutions.

E-business will impact on a firm's branding practices in ways described above – i.e. through first- and/or second-order effects. Managers, then, need to plan adequate responses, either through radical transformation – re-branding – or by judiciously incorporating e-technologies to their existing branding plans. But,

given the emerging nature of the phenomenon, how should a manager go about predicting which set of effects is more likely and therefore which response more appropriate?

III. Redefining Value Package

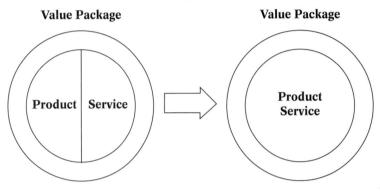

Figure 12 – Second-Order Effects on Delivery (C)

The '4 Cs Model'

Figure 13 presents the '4 Cs Model', which compares First- and Second-Order Effects and associated branding responses on the dimensions of Choice, Change, Complexity and Community.

	FIRST-ORDER EFFECT **Re-Branding** *Change Business Model*	SECOND-ORDER EFFECT **E-Branding** *Need Strategic Adaptation*
Choice	Customers desire substantial increase or decrease in brands to choose from.	Customers favour the available range of brands.
Change	Customers have high expectation of change in functionality/benefits deliverable by brands.	Customers expect their requirements and brand functionalities to evolve over time.
Complexity	Customers desire a step reduction in usage/transactional complexity.	Customers desire existing systems to work better.
Community	Customers desire sharing brand experiences and expectations among one another.	Customers prefer to keep their brand experience private.

Figure 13 – Comparing First- and Second-Order Effects

Certain industries are characterised by a 'crisis of **Choice**'. That is, customers perceive that there are either too many brands

or too few to choose from. Industries in the former state include auto insurance services, while an example of the latter state is shops selling speciality and rare books in a given region. E-business, under the latter, has a tremendous potential for unleashing greater choice by dropping entry barriers and allowing new firms to satisfy hitherto unfulfilled needs. Thus it is possible, now, to employ search engines such as the Frugalfinder to scan used bookshops in three continents and fill rare book orders within a very short time. In the former, where customers are overwhelmed by many similar brands with only minor variations, reintermediation might lead to emergence of aggregators who would act as 'decision surrogates' or 'smart shoppers' on behalf of customers. Already, specialised real estate services are aiming to narrow down residential alternatives to a select few options matching a customer's requirements from lists scoured from all agencies operating within a region. A similar-value proposition is the basis of many of the emerging e-procurement exchanges.

When customers across segments have high expectation of **Change** in product functionality, marketers may be prompted to embark on radical branding transformations in place of 'normal' incremental changes. Nowhere is this more pronounced than in the software industry. High expectation for change, of course, introduces a new dimension in branding: investing the brand with dynamism and a willingness to be innovative. Specifications become less important than core values that embody change and the challenge to be at the cutting-edge. It also implies a different product development regime, one that plans for obsolescence just as effectively as market entry. Hewlett-Packard and 3M have both established such brand positioning. In the e-world, Amazon.com has included such values as part of its brand.

A third aspect that points towards potential first-order effects is **Complexity**. When customers' experience of an industry is characterised by ungainly procedures, delays, or uncertainties, there is an inbuilt motive to reduce complexity. This could take several forms: customers may be frustrated by inherent difficulty in product use, or confused by the lack of relevant information. Complexity could result from uncertain effects of consumption, or ambiguity with respect to a brand's price/quality offer. Transactional delays as a result of system inefficiencies or shortages could also add a tier of complexity. Obviously, branding under these conditions needs to seriously address expectation and experience, redesigning the pillars to locate the brand in a strategic space that allows customers to appreciate its values

more fully. It is noteworthy that a significant number of re-branding exercises have resulted from perceived complexity-related problems. In many business-to-business transactions, routine purchase of components is now being moved over to the Net, to avoid delays in working with purchasing departments and lengthy sales protocols. Equally, in the consumer durable/non-durable and services domains, there is a growing push towards Net-based transactions, where underlying information systems are seen as key in delivering the value chain (e.g. travel reservations, investing, account management).

Finally, there are industries where customers desire more than a brand. They may desire equally a sense of **Community** with other customers to share consumption experiences, pride of ownership and dissemination of product information. Need for a brand community, then, has critical implications for branding. Not only must the brand embrace shared values of its users – not simply standing above as a value provider – but also be seen as an equal participant in the brand-customer relationship that generates ongoing value. Further, it needs to be sensitive to the impact of such user involvement on expectation and experience. Needless to say, such impact could favourably match management's plans regarding the brand, or cause it to depart towards uncharted territories. Amazon.com has won much loyalty from customers by permitting them to share comments through product reviews. The example of Harley Davidson is a more intriguing one. Self-organised chat rooms frequented by Harley enthusiasts turned into meeting places for motorcycle gangs, turning off non-gang customers who were equally enthusiastic about their preferred brand but who did not wish to be identified with gangs. In any event, urge for a brand community creates conditions for creatively rethinking the branding proposition.

Our discussion of the '4 Cs Model' focusing on choice, change, complexity and community has emphasised re-branding. However, there are plenty of e-branding opportunities. When customers have a fair and manageable number of brands to choose from, they are likely to prefer e-technologies that could enhance communication effectiveness and delivery quality. Similarly, even if customers prefer to enjoy their brand experiences in private, marketers may use this as an opportunity to secure direct feedback through e-channels. The four Cs then, should allow a firm to explore the evolving nature of its markets and come to informed intuitions regarding the nature of potential change – first- or second-order – and the appropriate response, e- or re-branding.

Conclusion:
The Future for Branding

So, to return to our questions at the start of the chapter, will e-business sound the death knell of branding? Will the Internet become the ultimate brand? Or will branding retain its time-honoured flavour, albeit with embellishments from e-business? To draw an analogy with Marshall McLuhan's famous postulate on the media revolution a few decades ago (*'The Medium is the message'*), the argument in this chapter has been that neither the Medium (e-business in this instance) nor the Message (branding) can alone determine the future. There are many scenarios involving transformations. The managers who explore those scenarios, identify correctly the relevant implications for their businesses and act effectively will be the ones who determine the future for brands.

NOTES
1 See Magretta, J., 'The Power of Virtual Integration: An Interview with Dell Computer's Michael Dell', *Harvard Business Review*, March–April 1998, pp.72–84.
2 For an in-depth look at media effects on the HOE, consult Rossiter, John R. and Percy, Larry, *Advertising Communication and Promotion Management*, McGraw Hill, 2000.

New Business Models – The Challenges of Transition

Karl Moore and Keith Ruddle

Our starting place is to remind ourselves of the nature of the new economy and how widespread it will become. As we have seen in the Introduction and earlier chapters, many believe that e-business is one of the central planks of the new economy, along with knowledge and co-operative strategies. However, others remain unconvinced, arguing that in their industry or region e-business will at best be a long time coming and 'old economy' approaches will remain successful for a number of years. This can set up dissonances and insecurities in organisations, based on uncertainty about how to organise, about the scale of the change eventually needed and, if that is large, about how to navigate through to being an effective e-business.

The central thrust of our research fits with this book's Introduction: that e-business is here to stay and in a big way. As we see in Chapters 1 and 5, B-to-C is introducing new channels to many businesses and causing many industries to rethink their existing approaches to reaching end users. Nokia in Singapore was to be found, in 2000, introducing an Internet-based service which allows their end customers to purchase their cell phones

directly from Nokia. This means change in their relationships with their existing channels: phone companies, phone shops, department stores and other retailers. Existing distributors recognised the need for Nokia to adopt a B-to-C channel but were still restive as their world shifts underneath their feet.

As Chapter 6 makes clear, an even more fundamental set of changes for existing organisations is occurring in B-to-B, which involves changing trading processes and/or the refashioning of internal business processes using e-business approaches. British Airways has been doing both. BA is creating e-procurement as a way of both cutting costs in sourcing activities and helping to free up valuable purchasing specialists for more strategic sourcing tasks, such as vendor negotiation, relationship management and more thoughtful analysis of current purchasing activities. In a relatively short period of time this will result in price pressure on vendors, reduction in the number of vendors and a fundamental change in the job of purchasing people within BA. Not only is BA changing its work with outside suppliers, it is also applying the logic of e-business to internal processes and work. For example, its E-Working project piloted new ways of working, using intranets to streamline internal processes like pilot and crew scheduling, and sharing knowledge among aeroplane mechanics on a global basis.

In this chapter we bring together two themes. The first is five different ways of organising that we are witnessing among companies in their various moves to e-business. Based on over a hundred interviews conducted with leading large firms in late 1999 and 2000 in Europe, North America and Asia, we identify five emerging models, and point to the strengths and weaknesses of each in relation to engendering the Net culture necessary to realise e-business effectively. We also suggest the general evolution paths that will, in our view, lead to a more generic model developing over the next three to five years.

The second theme is the organisational transformation that these moves to e-business imply. This theme was signposted in the Introduction, but is implicit throughout the book. Transformational shifts are, in fact, not new. In all cases they represent massive challenges, but especially where organisations are large and have developed cultures and ways of operating that have, in the past, experienced some levels of success. In this chapter we draw upon research into journeys of transformation made by twenty-five major corporations. The purpose here is to provide frameworks that help us to understand these journeys and assist

in the management of such journeys into the e-world. The focus will be on the type of transformational change style needed to move to e-business. As we shall see, this requires specific characteristics of leadership, navigation, ownership and enablement that are radically different from those frequently attempted in the 'old economy'. The chapter then points to the paradox for large firms that are evolving through the five ways of organising discussed earlier in the chapter. They need to balance both old and new ways of changing. Navigational leadership emerges as a key capability for the firm and the chapter concludes by pointing to what constitutes this capability, and how it can be learned and facilitated.

The E-Culture Challenge

Insightful executives are increasingly recognising that e-business culture may well become *the* business culture in most industries and countries within the next three to five years. This issue receives much more discussion in Chapter 8. For our present purposes it is enough to point to the characteristics of e-culture that emerged from the organisations we studied. The characteristics that emerge seem to be sixfold (see also Figure 1):

- Operates @ Net Speed – central to e-culture is speed, speed and speed. Things are just done much faster than in traditional firms. A team from one large consulting company related how they were working jointly with another large consulting firm on a project for a client. One afternoon they had discussed setting up a portal for one of the client's functions; on their return to the client the next morning they were astonished to find that their competitor had set up a prototype of the portal overnight. They reflected that their traditional approach would have taken weeks of activity to reach the same point. They had learnt something about e-business. Dot.com firms view their ability to create and respond at high speed as a capability which big firms simply cannot match. One thinks of small, swift warships hammering away at massive, slow-moving galleons.
- Executes Dynamic Strategy – the key is responsiveness. E-culture accepts fast changes in response to a hypercompetitive

market, and is willing to build and launch new business models on a regular basis.

- Reaches Globally and Virtually – the Internet recognises few national boundaries, other than those of language, culture and brands. E-culture stresses worldwide learning, customer segments in many countries and 24×7 service.
- Adopts New Technology – as an enabler of e-initiatives. Technology is not the be-all but awareness of what is currently possible and economically appropriate is important. It is helpful for a good cross-section, including senior executives, to become technology enthusiasts.
- Engages in Internal Collaboration – cutting across traditional functional silos, multifunctional teams are the norm in e-culture. Speed is all important and wearing your functional hat too firmly will delay getting product to market. Teams are formed and focus on their goal, and then disband just as rapidly.
- Integrates with Partners – in the new economy, no one firm can do it all. Small firms see this as self-evident, large ones are learning it at a slower rate. Working well with other organisations is a demanding skill and one that does not come naturally to those who grew up in the competitive environment of the seventies, eighties and nineties.

It should be stressed that in the organisations we studied, e-culture did not always emerge as a positive attribute. Partly this was because its characteristics inevitably clashed with most existing cultures we found in large organisations. But we noted, too, that even in stand-alone or quasi-autonomous Internet-based business units senior managers pointed to the need also for experience, financial acuteness, and often a mix of backgrounds and approaches on the part of employees, rather than one unified 'e-culture'. For example, several cited high-profile Internet start-up failures were partly caused by the lack of some 'old economy' managerial practices. The cultural challenge that our companies faced was invariably the same, though experienced to different degrees depending on the mode of organisation adopted. The cultural challenge can be portrayed as: how do we leverage the strengths of e-culture and assimilate these with those of existing cultures in our organisation, without negative consequences arising from cultural dissonance? With this short background on e-culture in mind we will now describe the different ways in which firms are choosing to organise their

e-initiatives. As we shall see, ways of organising themselves can provide effective business answers to this question.

★ *Ways of Organising*

- Kingfisher, a large European retailer has formed four new e-commerce units. Each of these units reports directly on a monthly basis to a select committee, the Chief Executive, Sir Geoffrey Mulcahy and the finance and strategy directors. Each unit lines up with the major UK businesses Kingfisher owns: B&Q, Comet, Superdrug and Woolworths. These new units will benefit considerably from access to the powerful brands, access to the purchasing clout of its larger sister, but are stand-alone to allow for possible IPOs to benefit from the much higher share prices Internet stocks receive versus retailer shares.

- The Oriental Chinese Banking Corporation (OCBC), a large Singapore-based bank, has formed the first stand-alone e-bank in Asia. This new venture offers products from a number of OCBC's competitors, as well as its own products. It is run as an autonomous division. Concurrently, OCBC is running major e-commerce projects, reporting to the director of strategy.

- At Volvo Cars, marketing is responsible for e-commerce within the firm and is diffusing it throughout the organisation, working closely with country organisations and dealers. A manager in the e-commerce area admits that she is finding the process frustrating at times, as the Net speed of start-ups is hard to replicate in a big firm.

- The first Internet bookshop in the UK was sold a couple of years ago to one of the largest booksellers in Europe. The founder feels that his start-up is being ruined by 'help' from its new head office and is much less profitable than it could be if he were still running it!

- Nokia has formed groups within each business area to focus on e-commerce opportunities with customers and, perhaps more important, on internal processes. The managers responsible for these initiatives are located across the globe and are generally at a senior level.

- A leading North-American telecom firm has been enjoying

considerable growth from both organic growth and acquisitions. Its approach to e-commerce is unusual. New acquisitions are brought under the umbrella of a new organisation called Telecom II, where they are transformed to the new e-businesses approaches. The existing organisation will continue to operate in the current relatively 'non-e' fashion. In time, as Telecom II grows in experience and critical mass, it will merge with the parent to 'infect' it with e-culture.

These vignettes capture the considerable variation in the ways large firms are organising their e-commerce efforts. However, when we analysed the large firms in our study, we found them adopting one of five approaches to organising. These are shown in Figure 1.

Key Issues	Greenfield in Parent Firm	Semi-Autonomous in Parent Firm	Integrated in Parent Firm Functions	Integrated in Parent Firm IT	Parallel Organisation
Impact on Owner Firm Culture	Very Low	Low	Medium	Low	Potentially Higher in the Longer Term
Contribution to Shareholder Value	Potentially High	Low (today)	Low (today)	Low (today)	Medium
Retaining Net Culture	High	Medium	Low	Low	High
Attracting/retaining Key Employees	High	Medium	Low	Low	Medium
Alliances	High	Medium	Low	Low	Medium
Degree of Management Control	Low	Medium	High	High	Medium
Examples	Kingfisher	OCBC	Volvo Cars Nokia	Nordic Telecom	Telecom II

Figure 1 – Five Ways of Organising for E-Delivery

The six key dimensions on the right side of Figure 1 assist senior managers to decide the best approach for their firms. Each of these six dimensions involves a central issue:

- The first dimension is *Impact on Owner Firm Culture*. Belief about the importance of e-business for your firm is a pivotal point. If a CEO thinks it is the wave of the future, and indeed of the near future, then it may be considerably more important to achieve the transformation of your organisation into being an e-firm than merely to generate some additional profitability from e-commerce in the short term.
- The second dimension is *Contribution to Shareholder*

Value. Predicting the future price of Internet stocks is a quagmire but, at least for now, today's Internet stocks enjoy considerably higher P/E multiples than most large firms. How to convert a firm's multiples to Internet multiples is a question tantalising CEOs. One approach was that of Kingfisher in 2000, setting up separate organisations which City analysts will easily recognise as Internet plays – and hopefully value them accordingly. They enjoy the added benefits of links to dominant brands and access to large-firm supply chains.

- *Retaining Net Culture.* A central concern is that the culture of the parent firm will effectively 'nip' the buds of Net culture. For many firms, Net culture is still a 'fragile flower', which will be overwhelmed by the parent firm's traditional ways of doing business.

- The fourth and fifth dimensions are *Attracting/Retaining Key Employees and Attractiveness to Alliance Partners.* If a firm retains Net culture, can offer equity sharing and has a non-hierarchical organisation, then it will find it easier to retain and attract hard-to-recruit young and e-capable staff. Alliance partners often find attractive the opportunity to co-brand with the powerful brands of large firms but, typically, are concerned about the speed of action of large firms.

- *Degree of Management Control.*[1] Again, the pivotal issue arises as to whether e-culture is perceived as the way of the future. If it is, senior managers will want to be able to manage and control their firm's e-initiatives. No CEO is likely to want to confess to his/her Board that they think e-business is very important but are not putting senior team time and energy into it.

On the horizontal axis of Figure 1 are the five different approaches being employed by large firms.

- *Greenfield* – this is when a firm puts its e-business activities into a separate organisation and isolates it from the parent firm with linkages typically only through the head of the new unit. Often, as with Kingfisher and part of OCBC, they report in to the CEO or other senior executive. The advantages of this model are that it allows for a spin-off with an IPO; it is a good way of retaining Net culture unstifled by the parent firm culture; it is often excellent for attracting new people and retaining staff who may be tempted by dot.coms; it is also

potentially attractive for alliance partners who want access to parent firm brands but without the hassle of big-firm hierarchy.

- *Semi-Autonomous in Parent Firm* – the e-business side of the company has more linkages than the greenfield approach but fewer than the fully integrated model. This is a halfway house, which is appropriate when there is considerable support among senior management for e-initiatives and where the corporate culture is more open to innovation.

- *Fully Integrated into Firm in Functions* – e-commerce reports in to functional and business units heads. Volvo and OCBC take this approach. The advantages are twofold – senior management is more apt to be fully engaged 'e-ing' the firm; and e-culture may diffuse more fully through the firm, transforming the firm into a twenty-first century firm. The disadvantages are serious ones. In today's stockmarket few large firms, Ford and GE being prominent exceptions, have gained much in share price from their e-business activity. Perhaps analysts will be more open in a year or two. The critical issue of Net culture is a continuous one. Most observers believe that large firms' traditional cultures will overwhelm net culture rather than the reverse. Strong leaders, such as GE's Jack Welch and Ford's Jac Nasser, may be able to lead their firms to take on broad Net culture, but the jury is still out. Attracting staff, keeping them and attracting alliance partners are all in doubt with this model. In spite of these problems, the firms we researched tended to feel that this is the way forward.

- *Fully Integrated in Parent Firm IT* – A variation on the fully integrated model is one where IT leads the way. The idea here is that technology is sovereign. A leading Nordic telecom company, a former monopoly, is taking this approach. However, some of their managers question the business impact e-initiatives will have without business units directing development. The technology tail is wagging the business dog. This approach may work if the IT department is business-orientated.

- *Parallel Organisation* – This is an intriguing model, which we have seen so far in only one firm among the dozens we have studied. The company is a large North-American telecom firm expanding rapidly through both acquisition and internal growth. One of their 'rising stars' has been appointed to run a new group, Telecom II. This new organisation will be e-enabled – piloting and experimenting with e-approaches and

with e-culture from its start. New acquisitions will become part of the new division. This firm believes that new acquisitions are a good place to start with the transformation which comes from the wholesale embrace of e-world approaches because the acquired firm is already anticipating the major change of becoming part of a much larger firm. In time, the two organisations will be merged, in the hope that the e-culture part will 'leaven' the mother firm with its new e-approaches.

What does the future hold? So far this chapter has outlined five approaches currently being utilised by a number of large firms around the world. Considering our six critical issues, each model has considerable strengths and weaknesses. Deciding which model to adopt depends on your view of the relative priority of the six critical issues. What the competition drivers are in your industry, the history and capabilities of your firm, and senior executives' view of the future are the key factors that affect your stand on the six issues.

In industries which are already impacted by e-business – book, electronics and airlines, for example – it may make managers consider going straight to the fully integrated model.[2] To do so means not merely fine-tuning the organisation but transforming its culture – no small task, as we reveal below. Unless the CEO and top team support and, preferably, champion e-business, proceeding more slowly may be better.

Figure 2 shows the five models. The size of the arrows suggest what we see as the evolutionary path for most firms.

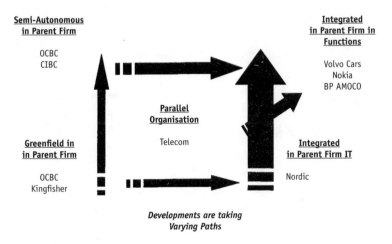

Figure 2 – E-Commerce Organisational Development for Large Firms

We believe that the end point will be the Fully Integrated model but for most firms this may, and probably should, be in three to five years' time or even more. Firms will start out at other points and may well pass through one of the other models as appropriate midway stations. At the same time as reorganising, they will also be looking to manage a much wider set of changes and we now turn to the issue of how to do this.

The Transformational Challenge

In this chapter so far we have seen how larger firms are organising in different ways to embrace the e-economy. For many such companies the spectre of operating at Net speed has massive implications for the fundamental architecture of running the business. In many cases the old ways of working – processes, structures, culture, internal control systems and human resource mechanisms – have to be transformed to embrace a new paradigm. A typical somewhat popularised view on such a shift in organisational paradigm is captured in Figure 3.

FROM	TO
Operational inputs and targets	Purpose and higher-level outcomes
Organising by function	Thinking process and task
Centralised hierarchy	Decentralised networks
Centre as decision-maker	Centre as enabler and adviser
Supplier – customer	Partnership and alliances
Specialist individual skills	Teams aligned around task
Rewards for task	Team recognition for outcome
Not-invented-here	Networks of trust
Centralised physical functions	Virtual centres of excellence

Figure 3 – Organisational Shifts for the E-World

For the existing top leadership, transformation inevitably means venturing into the unknown – implying in the shift itself the need to adapt and adopt new styles of leadership and new approaches to change. Mechanisms used to enact change from the top in the past may not be appropriate in the more dynamic and unpredictable e-economy.

Transformational shifts are not new. The experience of many large global firms in the 1980s and 1990s – such as ABB, British Airways, IBM, AT&T, Ford, BP Amoco, SmithKline Beecham, Shell and others – have seen in many cases periods of shift, flux and transition, driven by both external context (the competitive markets) and internal discontinuities (crisis, changes in top leadership, mergers etc.). Many of these journeys of change have seen periods of revolution and then more traditional evolution or consolidation. With the advent of the e-economy, such large firms may be entering a period where uncertainty, change and flux are genuinely permanent features of life.

Does such a change require a new and dynamic approach to transformation and change? We have already learnt a great deal about transformational change and how it can be managed. We now describe what we have found.

Understanding Journeys of Transformation

Research at Oxford throughout the 1990s and into the new decade looked at the leadership of transformation in twenty-five major firms experiencing periods of significant transformation and shift.[3] In many cases such change was moving to global operations, enabled by increasing knowledge and information. In each case the journey of change was unique, passing through stages where the top leadership actions were adjusted or changed because of the shift in context and type of change needed. Examples included:

- Major long-standing UK-based insurance companies, such as Royal and Sun Alliance, General Accident, and Legal and General, which after many years of stability confronted industry downturn, new-entry competition from direct

channels and radical new ways of dealing with customers.

- Global consumer and healthcare companies, such as Smith-Kline Beecham, Pfizer and Nestlé, moving to new global models of operation to exploit brand and product innovation based on new ways of sharing and innovating.
- Technology-based multinationals, such as IBM and Siemens responding to global shifts in markets and competition, seeking global scale but local responsiveness.
- Privatised industries in the UK, such as Thames Water, Southern Electric and AEA Technology, which found themselves forced to achieve operational excellence with reduced costs but then made the shift to more responsive market and customer growth.

By plotting changes in context and content of change over time we are able to provide a framework in which top management can understand where they have come from, where they are and how the actions they might take to move to the next stage can be adjusted. Figure 4, adapted from Pettigrew,[4] explains a longitudinal journey of transformation in terms of the context of change (both internal and external), content of change and journey management process involving the top management team. The interrelationships, dependencies and mutual configurations of these variables over time provide the fundamental observation and explanatory lens for an organisational journey.

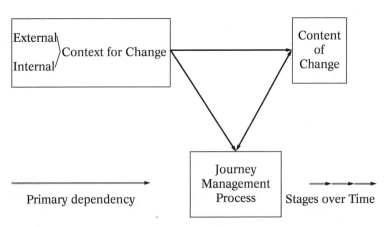

Figure 4 – Framework for Understanding Transformational Journeys

The primary relationships are important for analysis. First, *context* at a point in time provides both the external drivers or

factors influencing the direction for change (the why), as well as a number of internal organisational constraints or influences that may affect both the target for what might change over time (the *content* of shift in strategy and structure) or the way the change happens (the journey management process). Secondly, the *content* of the change, in its type, focus, degree and urgency of shift, is likely to influence the journey management process. As a corollary, the way in which the process is carried out may well influence the details of the result.

The triangular framework can be applied over time, either at a high level to an overall journey for a significant period of organisational life, or for analysis of shorter periods or stages of the journey.

Framework for Journey Management Process

We have also been able to develop a simple framework to describe a Journey Management Process (Figure 5). Originally developed in practice with clients of Andersen Consulting, it was helpful in understanding all the change actions that were important to achieve progress on a number of fronts. Four dimensions of Leadership, Navigation, Ownership and Enablement are used to describe actions in four 'quadrants' of a change management process. In looking at the roles, actions and processes involving top management, this model has top-down and organisation-wide dimensions, as well as notions of demand and supply of change.

The demand-side actions are those carried out involving the top leadership group as well as the wider line organisation – who will largely be the acceptors, absorbers, executors or operators of the changed organisation. The supply-side actions are particular mechanisms or projects configured especially to help manage or enable the change. Vertically, the top-down quadrants are those actions with significant involvement from the top team or senior management dedicated to the transformation efforts. The lower quadrants will generally refer to organisation-wide and detailed activity involving a large number of people:

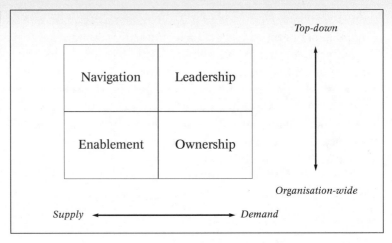

Figure 5 – Framework for Isolating Journey Management Processes

- **Leadership** actions concern the behaviour, skills, style and actions of the CEO and the top team to set direction, create vision, plan and communicate change, use power and make decisions, work as a team and sponsor change initiatives.
- **Navigation** actions and processes concern special mechanisms, structures or systems used by the top team to guide, co-ordinate or control transformation. This might, for example, suggest that at certain points in a journey a proactive, almost professional approach is employed to stay focused, integrated and in balance, implying planned and architectural control over change. Project management and measurement systems may be used here such as programme results and outcomes, and a wide spectrum of operational and strategic measures. The scorecard notion helps in looking at <u>which</u> areas of measurement are used or appropriate for different types of transformational journey.
- **Ownership** activity includes processes to create demand for change and connect organisation-wide initiatives to the top. This might include planned involvement in cross-functional teams, self-diagnosis and improvement activity, communicating the rationale for change aimed at mobilising commitment, sharing vision, fostering consensus, spreading revitalisation, institutionalising new cultures and values, as well as learning.
- **Enablement** implies special project or infrastructure activity to support transformation and change initiatives, very often conducted by task forces separated from the day-to-day business. This might include process and organisation redesign,

IT projects, training programmes, and special Human Resource and restructuring projects (see Chapter 8). For support for more sustaining change it would include facilitation and infrastructure for knowledge and self-learning. It is also in this arena that external change agents may be found in areas such as organisational development and change management.

In any stage and change process, one would expect to find activities being carried out that fit in each quadrant. We can define here a journey management style as a particular configuration and interrelationship of activities in all four quadrants.

Contrasting T-Change and E-Change Styles

For leadership teams faced with the need for a radical shift the research in the twenty-five companies demonstrated two different styles of leading change – depending on the context and situation. For many changes in the 'old economy', leaders often adopted a style suited to predictability and planability – driving transformation from the top down. In contrast, in a world where the change itself was unpredictable, ever changing and often experimental in nature (such as with e-working and e-enablement), a different style of change was embraced – with very significant implications for the role of top leadership. We might for shorthand call these two styles T-Change (traditional top-down) and E-Change (e-enabled and enterprise-wide).

Figure 6 demonstrates this contrast using the dimensions of the earlier model of the Journey Management Process. Both styles are evident in journeys where radical change takes place over a relatively short space of time. Programmatic leadership (as a style) appears to be substantially top-down planned and prescribed change, whereas transformational leadership appears to be a mixture of a top-down leadership of a more visionary kind connecting with emergent and self-initiated organisation-wide change activity. The shift between one style and another – for reasons of context and intent – provides some data on how organisations reconfigure change processes and learn new styles. For a large organisation dealing with both 'bricks and clicks', like those described earlier in the chapter, this might provide one key to future shifts.

	T-Change (Programmatic Leadership)	E-Change (Transformational Leadership)
Contextual Conditions		
– external	– short term pressure for radical improvement – predictability in planning horizon	– longer-term shareholder value
– internal	– bias to risk management, rules, order, hierarchy, structure – proven business models – traditional processes	– bias to entrepreneurship, values and behaviours – new, exploratory business models – potentially e-enabled processes
Strengths		
	– delivery to target, certainty – efficiency of implementation, so complete major programmes in short time	– sustainability in future world of uncertainty and flux
Leadership traits		
– role of CEO and top team	– deciding strategy and tactics, setting plan, monitoring	– articulating purpose, encouraging values and behaviours
– method of setting direction	– detailed analysis and planning at top	– scenarios, strategic intent, options – wider strategy formulation process
– sponsorship of change	– hands-on project management	– providing encouragement and backing to others
– key behaviours	– dictatorial, directive, prescriptive	– collaborative, persuasive, listening, teaming
– communication focus	– internal down the hierarchy: on targets	– vertically, horizontally and outwards: on behaviours and purpose
Navigation traits		
– overall programme co-ordination	– full-time senior programme director and team – centralised detailed schedules and networks – detailed task planning 'war room' approach – chief executive chairs hands-on meetings of programme	– issues addressed by top team as part of normal business – small central support to facilitate information exchange – scenario revisiting – middle managers provide co-ordination
– nature of central targets and measurements	– largely financial, operational and process targets – outcomes, detailed inputs and milestones	– balanced scorecards, including people and learning – strong accountability to high-level outcomes only
– control style	– micro-monitoring based on detailed measures	– macro-management aligned to purpose and outcomes
Ownership		
– extent of local involvement	– only involved extensively at point of implementation – follow new instructions and procedures – some seconded to full-time enablement teams	– extensive involvement, most people involved in change activity as part of their jobs – balanced scorecards self-assessed
– local change initiatives	– few unless specifically connected to programme	– learning activity, breakthrough and continuous improvement cultures – self-initiated within overall purpose and outcome – experiments encouraged and nurtured
– awareness and knowledge	– regular directed top-down communication – need to know basis	– regular two-way vertical and horizontal exchange of information – wide knowledge of overall business purpose
Enablement		
– typical priority enablement projects	– work and task redesign, new structures, systems architecture, measurement systems	– process reinvention, competence and skill development, rewards and performance mechanisms
– support and approach to projects	– full-time teams, use of external content experts and resources, line representatives – centralised functions provide expertise and resource	– facilitation to line, support for learning-by-doing. – promulgation of best practice and knowledge – centres of interest, practice and peer groups

Figure 6 – Contrasting Journey Management Styles for Radical Change

Examples of T-Change, a programmatic approach, can be found where top management used existing well-tried mechanisms to drive change. The insurance companies

attempting to move from crisis to a new customer orientation in the early 1990s typically set up strong centralised programmes and action teams. Similarly, in the early 1990s utilities such as British Gas and Thames Water employed centrally driven 'engineering'-style change to reduce costs and update processes – employing well-proven management practices and project-based methods.

For examples of E-Change an enterprise-wide approach more suited to a flexible and fast-changing e-economy, we can turn to other examples of change management process in the 1990s and into the new decade. Charles Schwab, as described in the Introduction, is one such. Here the integrated and holistic nature of the transformational leadership style appears to be key in order to harness and connect top-down intentions with emergent organisation-wide activity. Some of the distinguishing characteristics include:

- **A visionary leadership role and behaviour for both the CEO and the top team of management**. Although the CEO can be key to articulating and orchestrating the vision and direction, for sustaining transformational behaviour throughout the organisation a larger senior group needs to take on the role of coaching, communicating vision, sponsoring change, and acting as role models of new teaming and empowering behaviour. The Principles of Leadership used at Siemens (Figure 7) demonstrate this – and are implemented with many business leaders working in peer groups to support each other.

Figure 7 – Siemens Principles of Leadership

In our research these leadership characteristics were often described alongside not only a new or changing role for the CEO and top team, but a more involving and empowering process down in the business:

It's a totally different style for the chief executive. It requires total involvement on middle- to long-term issues and less hassle about the monthly sales figures . . . much more of a total involvement in all strategic issues that previously would have got lost somewhere in the morass. The old culture was you negotiated the budget once a year and then you ran away . . . now at our group management committee we only talk about numbers at the end of the meeting . . . the meeting is about strategic issues that will really affect the business. John Robinson, – Chief Executive, Smith & Nephew

I see my role primarily as defining business scope and purpose . . . a context for the manager within which he understands how he fits . . . a dramatic style change between the way I've run these companies and the way the other guys have run them previously . . . they kicked the tyres, personally approved the tender submissions . . . they [the managers] feel part of it, they can contribute . . . I walk around with my mouth shut and my ears open encouraging them to say. Bill Alexander, Chief Executive, Thames Water

- **Navigational mechanisms**. Outcome-based balanced scorecards are integrated into the day-to-day management. Collaborative processes for issue management and co-ordination are again integrated with the line executive team. In our research, a number of companies were introducing the use of balanced scorecards – aiming to allow management teams down in the organisation to develop outcome measures to guide change actions over time. A wall chart (Figure 8) found in IBM UK in the mid-1990s period of transformation shows how managers are encouraged to develop a number of indicators of stakeholder success. In this case relationship management was the critical area for change.

In E-Change particularly critical are experimentation, innovation and learning. In the research some companies linked innovation to the ability to transfer knowledge. Focus on board level involvement here is key – to ensure that e-initiatives are legitimate and recognised (see also Chapter 7). Examples

included: measurements of customer perception of innovation (Citibank), usage of open learning centres by employees (Norwich), outcomes of numbers of improvement opportunities generated per employee (Milliken), percentage of the business and employees actively working on project improvement and innovation projects (Norwich Union), percentage and amounts of spend in categories of new product development (Smith & Nephew), team evaluation and awards for idea development and knowledge transfer (SmithKline Beecham). Similar balanced-scorecard measures can be applied to e-initiatives.

	1994	1995	1996	1997
Customer View	• IBM seen as product vendor, not a solutions provider • Hard to obtain a proposal quickly • Difficult to be an IBM customer	• Better solutions through use of Conditions of Satisfaction • Improved response • Greater flexibility	• Broader range of high-quality solutions • IBM delivers on its promise in time • Ease and consistency in doing business with IBM – worldwide	• World-class solutions through continuous improvement of processes, skills, tools and data • Responsiveness and speed of execution common throughout IBM • IBM seen as Number 1 partner for business solutions through IT
IBMer View	• Many workaround inventions and few process designs • Too many, and inconsistent, tools/methodologies • Hard to find resources/skills • Reinventing the wheel each time • Individualism is promoted	• Common processes are taught and are executed worldwide • Use of a consistent set of tools and the Information Warehouse is established • Access to a structured skills inventory • Start capturing Intellectual Capital • Teamwork is possible and encouraged	• Best of breed professional practices are the norm for every IBMer • Tools are improved and the Information Warehouse contains the data needed to run our business • Best skills applied to each situation • Re-use of Intellectual Capital is effective • IBM is a company managed by process	• We can be used as a reference for successful business process re-engineering • We sell the solutions we use • Fluidity of Resources is achieved worldwide • Intellectual Capital is IBM's primary asset • Pride of being an IBMer is back

Figure 8 – Stage Targets on IBM Employee Wallchart

- **Inclusive ownership of change.** E-change styles demand extensive enterprise-wide involvement and a bias for experimentation, self-initiative and improvement. 'Breakthrough' cultures that can manage in uncertainty and stimulate change have been emerging in some larger companies in the late nineties. Examples here might be the whole Simply Better Way (Kaizen-based) change culture and architecture at SmithKline Beecham – ideally suited to a potential new e-economy if it could be sustained. Similarly, the late 1990s performance and breakthrough culture at BP Amoco under CEO John Browne might be another example – a company also moving heavily into aspects of e-business in the new decade. In our research such rapid breakthrough enterprise was rare. More popular were more evolutionary processes of self-improvement or change embedded down in the organisation ('bottom-up' or heavily in the Ownership dimension). These would be TQM or EFQM (quality management) continuous improvement processes (for example at Milliken, Courtaulds, Norwich Union, Nestlé).

These were generally described as longer journeys of change, for example:

> Much more on the whole EFQM type model ... that started about 1983 as a fairly inquisitorial sort of thing and has developed over the years, much faster over the last three years than the previous ten ... very much a system that starts with a self-assessment of the business ... then goes into the team discussing the outcomes of that self-assessment ... then focuses on some issue which needs improving and working together ... we've developed our tools along the way ... constant striving for operational improvement ... Courtaulds Operations Director

Where such embedded processes were used in a period of dramatic shift there were tensions and conflicts with some of the more urgent top-down imperatives (reported at Natwest Bank and Nestlé). Only in a few cases (for example, SmithKline Beecham with Simply Better Way) did there seem to be strong congruence between the organisation-wide activity and the top-down direction setting (SmithKline Beecham's 10:3:1 planning process).

- **Enabling support for change**. Investments need to be made primarily in facilitation, knowledge and skill development, that can help to leverage the whole organisation to bring changes into the business. The knowledge-sharing infrastructures developed in SmithKline Beecham, BP Amoco and, more lately, in Royal and Sun Alliance and Shell, for example, have been aimed at facilitating sharing and improvement from learning and breakthrough.

Emergent Characteristics of Successful Transformation

From our observations of transformation we can generalise about critical factors for a successful shift from a historical state, through a journey of radical organisational shift to a new, more fluid e-environment. Such a list of **journey success conditions** for moves to e-business must include:

- development of a climate and readiness for change, an ability

to break out of inertia and historical context, either from within or from an external stimulus and crisis.

- evidence of a clear, well-articulated, understood and widely owned strategic intent, purpose and vision.
- energetic and visionary leadership in the top team (but not just the CEO), with a particular focus on new customer propositions, values, behaviours alongside target outcomes, to engage the organisation in charge.
- continuous attention to interpret, understand and influence organisational context that will itself influence stages of the journey and progress.
- an alignment of the whole journey management style (mix of leadership, ownership, enablement, navigation actions) that is appropriate for the context and targets for change.
- a continual focus on systems and holistic thinking to align intent with behaviour, strategy with operations, rewards, performance measures and structure.
- an ability to set, navigate and adjust a journey path that is flexible and nimble, taking into account the unexpected exogenous and endogenous events along the way.

The Paradox for Large Firms – Balancing the Old and the New Ways of Changing

These success conditions may well be elusive to some of the larger firms moving from old habits and ways of working. Our examples earlier start to illustrate some of the difficult challenges for leaders finding themselves having to develop and deal with the consequences of a 'bricks and clicks' strategy. Which styles of change and leadership to adopt? When? Let us look at some examples. In the year 2000 two well-studied enterprises, British Airways and BP, were both investing quickly in the next stage of their journeys to embrace the e-economy.

For BA, historical transformation in the eighties of the front-line staff was given plaudits. In the 1990 some reversion to old introspective structures has been noted. The organisation in 2000 remained, with cults of professional tunctions, centralised

decision-making, strong head office departments and a propensity for rules, detail and procedures. Much of this has also been responsible for its success in managing a safe and well-respected airline. To move to the new economy, can and should the top management style be adapted to embrace new models of change?

For BP, the successful performance culture implemented in the 1990s relied on over 150 strong, energetic and accountable BULs (business unit leaders) to drive a decentralised business – with old central functions now largely dismantled. Investments in knowledge networks in the early 1990s facilitated peer exchange for improvement. Theoretically, by 2000, the organisation was ripe and fit to move to the next stage of an e-enabled enterprise, to take advantage of B-to-B and other opportunities. The paradox here, though is that with a decentralised philosophy, how could new e-based ideas get promulgated fast enough? Could the current incentives and targets be used to drive e-enablement from John Browne downwards?

For both these organisations the challenge for leadership in the future will be in how to adopt programmes and styles of change appropriate to both the past and the future. Here we can turn again to experience of transformation in the 1990s for help.

Towards 'Navigational Leadership' Capability

For large firms the real skill lies in keeping the strengths of the old with those of the new. This suggests a higher set of conditions is needed for what we might describe as a continuous **'navigational leadership style'**. Such a style might be thought of as a 'meta-style', compared with those discussed earlier, because one of its particular ingredients would be an organisational capability to identify when and how to switch between styles. Elements for moves to e-business include:

- organisational 'antennae' to be able to interpret and influence context continuously and switch to a new way of changing;
- a broad leadership capability among a wide group of executive and senior management that has a bias for experimentation, learning and adapting;

- an ability to lead the organisation through a combination of purpose and values via a clear navigational process of balanced outcomes and targets that reflect the path of the journey;
- an ability to set paths, and balance choices of pace, sequence, timing, synchronicity, and interdependence of change initiatives;
- an ability to choose appropriately between the separation and integration of change projects and the day-to-day line business, similarly choosing between the different methods of co-ordination and management of such initiatives.

Such a 'navigational leadership' style would also imply new roles and skills for both top leadership and the central management of the organisation.

Towards New Tools for 'Navigational Leadership'

Any frameworks and tools discussed here will be less a linear prescriptive guide along the lines of 'ten steps for managerial action' and more a set of diagnostic aids (using our navigational metaphor, the sextant, compass, the experience of previous exploration journeys and the navigational chart of the current journey) for the whole leadership team. In this context, the comments made in 1997 by Heifetz and Laurie on adaptive leadership are worth quoting:

> Leaders have to stop providing solutions . . . the prevailing notion that leadership consists of having a vision and aligning people with that vision is bankrupt because it continues to treat adaptive situations as if they were technical . . . adaptive situations are hard to define and resolve precisely because they demand work and responsibility of managers and people throughout the organisation . . . they are not amenable to solutions provided by the [top] leaders . . . leadership has to take place every day. It cannot be the responsibility of the few. A leader from above or below has to engage people in confronting the challenge, adjusting their values, changing perspectives and learning new habits.

This brings us fully back to the emerging navigational leadership style suggested in this chapter for a new e-world of change.

In seeking attributes of successful journeys of transformation, conclusions are often contentious because of issues of cause, effect, measurement and perception. On the evidence here, confirmed with the top management involved, the importance of success conditions such as clarity of strategic intent, alignment and the presence of visionary leaders are key traits. It is clear, however, that the leader needs to connect with context and action.

The research, though, suggests that, for a sustainable successful transformation in a contemporary environment of flux and change a broader leadership capability needs to be pervasive. It is not just the top leader but the wider management team that must embrace a navigational leadership capability. As such a new theory is suggested here, based around organisational ability to self-assess context, diagnose situations and the appropriateness of new directions, set and adjust paths, and adjust along the route. These characteristics need to be embedded in new management processes and behaviours.

★ *Conclusion*

In our studies we have observed major organisations take different routes towards reorganising and changing themselves as they have moved uncertainly towards a 'bricks and clicks' strategy for the development of e-business. The issue of how far an e-culture should be adopted, and how far other cultural elements and practices need to be part of such 'bricks and clicks' strategies, was flagged as a major challenge. We have pointed to five main ways of reorganising that firms have been adopting and also suggested a model of the likely evolution of these reorganisations towards the fully integrated model. This is what it will take to achieve Stage Four of the model presented in the Introduction (Figure 2).

The second half of this chapter has aimed less at offering rules for the success of transformational change and more at shedding light on the complex process of guidance and navigation in the context of change. Understanding how top management should act in the new e-economy is still new. Recent notions of adaptive leadership that fit closely with the ideas of navigational leadership are plainly appropriate in a world of such complexity and uncertainty.

For CEOs and researchers seeking answers a number of challenges are relevant. Firstly, as the occurrence of such leadership styles increases, it will be easier for us to see how they are learnt and conducted in practice across different contexts.

Secondly, as the business and environment of the large enterprise becomes increasingly turbulent and complex, our understanding of change processes must take into account theories such as complexity, chaos and disturbance. The use of physical and life sciences as analogies or explanatory tools in thinking about organisations will be of real interest and help here. It remains for all those who engage in and think about strategic change management to step up to the task and demonstrate their own forms of adaptive and navigational leadership in taking knowledge and practice into the twenty-first century.

NOTES

1 The importance of the view of management towards e-culture is found in Venkatraman, N., 'Five steps to a dot.com strategy: How to find your footing on the Web', *Sloan Management Review*, Spring 2000.

2 An article which argues the case for going straight to a fully integrated model is Gulati, R. and Garion, J., 'Getting the Right Mix of Bricks and Clicks', *Harvard Business Review*, May–June 2000.

3 Ruddle, K., 'Understanding Journeys of Transformation', unpublished D. Phil. thesis, Templeton College, Oxford, 2000. See also Ruddle, K. and Feeny, D., 'Benchmarking Organisational Transformation and Peformance', Executive Research Briefing, Templeton College, Oxford, 1998.

4 Pettigrew, A. 'Contextualist Research: A Natural Way to Link Theory and Practice' in Lawler, E. (ed.), *Doing Research that is Useful in Theory and Practice*, Jossey Bass, San Francisco, 1985.

New Roles for Intermediaries

Jonathan Reynolds

Retailing, or transactional services, has always been considered a 'killer application' in any form of electronic marketing activity to consumers.[1] This has been the case for several decades: even when the kinds of market conditions that characterise the new economy were merely a gleam in the eye:

> It is not difficult to see investment in teleshopping and other non-store methods becoming as attractive an option as vertical integration or international expansion strategies. It is not so much a case of whether teleshopping will happen, but when.[2]

Yet at the same time commentators have often disparaged the merits of the sector, claiming that retailing's relative lack of professionalism, poor record on innovation and overt conservatism – as well as its excessively domestic concerns ('retail is detail') – make it somehow unfitted to make the transition. As if to confirm the pessimistic asides of its critics, retailing has indeed come slowly and apparently grudgingly to e-business. As late as 1997, only eleven of the top hundred retailers in the US had any kind of Internet presence.[3] In a recent survey by industry group CIES, for example, home shopping was ranked ninth of the priorities on European retail CEOs' agendas.[4]

This chapter provides a summary of the competitive landscape

as it is currently emerging in relation to established retail firms and the new intermediaries. It raises questions that retail companies need to address if they are to make informed decisions as to their positioning in relation to e-business. In particular, it challenges retailers to consider the implications of e-business for the value of their 'bricks and mortar' investments and to assess the impact of the international dimension of business unconstrained by place. It concludes by identifying three advantages enjoyed by established retailers in relation to their newer and more nimble competitors.

The 'Pure-Play' Challenge

Technology has played a powerful role in determining the scale and character of retailing. For example, IT used in connection with sales-based ordering (SBO) or efficient consumer response (ECR) already allows traditional retail intermediaries to achieve significant cost reductions and raise barriers to entry. Dawson identifies three distinct approaches, which have led to more profitable enterprises.[5]

- Knowledge-based (finding more creative ways to run the business).
- Alliance-based (using co-operative initiatives between firms to generate new competitive positions or to reinforce existing ones).
- Productivity-based (focusing assets and resources on key business areas to achieve cost substitutions).

The restructuring of marketing channels to the consumer by means of such phenomena as the Internet certainly offers opportunities for conventional retailers to progress by means of all three of Dawson's approaches. However, it also holds the threat of new entrants to conventional markets, so-called 'pure plays', challenging traditional intermediary niches.[6] This has been termed *disintermediation*. For example, Ducati, the Italian motorcycle manufacturer, marketed its MH900e, a special edition bike, solely through the Internet, bypassing its traditional outlets, and sold out in a matter of days.[7] In practice, the reality of channel proliferation and new opportunities for different kinds of

organisation to add digital value[8] may result in an effective *reintermediation* of channels with new players and new configurations and networks of actors.[9] These will include the more nimble and far-sighted of established retail businesses. find.co.uk is a new intermediary that has inserted itself between specialist comparison sites in financial services. Visit their site and they provide access to a range of other specialist financial advisory sites that provide such services as mortgage comparison, credit card comparison and personal loan comparison.

However, in the initial vacuum created by the relatively low level of action from traditional intermediaries, pure plays have flourished, benefiting from exclusive access to the rhetoric, as well as from unoccupied niches in the market space (see Table 1). Some, such as Boo.com, have been unable to exploit the opportunities with a sustainable business model. However, those pure-play operations that have survived cash flow and general management problems have demonstrated beyond doubt that there are both new kinds of markets to be assembled and exploited, as well as new kinds of intermediary roles which would be difficult, expensive or impossible for legacy retail businesses to undertake through conventional channels to the consumer.

	Businesses	**Consumers**
Businesses	*B-to-B* GlobalNetXchange RetailLink	*B-to-C* EToys.com Designers Direct
Consumers	*C-to-B* Adabra.com Ybag.com Letsbuyit.com Priceline.com.	*C-to-C* EBay.com QXL.co.uk

Table 1 – A Typology of Market Space Niches, with Retailing Examples

New Kinds of Markets, New Kinds of Intermediaries

A classic example of such reintermediation is the notion of the *metamarket*, occupied by a *metamediary*, developed by Sawhney and others.[10] Such new intermediaries take advantage of the Internet's more effective capability for linking and aggregating information and knowledge related to certain kinds of activities in a way which is not possible (or is more difficult) conventionally. Sawhney's metamediaries:

- offer a rich set of related activities that can be clustered together;
- are important in terms of their demands on customers' time and their economic impact;
- require customers to deal with many product and service providers across several industries;
- are in markets containing integrated middlemen who currently provide channel flows inefficiently and where the buying experience is unpleasant.[11]

New intermediaries of this kind can be found servicing a range of 'new' consumer markets: childbirth (www.babycenter.com); car-buying (www.edmonds.com); weddings (www.weddingchannel.com) and gardening (www.garden.com). They have the potential to capture the totality of consumer behaviour in respect of one broad market sector, while acting as gatekeepers within the channel in relation to the activities of contributory players.

New Kinds of Customer Relationships

New entrants are also creating the possibilities of new kinds of relationships with customers, mediated via technology. Table 2 summarises the kinds of features being exhibited by contemporary web sites, which offer new or complementary opportunities for

enriching relationships between retailers and customers (and sometimes between customers and customers).

Category	Example
Notification	Lastminute.com
Recommendation	Internet Bookshop
Merchant brokering	evenbetter.com
Negotiation	Kasbah
Reputation mechanisms	Consumers' Association web trader

Table 2 – New Kinds of Customer Relationships (Source: after Maes, 1998) [12]

The increasing acceptance of e-mail as a means of interpersonal communication signifies real direct marketing opportunities. Companies such as www.amazon.com, www.lastminute.com and conventional goods and service suppliers are using the medium extensively as a *notification* channel. More sophisticated intermediaries use software applications to track user behaviour and store user preferences, in order to make relevant *recommendations* to customers. Amazon sends customers messages to notify them of new books and CDs by writers or artists they have bought previously. It then uses sophisticated reviews to recommend the new item to the customer. New intermediaries have become established with the sole purpose of *brokering on-line retailers* to the end customer. www.evenbetter.com, for example, has won several awards for its pioneering price comparison service. It is also possible to envisage software development which permits consumers, or groups of consumers, to *negotiate* with suppliers direct. The experimental Kasbah service at MIT Media Labs derived haggling rules from North-African markets and souks to generate negotiating profiles, sticking points and haggling styles for individual consumers, who send off their avatars to discuss prices with similarly virtual retail agents. Priceline.com already offers consumers power to propose offer prices for airline seats, hotel rooms and groceries.

Dynamic Pricing

One of the biggest threats electronic commerce poses to conventional retailing is the shift it brings about in pricing dynamics. Until recently this threat has been rather more apparent than real in business-to-consumer markets; particularly so while on-line consumer markets remained relatively modest in size. The biggest growth has been seen in business-to-business markets. More recently, however, we have seen start-up companies exploiting the potential offered by the Internet to bring consumer buyers and retailer (or manufacturer) sellers together in new and innovative ways involving *variable (or dynamic) pricing strategies* of one kind or another. These are organisations which play an intermediary role in matching consumers with business or consumers directly with other consumers.

There are four broad types of dynamic pricing strategies available to businesses moving into this market place (Table 3).

Strategy	Description
Auctions	A seller or an intermediary for the seller entertains bids from a number of potential buyers and controls the auction.
Reverse Auctions	A buyer or an intermediary for the buyer entertains bids from a number of potential suppliers and controls the auction.
Dutch Auctions	The price of a product or service is reduced by an auctioneer intermediary until a buyer is found.
Collaborative purchasing or exchanges	A neutral party operates an exchange, and sets ground rules for many buyers and sellers. A fee is levied for each transaction conducted.

Table 3 – Pricing Strategies for C-to-B and C-to-C Businesses

Most of these forms of variable pricing are commercially implemented on the web at present. Unlike regular transactional sites, dealing with a straightforward sale of a fixed price item, sites whose strategies centre around dynamic pricing have

particular challenges. Not least is the need to provide more effective customer support than single-format sites. For example, they may have to be on hand to explain the complex purchasing rules surrounding the site or the progress of a particular transaction. Or they may need to answer questions about shipping or delivery when the product is being shipped not by the intermediary but by the original supplier. There are also important cultural considerations about consumer trust and confidence in approaches, which will affect certain markets unused to haggling or negotiation on price.

Priceline.com (www.priceline.com) originated as a seller of surplus airline seats in 1997. The company's founder developed bespoke 'name your price' demand software, which was extended into hotel reservations and car buying in 1998, and into home mortgages and equity loans in 1999.

Buyers must name their preferred price for a product or service, with subscribing suppliers having to respond to a buyer's offer within a fixed time. If the supplier accepts the buyer's offer, the buyer is committed to the transaction. Offers lower than thirty per cent below the lowest asking price are not considered 'reasonable' by the company, but it was only able to satisfy thirty-five per cent of even 'reasonable' bids in the first half of 1999. The company generates marginal revenue on each transaction and a flat fee for car sales. Japanese manufacturers dominate Priceline.com's latest 'Top Ten' list. Most recently, Priceline.com has licensed its service and technology to WebHouse Club in connection with grocery sales in New York, New Jersey and Philadelphia. This most interesting extension has generated 40,000 members in its first month of operation. Over half a million items are priced at over 1100 area supermarkets outlets, including A&P, ShopRite, Grand Union and d'Agostino.

Collaborative buying was once considered the domain of tree-hugging environmentalists, according to political satirist P. J. O'Rourke. The practice is evidently becoming more commercial. Letsbuyit.com (www.letsbuyit.com) is a fast-growing Swedish-based on-line buying co-operative. The business was founded by Johan Stael van Holstein, one of Sweden's Internet pioneers and a founder member of the Icon Medialab. Rewe's Pro Sieben TV network (which also operates the German home shopping channel HOT) has a twenty-five per cent stake in Letsbuyit.com. The site offers savings of up to thirty per cent on goods ranging from toys to electrical and sporting goods. With some 5000 products on its Swedish site and around 100 in Britain and Germany, the company sees a pan-European opportunity, with staff in seven countries and sales planned to grow from $4 million in 1999 to $54 million in 2000 and $700 million by 2003. Customers sign up for free membership and items are sold once a minimum number of buyers have signed up, against a sliding price scale. 'Our aim is to destroy the existing value chain, cut out the middleman and connect the member to the manufacturer, claims the company's president, John Palmer. Members suggest seventy-five per cent of products listed. The site recently shipped 4000 Christmas trees to Swedish homes at SKr39, discounted from the usual SKr200.

Other collaborative buying sites include Adabra (www.adabra.com) and the recently launched Ybag (www.ybag.com).

Business-to-consumer pricing strategies are in their infancy. Shopping at auction sites can be frustrating as underbidding or out-of-stocks occur. Sites so far adopting such strategies require that consumers place their trust in relatively unknown intermediary brands. Some Western cultures are unused to the practice of haggling or negotiation (a reluctance which, of course, has been encouraged by conventional retail intermediaries within those markets) and must learn new rules of purchasing. The Internet allows nearly every industry sector to leverage variable pricing as a competitive weapon – to reduce excess inventory or to meet demand more dynamically. The so-called 'ripple effect' of this will be significant. Existing retailers' lack of flexibility in incrementally adjusting price levels (so-called 'menu costs') will count against them, although consumer's continuing reliance on a few known and trusted on-line brands may work against a fully frictionless environment.[13] Those holding (either physically or in title) excess inventory will be especially disadvantaged, although a number of such businesses are now investigating the use of the Internet for clearance auctions, through a shared marketplace or by means of third parties (such as www.CloseOutNow.com, founded in May 2000).

Conventional Retail Responses

The majority view among informed commentators is that despite the rhetoric, e-commerce's impact on retail will be incremental rather than immediately transforming:

> Retailers trading out of stores have successfully met the challenge of previous high-growth formats. Mail order companies, telephone sales and television shopping channels have all done little more than chip away at the market share of property-based retailers.[14]

This view is unsurprising, not least because of the importance of confidence in maintaining and enhancing the value of 'bricks and mortar' retailing in the minds of all stakeholders, particularly property investors and real estate professionals. The conservatives had many of their prejudices reinforced at the end of 1999 and into the first quarter of 2000, as high technology and Internet

stocks experienced the first of a number of significant downward corrections.

> This was supposed to be it. The big one. This [1999] would be the Christmas that would see the US, as a collective purchasing whole, forsake its love affair with the shopping mall and get down and dirty with the Internet. Yessir! We were going to see records not just broken, but splintered into a thousand pieces – scattered in the wake of US consumers riding in the fast lane of the information superhighway (*Los Angeles Times*).

Yet estimates suggest that, while US consumers spent between $5 billion in the lead-up to Christmas 1999 (just over twice as much as in 1998), on-line nevertheless accounted for only a little over 1.4 per cent of total US retail sales in 1999 ($31 billion of $2.7 trillion) compared with just under one per cent in 1998. UK on-line retailing turned over in the order of £200 million in pre-Christmas trading – equivalent to on-line sales in the whole of 1998. However, the company which made these estimates, E-Insight, suggested that these retailers also lost some £75 million over the period. Heavy discounting and marketing costs were largely to blame, with electrical retailing suffering particularly badly. Other estimates put UK on-line trading at nearer £400 million during the period. Both estimates mean that 1999 Christmas on-line accounted for only between 0.9 per cent and 1.3 per cent of total retail sales.

Even the best-favoured sector, on-line book retailing, only achieved a maximum market share of around four per cent in the UK during the Christmas period, according to book trade organisation BookTrack. Despite major marketing efforts in the whole eight-week lead-up to Christmas and much media hype, conventional shops still overwhelmed the five major Internet retailers – selling over 30.8 million titles, compared with fewer than half a million on-line; a market share of only 1.6 per cent. Hardly 'the big one', although impressive from a standing start.

However, despite the dampening effect of recent events, the Internet threatens to undermine the traditional defences of established retailers. The perceived high cost of retail property (at least in parts of Western Europe) is suggested as being one of the chief barriers to retail internationalisation. The argument runs that economies favouring overly restrictive planning regulation (especially those in Germany, France, UK and the

Netherlands) give rise to congested and overtrading retail space that, in turn, commands artificially high rental levels. For example, a recent survey by Management Horizons Europe suggests that US consumers have access to some eight times as much shopping space per capita than UK shoppers.[15] Partly as a consequence, the authors observe, average rental per square foot of speciality retailing tends to be twice as high in the UK compared with the US. Further, particular national constraints add to this inequity: the predominant UK climate favouring five-year upward-only rent reviews (rather than turnover rental arrangements) exacerbates a consistently upward spiral in property costs.

The role of e-commerce in circumventing some of these barriers cannot be discounted. A wider potential impact on confidence should not be ignored:

> The Internet tends to disperse and decentralise human activity, while the value of real estate stems from the economy's need to concentrate and centralise human activity. That suggests that the Internet will tend to 'cannibalise' retail sales away from store-based retailers, thereby reducing the underlying value of retail real estate.[16]

By mid-2000, the UK had witnessed something of a flight from investment in retail property as investors sought less uncertain destinations for funds. It has not been difficult for these stakeholders to calculate the knock-on effect of even a five per cent market share captured on-line upon traditional retailers' margins, profits and their continuing ability to afford high rents in regional malls.

In reality traditional retail will not be instantly transformed either by the opportunities or the threats of e-business. There will just be more opportunities and more risks, which will be unsettling for all. While many of the opportunities and risks are potential rather than actual, retail businesses and real estate investors will want to think through the implications of this scenario. We consider five possible sets of effects below.

THE IMPACT ON EXISTING SPACE REQUIREMENTS

Retailers express most concern about a growing phenomenon known as the 'showroom effect' – where customers touch and feel the product in the store, and then return home to purchase cheaper on-line. Increasing price transparency makes it difficult for many retainers within high-value merchandise categories (such as vehicle sales and electrical goods) to avoid invidious price comparisons and close the sale. A number of retailers have already dropped shop floor prices to reflect Internet levels. Some (but not all) have started to extend 'never knowingly undersold' guarantees to Internet comparisons. In the long term, these sorts of strategies may prove barely sustainable in the light of the very different cost base under which the conventional retailer operates. Certainly, they have contributed to the price deflation now common in many Western economies. Should the 'bricks and mortar' operators seek to rebuff non-genuine browsers, or will they want to develop their own smaller specialist showrooms to offset the cost of competitive on-line price positioning?

It is often suggested that the resort of the conventional retailer in the face of on-line competition of this kind is to reposition the business through investment in leisure and entertainment retailing. Many see this as an effective and affordable antidote to the blandness of on-line retailing. But is it? The experience of leisure retailing within Western Europe demonstrates that there are some significant commercial challenges and almost as much rhetoric as there is in the case of on-line retailing.[17] And what real estate implications arise from any shift in this direction?

The effects upon the traditional shopping hierarchy of on-line retailing are therefore potentially very significant. Any lack of investor confidence in conventional retail property is likely further to reinforce, for example, investments in the lowest-risk locations. What happens to the smaller 'caught in the middle' centres across much of Western Europe, for example, the existing top seventy shopping centres in the UK, or the super regional shopping centres in the US marketplace? Are stores in the smallest centres favoured as drop-off or collection points?

How will conventional retailers engaging in on-line activity seek to use their existing stores (if at all) as return points? The US experience shows (as in the case of Gap) that being able to use existing real estate for returns is a competitive advantage for established businesses over new on-line entrants.

THE GEOGRAPHICAL IMPACT

Many on-line trials (most especially in grocery goods) have tended to be focused in urban areas, 'creaming off' revenue from densely populated and easy-to-service markets. Boston, for example, boasts some ten on-line grocers at the time of writing. What are the effects of this concentration of competition upon the differential opportunities for consumers in different geographical areas? Conversely, in more physically extensive rural areas, how will on-line retailing manifest itself physically? What tangible resources will be required to maintain a profitable and cost-efficient distribution system?

THE IMPACT BY SECTOR

Will on-line trading's differential effect on product groups affect the pace and site locational requirements of existing retails? If so, how? Will department stores need to focus on fewer, higher margin, more tangible and experiential departments, for example? Conversely, while software retailers such as Egghead have closed their physical retail outlets, we have seen no real slowdown in physical bookshop development in the face of extensive on-line market growth.

Will the notion of 'dynamic trade' in e-commerce (a sort of 'just-in-time' principle for the consumer) have a knock-on effect upon other channels of distribution and, if so, what are the implications for the size of and split between retail selling and non-selling space within conventional stores?

NEW PROPERTY REQUIREMENTS

The natural reaction of the property industry faced with the challenge of e-commerce is to indicate a greater need for distribution centres. Companies like Entertainment UK, an entertainments products distributor, is currently building itself a major new state-of-the-art distribution centre to enable it to better handle the personalised distribution (see Chapter 9 for further discussion of infrastructure development issues). FDPSavills estimate some 8 million square feet will be required in the UK alone over the next five years, but is this the only (or indeed the most significant) new property requirement?

Will 'showroom effects' affect store size or format? Will retailers be able to open in smaller towns previously

uneconomic, because of a new 'extended market' and increased activity as a result of the need to handle returns of Internet-purchased goods?

Will there be other ways for real estate investors to make money? For example, Taubman Centres (the sixth-biggest REIT – Real Estate Investment Trust – in the US) has recently purchased a stake in an on-line mall.

THE IMPACT ON SUPPLY CHAINS

As contributions elsewhere in this volume make clear, business-to-business exchanges have become increasingly fashionable vehicles for investment and development. *The Economist*[18] estimated that in the first quarter of 2000, some 759 B-to-B exchanges were in existence, dealing with commodities ranging from agricultural feed (www.rooster.com) to petrochemicals and pharmaceuticals. Single industry-wide exchanges have been seen as important in achieving cost savings – so important that businesses normally in competition have been happy to suspend their differences to achieve mutual benefit. Such exchanges particularly favour those sectors where concentration is high and there are relatively few buyers. The formation of a motor components exchange between Ford, General Motors and Daimler-Chrysler therefore made sound business sense (see Chapter 10).

Retailing, where supply chain efficiencies – particularly in the grocery sector – are highly prized is not so highly concentrated as some of the markets targeted for exchange applications and there is less overwhelming logic for mutual buying pacts which suppress competitive instincts. Suggesting that European retailers have until recently been shielded from large-scale globalisation pressures, Hubbard and Kelly propose that mergers, acquisitions and partnership arrangements are now being pursued for a number of different reasons: 'For food retailing, size matters in securing purchasing power; in non-food, size is important only when delivering supply chain success.' Hubbard and Kelly conclude that the correct choice of partner is critical in determining such success. March 2000 saw the launch of an exchange jointly owned by Sears of the US and Carrefour-Promodès of France, together with software group Oracle. GlobalNetXchange will initially put together purchases made between the two parties from over 50,000 suppliers and totalling $80 billion annually. It is no accident that one of the founding partners in this first retailing exchange is a global grocery retailer and that two subsequent members, J. Sainsbury in the UK and

Ahold of the Netherlands, are in the same business. The members stress the benefits as follows:[19]

- greater efficiencies and cost savings in buying on the web;
- collaborative buying opportunities for non-resaleable goods;
- more efficient planning and forecasting in supply chain;
- increased range and choice of sourced goods, particularly in own-label goods.

Implications and Conclusions

In one sense, the Internet provides simply another means for retail businesses to internationalise.[20] There is no reason why practitioners should not simply extend the conventional tool-kit used to evaluate potential markets into an electronic dimension.[21] We may nevertheless expect to observe a differential distribution of risks and benefits associated with internationalisation through electronic as against more traditional means.

A number of competitive advantages may exist to offset – albeit in some cases temporarily – the apparently greater expertise and experience of new entrants to the channel from non-domestic markets. We identify three, below.

ADVANTAGES FROM ESTABLISHED STAKEHOLDER NETWORKS

Advantages from established physical infrastructure (or 'grounded capital')[22] are unlikely to be sustainable in the long term. While warehousing in appropriate locations, relationships with distribution companies and logistics skills appropriate to the market are already part of the set of competencies offered by domestic retail businesses, these are open to gradual encroachment. Further, it will prove just as difficult (if not more so) to translate this infrastructure into one more appropriate for e-commerce as it would be for new entrants to start from scratch. The grounded capital advantage has not prevented operators such as Lands' End and Amazon.com from purchasing appropriate infrastructure, although the current evidence is that many established e-commerce operators outside Europe have a poor understanding of this infrastructural barrier.

CULTURAL AND LOCAL MARKET ADVANTAGES

A second advantage is consumers' preference for familiar cultural conditions. Within Europe the consumer will remain reluctant to depart from known national retail brands, which are generally associated with culturally relevant values and beliefs. This advantage is often portrayed as one of local market knowledge, where the domestic retailer is, by definition, best placed to understand and anticipate the needs of their marketplace. Already, we have some limited evidence that European on-line consumers do seem to prefer local merchants – when they are available – rather than US vendors. According to Jupiter Communications, in 1997 only five per cent of European shoppers polled bought from European-based retail sites; in 1999, some fifteen per cent bought locally.

RETAILERS AS ELECTRONIC INTERMEDIARIES

The changing character of the electronic channel provides a third set of potential advantages. The US has witnessed the growth of gateways or portals into the Internet originally dominated by companies such as AOL, but now increasingly by web properties such as Yahoo!, Geocities and the Excite Network. These companies effectively determine the access of individual users to the Internet and the relative visibility of sites. As gatekeepers, they have the potential to act as the first-contact intermediary for the end user. This is a significant opportunity for European consumer-facing businesses.

Aside from the exponential growth of so-called 'free' Internet service providers (there are over 150 such in the UK alone) European retailers have begun to explore the sector. In the UK, Dixons, the Arcadia Group and Tesco have been particularly active. The Arcadia Group's Zoom portal gives access to the group's fashion brands and partnerships with designer labels. In France Kingfisher/Group Arnault's Libertysurf ISP operation promises to offer a pan-European service. Gatekeeping in this way provides a number of opportunities for retailers. Those who operate gateways can control the extent of brand visibility of others, can take advantage of trust earned through conventional channels and can capture data in ways which can be integrated with existing data warehouses within conventional channels.

However, as Table 4 shows, and despite the encouraging evidence from Jupiter Communications above, European consumers show little reluctance in embracing US Internet brands to access the channel. It is instructive to note not only the commonality between countries in occurrence of names, but also how few truly domestic, home-grown sites appear among the top twenty-five web properties in Europe's three largest markets.

Rank	UK	Unique visitors '000	Reach (%)
1	Yahoo!	2687	34.4
2	MSN	2642	33.8
3	Freeserve.co.uk	2524	32.3
4	Microsoft	2211	28.3
5	AOL	1930	24.7
6	Lycos	1479	18.9
7	Demon	1447	18.5
8	Geocities	1420	18.2
9	Passport.com	1309	16.7
10	BBC	1293	16.5

Rank	France	Unique visitors '000	Reach (%)
1	Wanadoo	1119	47.9
2	Yahoo!	877	37.5
3	Microsoft	705	30.2
4	AOL	623	26.6
5	Multimania	593	25.3
6	Voilà	579	24.8
7	Club-internet.fr	504	21.5
8	MSN	470	20.1
9	Free.fr	377	16.1
10	Altavista	375	16

Rank	Germany	Unique visitors '000	Reach (%)
1	T-Online	3612	68
2	Yahoo!	1767	33.3
3	AOL	1566	29.5
4	Microsoft	1404	26.4
5	Lycos	1345	25.3
6	Netscape	1082	20.4
7	MSN	993	18.7
8	Tripod	841	15.8
9	Fireball.de	815	15.4
10	Geocities.com	755	14.2

Table 4 – Top 10 Global Domains, UK, France and Germany, January 2000, Source: MMXI Europe BV, 2000

The evidence that European retailers can use existing barriers, or generate new defences against non-domestic competition through electronic channels is yet to be discerned. The advantages outlined above can arguably be eroded through the activities of new entrants offering new choices and competitive prices to consumers, in just the same ways as conventional non-domestic competitors have done within European markets already. Whether existing market shares are eroded as a result of on-line competition will be similarly a

consequence of the domestic retailer's ability to command a defensible position in the marketplace in terms of brand trust, value for money and price competitiveness.

We are likely to see much consolidation as on-line players such as Boo.com fall by the wayside, having failed to convince their prospective customers or their investors of the merits of their offer or performance. It is likely that there will be many joint ventures and partnerships, and not a few acquisitions, in the future. But of course, this means stronger and more effective competition for existing retailers in years to come. At the time of writing, we can start to see these competitive pressures building further.

NOTES

1. Quelch, J. A. and Takeuchi, H., 'Non-store Marketing: Fast Track or Slow?', *Havard Business Review*, 58, 1981, pp.103–12.

2. Davies, R. L. and Reynolds, J., *The Development of Tele-shopping and Teleservices*, Longman, Harlow, 1988.

3. Morganosky, M., 'Research Note. Retailing and the Internet: a perspective on the top 100 US retailers', *International Journal of Retail & Distribution Management*, 25, 11, 1997, pp. 372–7.

4. CIES, 'Top of Mind 1999', *Food Business News*, December 1998.

5. Dawson, J. A., 'Retail Change in the European Community', in Davies, R. L. (ed.), *Retail Planning Policies in Western Europe*, Routledge, London, 1996.

6. Reynolds, J., *Home Shopping across Europe*, KPMG, London, 1997.

7. Ducati will, however, use its distributors to carry out pre-delivery inspection and final delivery.

8. Rayport, J. F. and Sviokla, J. J., 'Exploiting the Virtual Value Chain', *Harvard Business Review*, 73, 6, 1995, p.75.

9. Sarkar, M. B., Butler, B. and Steinfeld, C., 'Intermediaries and Cybermediaries: A Continuing Role for Mediating Players in the Electronic Marketplace', *Journal of Computer-Mediated Communication* (http://www.ascusc.org/jcmc/vol1/issue3/sarkar.html), 1996.

10 Sawhney, M., *Meet the Metamediary*, http://sawhney.kellogg.nwu.edu/metamed/metamediation.htm, 1996.

11 ibid.

12 Maes, P., 'Software Agents and the Future of Electronic Commerce', Tutorial on Agents and Electronic Commerce, MIT (http://pattie.www.media.mit.edu/people/pattie/ECOM/), 1998.

13 Brynjolfsson, E. and Smith, M.D., 'Frictionless Commerce? A Comparison of Internet and Conventional Retailers', *Management Science*, April 2000. Working paper available at: http://ebusiness.mit.edu/papers/friction.

14 Cooper, M. and Rose, A., 'Agents' reports split over the Net's impact on retail', *Estates Gazette*, 12 June 1999, p.40.

15 Management Horizons Europe, 'Comparative Retail Costs', A report sponsored by the British Brands Group, MHE/Horizon Retail Design and Strategy, 1999.

16 Merrill Lynch, 'Real Estate. Minding the Store: Retailing will influence Real Estate' in *E-Commerce*, Global Securities Research and Economics Group, Merrill Lynch & Co., London, 1999.

17 Howard, E. B., *Leisure and Retailing*, Longman, Harlow, 1989.

18 *The Economist*, 'Shopping around the web: a survey of E-Commerce', 26 February 2000, http://economist.com/editorial/freeforall/20000226/index-survey.html.

19 J. Sainsbury, Press release, 23 March 2000.

20 Reynolds, J., 'Who will Dominate European E-Commerce? Threats and Opportunities for European Retailers,' *International Journal of Retail & Distribution Management*, Vol.28(1), 2000.

21 McGoldrick, P. J. and Blair, D., 'International market appraisal and positioning', in McGoldrick, P. J. and Davies, G. (eds), *International Retailing: Trends and Strategies*, Pitman, London, 1995.

22 Wrigley, N., 'Sunk Costs and Corporate Restructuring: British Food Retailing and the Property Crisis', in Wrigley, N. and Lowe, M., *Retailing, Consumption and Capital: Towards the New Retail Geography*, Longman, Harlow, 1996.

The Business-to-Business Boom

Graham Costello

Today, the world is excited by Amazon.com, ebay.com, rei.com and others in the retail B-to-C market space. But the largest segment of e-commerce is the buying and selling of goods and services by businesses to other businesses. Market studies show that B-to-B commerce will grow at a very rapid rate, becoming much larger than B-to-C commerce. IDC recently predicted that by the year 2002, more than three-quarters of all commerce facilitated on the Internet will be of the B-to-B variety. To give some sense of the difference, one 2000 estimate made the B-to-B marketplace $617 billion compared with $116 billion for B-to-C. Moreover, Forrester Research has predicted that B-to-B e-commerce will surpass US$1 trillion by 2003. Industry adoption rates will vary, but growth is expected to be strong in most sectors, but especially in computing/electronics, utilities, petro-chemicals and motor vehicles.[1]

The initial phases of B-to-B e-commerce were point-to-point solutions between trading partners. The second phase was hub-and-spoke B-to-B, where a major supplier or buyer established a network linking it to its business partners. Now we see improved interoperability of the Internet, enabling the linking of previously proprietary hub-and-spoke networks into multipoint-to-multipoint markets.[2] We will inevitably continue to witness a migration towards e-market exchanges (see Chapter 10), vertical portals and other communities of interest[3], which will facilitate value generation of one kind or another for players in the B-to-B space.

In this chapter we outline the economic laws that are making the difference and are influencing developments in B-to-B. The chapter describes these developments and then proceeds to discuss emerging new business models. We then look at four major case studies. These cover Amway's use of an extranet to facilitate its massive distribution network; IBM's initiatives on e-procurement and e-care for its business and its partners; Boeing's on-line selling of spare parts; and Chrysler's on-line integration with its suppliers. Finally, the chapter draws out the implications of these developments for the future of B-to-B and its role in the development of an e-business.

Economic Laws and their Implications

Three laws of economics are driving rapid growth in business-to-business e-commerce. These are Metcalf's law of network utility, Coase's law of transaction costs and the law of Socio-Technological Disruption. Let us look at these.

Metcalf's law states that the value of a network increases exponentially as the number of users increases. The value of a business network increases as more organisations connect to it. A technical example is the Internet itself. While connections to the Internet were limited to US Defence Department computers the network was valuable, but this value increased exponentially when universities connected to the same network and has increased exponentially again as commercial organisations have connected. It is likely that the value of the Internet will increase exponentially again with the advent of 'pervasive' computing, when every device has an Internet address and is connected to the very same pervasive and ubiquitous network.

In the business world, networks of suppliers, manufacturers and distributors combine to deliver an end product or service to customers. If only two of these parties are connected then they will achieve some value. But if the whole supply chain is connected to the same network then there are many more opportunities to create value through 'virtual' vertical integration.

Likewise, linking similar manufacturers to the same horizontal network enables them to share resources, intellectual capital and services, thereby creating value through 'virtual' horizontal integration.

The Internet enables these networks to form and re-form quickly, and 'just in time'. The result of this dynamic network formation is they will evolve rapidly to exploit inefficiencies and to create new value for their members. It is this speed of network evolution that is a key issue for businesses. The central issue for businesses is no longer product or technology evolution. Rather, it is the evolution of business models in the context of the network economy.

Coase stated that the boundaries of a firm occur where it is more efficient for an activity to be executed internally rather than contracted externally. Industrial age firms grew by internalising operations such as procurement, administration, human re-sources, distribution, customer relationship management, sales and marketing etc. They developed these competencies internally because it was simply too difficult or too expensive to have ex-ternal organisations do it for them. Coase and followers such as Oliver Williamson used transaction cost theory and information theory to help define the optimal boundary of an organisation.

In the information age the cost of communication, collabor-ation and integration approaches zero. Consequently it is simpler and cheaper to outsource activities to third parties who specialise in those activities. Businesses are outsourcing non-core activities so that they can focus their people, management time and capital on core value creation activities. Moreover, when transaction costs are low, small corporations can challenge established players. Of course, business life is not as simple as this and there are a range of considerations that come into play before sourcing activities externally. These are dealt with in Chapter 10.

An implication of Coase's law is that new on-line businesses will continue to be spawned that aim to capture the most profitable part of the business without incurring the incumbent's high internal administrative overheads. New Internet start-ups focus all their assets on growth activities such as product development and marketing. Consequently new competitors can rapidly emerge from obscurity such as Amazon, AOL, VerticalNet, iSyndicate, E-Loan, ipix and thousands more.

The law of Socio-Technological disruption states that wid-ening gaps between technological and social norms result in occasional 'value revolutions'. While technology increases

exponentially, social systems increase incrementally. This difference in growth creates occasional gaps between the capability of technologies such as the Internet and their use by social systems such as businesses. This gap creates opportunities for new entrants to capture value from the 'gap' to replace the old way of doing business.

The larger the gap the greater the opportunity for revolutionary business change. While historically these gaps have been created by new technologies such as the printing press, weaving loom, trains, automobiles etc., the latest 'value revolution' is being triggered by the Internet.

Businesses have long anticipated the benefits of better interoperability among constitutents and their assets. Networks based on SNA, EDI, Swift are examples. The difference today is that the threshold of investment in Internet networks has been reduced to the cost of a browser – and they are often free.

SOME IMPLICATIONS

These changing economics are dismantling physical value chains and reassembling them as market-centric virtual value chains.

Value chains are being dismantled. In the industrial era, corporations had clearly defined roles and corporate boundaries, but in the information economy, reduced cost and increased ease of co-ordination has broken down these corporate boundaries (see Figure 1). In some cases, design, manufacture, distribution and customer relationship management have become more highly integrated. The end result is that partners who play different roles in the value chain become more interdependent. Some companies such as Cisco have extended the size, scope and complexity of their enterprise by integrating their business partners into their virtual value chain (see also Chapter 10).

Alternatively, e-commerce can cause disaggregation of a value chain. Where the cost of searching for new partners and establishing trading relationships with them has been dramatically reduced, companies can be more opportunistic about whom they partner with. Trading relationships can be more short-term and spot-price sensitive. To this end we continue to see the formation of electronic trading exchanges, or e-market exchanges, such as Virtual Chip Exchange, e-Chemicals, PlasticsNet, Asset Banker.com and many more across a range of industries.

The result is that corporate boundaries are being broken down by lower co-ordination costs. While companies are increasingly specialising in core competencies.

In the industrial era, corporations had clearly defined roles and corporate boundaries . . .

Design | Manufacture | Distribution | Customer Relationship Management

. . . but in the e-Economy, reduced cost of co-ordination has broken down these corporate boundaries.

Design | Manufacture | Distribution | Customer Relationship Management

In many cases the value chain has disaggregated, with one party retaining responsibility for the customer relationship and aggregation of all other services.

Design | Customer Relationship Management | Manufacture | Distribution

Figure 1 – The Breaking Down of Corporate Boundaries

As the cost of communication and co-ordination reduces, it becomes more feasible to specialise and collaborate. Intellectual property can be separated from physical goods and relationship management. Corporate value chains can thus be disassembled as external providers offer better quality and more specialised services than those that can be provided internally.

New value chains centred around markets are emerging. Near perfect information and real-time communication are creating virtual markets. A useful way to view B-to-B e-commerce is to look at the value chain and distribution channel from the perspective of these new markets (see Figure 2).

The Internet is enabling increased specialisation and the introduction of new intermediaries. There are now agents representing buyers that search for the best products on the best terms. These buyer agents will gradually capture relationships with buyers away from suppliers. Likewise, there are agents representing the supplier of products and services. In the physical world this role is carried out by wholesalers who have market knowledge and access. Similarly, specialists are emerging who provide physical fulfilment and payment services to on-line companies. Context providers provide access and the industrial or functional context to simplify use by either the buyers or sellers whom they support. This whole system revolves around the market makers who bring buyers and sellers together, and maximise the efficiency of the market.

Viewing a physical value chain from this market-centric perspective highlights the opportunities for companies either to specialise or reposition themselves to capture increased value. Companies that are presently playing the role of both buyer agent and seller agent should consider how they are going to resolve this conflict of interests.

Low interaction and collaboration costs enable e-commerce specialists to attack inefficiencies and redundancies in channel systems.

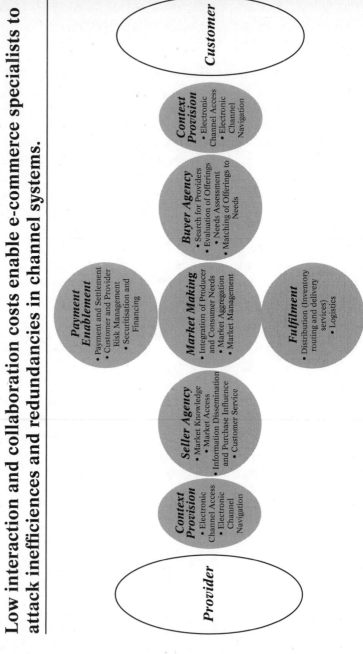

Figure 2 – The New Virtual Channel

Emerging Business Models

The e-opportunity described in Chapter 2 is certainly being grasped in B-to-B. New business models such as Portals, Internet Auctions, e-Supply Chains and Value Networks are proliferating.

Portals. These aggregate vertical segments or provide horizontal services. A portal is an on-line environment that provides users with access to information and services. B-to-B portals focus on specific industry verticals or specific business processes to create value by aggregating buyers and sellers, creating marketplace liquidity and reducing transaction costs. B-to-B portals create revenue through subscription, advertising, commission and transaction fees. Returns on scale increase exponentially with the size of the market created. While customer acquisition and retention costs are high, so are switching costs.

Vertical Portals aggregate buyers and sellers around a specific industrial segment. Figure 3 describes four examples. They create value by aggregating a fragmented market of buyers and sellers to create critical mass, build a domain of industry-specific knowledge, improve supply chain efficiency, create common industry-wide catalogues to enable better integration of systems and link to other vertical or horizontal portals as appropriate. The key success factor is to be perceived as the centre of industry expertise.

Horizontal Portals provide a single function or automate a specific business process across industries. See Figure 4 for four examples. They create value by reducing the cost of specific functions such as accounts payable, accounts receivable, or processes such as procurement. They can integrate multiple value chains across different industrial sectors. The key success factors are process knowledge expertise and automation. Implementation is difficult without some degree of process standardisation.

Vertical Portals aggregate buyers and sellers in a specific industrial segment.

Value Proposition

- aggregate fragmented market of buyers and sellers to create critical mass
- create liquidity in market
- improve efficiency in existing supply chain
- build domain knowledge and industry relationships
- create master catalogues and sophisticated searching
- add value from adjacent verticals

Characteristics

- domain expertise is essential
- customer acquisition and retention costs are high but so are switching costs
- returns on scale increase exponentially with size of market

Examples

- PlasticsNet.com – plastics manufacturers and producers
- eSteel – market between buyers and sellers of steel
- Intracorp.com.au – vertical portals around communities of interest such as sports business sportsbiz.com.au
- themis.com.au – Australian legal community of interest

Figure 3 – Vertical Portals: Examples

Functional Portals or 'horizontal hubs' provide a single function or automate a specific business process across industries.

Value Proposition

- reduce the cost of specific functions such as accounts payable or processes such as procurement

- integrate multiple value chains across different industry sectors

- achieve scale benefits

- develop domain of knowledge on specific process or function

Characteristics

- Degree of process standardisation is critical

- process knowledge and workflow automation expertise required

- need ability to customise business processes to respond to industry – specific differences

Examples

- iMark.com – buying and selling capital equipment

- Adauction – auctions of perishable on-line and print advertising inventory

- Optus CommerceOne – e-procurement for Australian businesses

- Telstra Streamlink/Sausage/Solution 6, SME ASP solution

Figure 4 – Functional Portals: Examples

Internet auctions. These create a cheap and easy electronic marketplace to exchange goods and services. B-to-B auction sites enable buyers to find sellers and to negotiate price and terms. Inventory is not held by the auction site but with the seller, while physical fulfilment of the goods and exchange of payment is facilitated by the auction site. Revenue is created through listing fees, commissions and advertising.

Auctions can be conducted in the normal fashion, where buyers bid until the auction is closed. If the reserve price is met, the highest bid wins. Alternatively, a wide range of formats can be implemented such as 'Dutch Auctions' and 'Reverse Auctions'. In Reverse Auctions buyers declare their requirement and sellers bid to provide on the required terms. A more formal process is the standard Request for Information (RFI), Request for Quote (RFQ), tendering process, which is increasingly implemented on B-to-B auction sites for major items or long-term contracts.

Dynamic pricing that reflects the true market price enables businesses to maximise profits when possible, and to ensure that they are not left with unsold perishable products and services such as advertising space.

It is possible to get carried away with the auction concept and it is important to retain a sense of what practical business issues have to be dealt with. Consider the case of IBuy.com (see Figure 5). It identified in 1999 a clear business opportunity. Small-to-medium enterprises required a means to trade products and services with other small-to-medium enterprises and Internet auctions seemed an inexpensive way to facilitate this type of flexible shopfront. IBuy built auction functionality and offered it to enterprises wishing to auction off products and services. The second stage was to build vertical portals around auction sites, while the final stage was to build geographically based and community-of-interest-based portals.

IBuy.com found that building Internet auction sites is relatively inexpensive, but signing up corporations to use the site is time-consuming and expensive in management time. The main lessons learned were that (a) marketing is key, (b) gaining access to the relevant business owners is a critical success factor and (c) don't underestimate the effort required to build momentum in a small business. Alliances are an important factor in helping rapidly to establish business partner networks that assist an online business to reach its required critical mass.

Internet Auction sites create a near perfect market where transaction costs are minimal and value can be captured through listing fees, commissions and advertising.

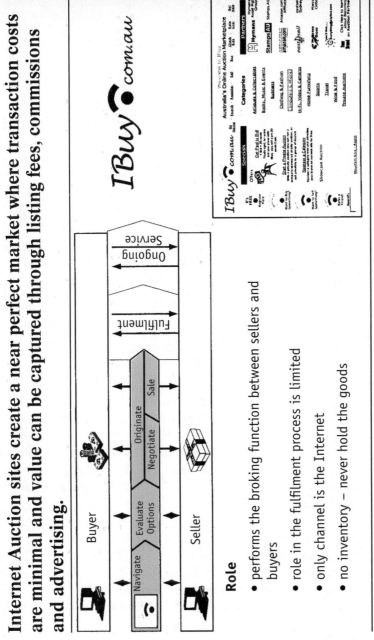

Role

- performs the broking function between sellers and buyers
- role in the fulfilment process is limited
- only channel is the Internet
- no inventory – never hold the goods

Figure 5 – Internet Auction Site: IBuy.com

E-supply chains. Supply chains can be optimised by electronically integrating trading partners. Efficiencies are achieved by introducing strategic sourcing, redesigning processes and implementing supporting technologies such as e-procurement.

Strategic sourcing rationalises the number of suppliers that a company deals with and the products that it obtains. Typically, in the order of six per cent of suppliers provide fifty-seven per cent of invoices for fifty-four per cent of spend. Therefore, concentrating on a few key suppliers and aggregating infrequent suppliers can assist in the ability to negotiate better terms, while reducing administrative overhead.

Procurement processes are generally inefficient with the average cost of an invoice often being in the vicinity of US$75. Automating this process through implementation of an e-procurement system can reduce administrative overheads while increasing integration with internal systems. In fact, properly executed e-procurement initiatives can often be the 'safe' e-business play that funds other higher risk–reward profile e-business opportunities. Also not to be overlooked is the fact that to take full advantage of strategic sourcing and e-procurement it is necessary to redesign processes that link trading partners. We give examples of redesigned e-supply chains below.

Value networks. These combine multiple linear value chains to build a network of greater value. An example is shown in Figure 6. Value chains link adjacent trading partners. B-to-B e-commerce enables this value chain to be extended to incorporate not only the end customer but also the suppliers who developed the source products and services. Integrating all these players removes inefficiencies in the value chain and consequently creates greater value to be shared (see also Chapter 10).

Linking extended value chains creates a network comprising other companies' customers and suppliers. These value networks enable efficiencies to be found throughout the extended network. They can also create additional value to the end consumer by aggregating products and services to satisfy customer needs in a holistic sense rather than simply to provide independent elements.

Given these developments, let us look now in more detail at four case studies of effective B-to-B implementation. These are set in different industry sectors and are Amway Australia, IBM, Boeing and Chrysler.

The emerging business landscape is characterised by the emergence of innovative organisational forms called Value Networks.

Example of Value Network

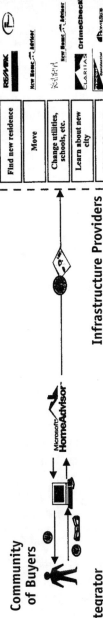

Community of Buyers

- Find temporary housing
- Find new residence
- Move
- Change utilities, schools, etc.
- Learn about new city
- Obtain Mortgage

Integrator

- Acts as agent on behalf of buyers or sellers in aggregating needs and enabling search and evaluation of options against buyer values/intentions
- Aggregates buyer and seller needs as trusted third party and performs market matching and clearing activities
- Performs governance and management functions

Infrastructure Providers

- Provides software solutions to enable specific business functions
- Provides systems and networks for e-commerce access and transport

Content Providers

- Sells goods and services to end customers

Figure 6 – Value Networks

CASE STUDY: AMWAY NETWORKS DISTRIBUTORS

With 2.5 million distributors in seventy-nine countries and more than US$5.6 billion in revenues, Amway is one of the largest distribution networks in the world. Amway Australia is experiencing twenty-eight per cent annual growth and processing 60,000 orders and 250,000 other transactions every month. In the past, orders and stock enquiries were handled through mail, fax, phone and electronic dial-up, necessitating computer entry that resulted in double handling and duplication of effort. With more than 90,000 distributors requiring information on product offerings, orders, sales points and more, processing and fulfilling these orders and requests became a challenge. In order to manage their business more efficiently, distributors were demanding information in real time, with immediate access to their sales performance data following the placement of orders.

Amway developed the Electronic Link Via Internet Services (ELVIS) extranet that makes up-to-the-minute information available to distributors anywhere, any time and streamlines order processing and fulfilment. Distributors order on-line, verify availability of products and remit secure payment via credit card.

Business costs and benefits. Within a year, one-half of all orders were being processed over ELVIS, reducing the cost of order processing by fifty per cent. Resultant savings in reduced order processing costs in the first year were US$1.26 million.

The organisation benefited in other ways as well. Distributors have more time to spend with customers; they also have more timely and accurate information about new products, stock availability and delivery. Further, real-time access to sales information motivates distributors to achieve monthly targets and the impact of each purchase is shown instantly on the sales points systems.

Lessons learned. Distributors were motivated to migrate to the new system, as Amway was willing to pay for the first twelve months of computer lease costs. The ELVIS project itself was brought from concept to pilot in twelve weeks and from pilot to full launch in a further twelve weeks. Some 125 distributors participated in the pilot programme prior to the system going live. Recently Amway Australia has launched direct sales to consumers with the distributors playing a marketing and fulfilment role, while still getting credit for all sales. This is a radical change in business model that would not have been possible if the distributors had not first gained confidence through the earlier project.

CASE STUDY: IBM, E-PROCUREMENT AND E-CARE

In 1993 IBM was suffering increasing losses despite also having achieved increasing revenue. IBM's market value was less than US$50 billion and the capital markets were not optimistic about IBM's future. IBM embarked on a mission to redesign itself. Transforming itself into an e-business was a significant aspect of that transformation. All business processes were re-engineered and migrated to the web where appropriate. There were seven major e-business initiatives that interfaced with different stakeholder groups:

- e-commerce (selling IBM products and services on the web);
- e-care for business partners (promoting loyalty and growth through web-based programs);
- e-care for customers (nurturing and supporting IBM customers via the web);
- e-procurement (streamline the procurement process and build partner alliances);
- e-care for employees (moving all HR processes and information to the intranet increasing the productivity, efficiency and skills of IBM employees);
- e-care for influencers (timely information for the press, analysts and shareholders);
- e-marketing communications (furthering the IBM brand through the web media).

This case study will outline the two key B-to-B initiatives, e-procurement and e-care for business partners.

e-procurement. In 1999, IBM's Global Procurement team committed to web-enable 10,000 IBM suppliers and transact US$11 billion in purchases with them – it has exceeded the supplier mark and the transaction goal is clearly in sight.

An application called 'A-Source' aids in controlling the cost of materials from IBM subcontractors. A standardised electronic bill of materials allows IBM to check the prices of components that suppliers receive. By leveraging the ability to quote and compare prices across the web, IBM is able to help its suppliers and itself obtain the best pricing and sourcing for parts.

IBM has also developed a search engine that helps to find new

suppliers. A recent pilot identified ten new sources for a product that it was thought could only be acquired from a single source. And now IBM is working to obtain the best possible price from the vendors and to ensure that back-up sources are available.

Another procurement application is making it easier for IBM to purchase technical services over the web. By building a knowledge database for qualified skills, IBM is shortening the cycle time to find those skills from ten days down to three days. This saves critical time for its business units and it reduces duplicate efforts made by suppliers responding to queries from multiple IBM business units.

e-care for business partners. Business partners are important to IBM since they resell IBM products, provide their own products and services to complement IBM's business, and depend on IBM as a supplier of products and services. A large percentage of these business partners are small-to-medium businesses that benefit from reducing complexity when dealing with IBM.

The interactions between IBM and its business partners were identified as a key opportunity area for web enablement. Therefore IBM embarked on an intense study that involved the business partners. They sat down with the business partners and IBM support organisations, and listened carefully to their issues and concerns to determine where they could be better serviced.

Initial findings revealed that individual IBM organisations built web sites that reflected the way *IBM was organised*, not the way a business partner buys products or needs information. Further, IBM had no business case to justify launching specific sites; IBM had multiple sites providing similar content; and IBM took too long getting sites up and running to support its business partners. In fact, IBM had 40,000 business partners looking for help on 150 IBM web sites, produced by 50 different organisations, covering 500 different products and functioning in different ways.

Improvements were focused in three areas: building new self-service applications to improve productivity; improving the supply chain shared with business partners; and creating efficiencies by eliminating redundancy and duplication. The result was Global PartnerInfo, which provides business partners with a single path to information covering IBM, Lotus, Tivoli and CorePoint. Global PartnerInfo drives commerce, collaboration and information delivery with a powerful, smart search tool.

Business costs and benefits. In the area of Web/EDI, IBM has reduced the cost of billing and inventory processes by enabling the electronic connection of roughly eighty per cent of its supplier base, with savings of approximately US$200,000 in 1998, growing to US$2.3 million in 1999.

E-care for business partners reduced order placing from thirty human interactions and four days elapsed time to 'one touch' and ten minutes. Additional benefits include a seventy-five per cent faster time to market, ninety-five per cent on-time delivery and a significant increase in measured business partner satisfaction.

Lessons learned. There comes a time when centralised control is necessary to extract value from B-to-B initiatives, and clearly devolution and decentralisation were hindering innovation at IBM. Focusing on business partner needs and integrating multiple systems through a common technical architecture achieved maximum value for both IBM and its partners. Also important, legacy systems can be web enabled. Viewing the trading network as an extended value chain enables the entire value chain to be web enabled, thereby releasing maximum value rather than making minor improvements at inter-organisational boundaries.

CASE STUDY: BOEING'S ON-LINE SALE OF SPARE PARTS

Faced with increasing costs of spare-parts management, as well as demand from airlines for a more efficient spare-parts management process, Boeing implemented an extranet that gave airlines access to Boeing internal spare-parts systems.

Boeing's spare-parts division implemented PART (Part Analysis and Requirements Tracking), an Internet-based interface, which allows customers to:

- enter orders directly to Boeing's system, avoiding clerical transcription time and errors, and resulting in fewer incorrect parts delivered;
- receive immediate acknowledgement that Boeing has received their order, eliminating the need for the customer later to match up and confirm acknowledgement messages with purchase orders;
- receive immediate response to information queries regarding part price, availability and order status;
- gain shipment status visibility throughout the delivery process through a direct link to package carriers' web sites.

PART generated over 150,000 transactions in its first six months and that volume grew to half a million by the end of the first year. Since going on-line, more than 200 customers of Boeing Commercial Airplane Group have started using the site to order jetliner spare parts, obtain price quotes, check on the status of shipments and request other information. The potential user base for the site is about 750 airlines and maintenance firms worldwide. More than 410,000 different types of spare parts are available to Boeing customers over the web site. Items range from small fasteners, brackets and machine fittings all the way up to large control surfaces, engine cowlings and landing gear. Boeing stores the items in seven distribution centres, supporting about 7000 Boeing jetliners in the world fleet. According to a senior manager of spares systems:

> The Boeing PART system provides a quick, easy, economical way for our customers to access the Boeing spares inventory database. It's intuitive, fully interactive and lets customers 'pull' information at their option. It greatly reduces the need for hard copies of airbills, shipping schedules and other documents.

By 2000 the web site accounted for about one-quarter of all transactions normally handled manually, including those received via phone and fax, and the proportion is growing steadily. This excludes transactions generated through electronic data interchange, in which mainframe computers operated by very large customers are linked directly to the Boeing database. A summary of the Boeing experiences is provided in Figure 7.

The web site is reached on standard computer work stations with Internet access. Customers register with Boeing for user IDs and passwords, and they need a web browser capable of handling a security protocol.

Business costs and benefits. Customers are more satisfied due to faster, 24×7 access to time-critical parts availability and order status information. Half of Boeing's customers, representing the vast majority of the revenue base, are using the e-business solution after just a year and a half. Boeing is also forging new relationships within its customer's organisations. Access to spare-parts availability and order status through Boeing's PART page is being put in maintenance engineering departments and hangars, not just purchasing departments.

Boeing's e-business solution, rated highly successful by the company, addressed its key business priorities.

Boeing's Successful e-business Experience

Business Priority	Business Value Achieved
Better Serve Spare Parts Customers	• Customers are more satisfied due to faster, 24/7 access to time-critical parts availability and order status information • Half of Boeing's customers (representing the vast majority of the revenue base) are using the e-business solution after just a year and a half • Boeing is forging new relationships within its customers organisations – Access to spare-parts availability and order status through Boeing's PART page is being put in maintenance engineering departments and even hangars, not just purchasing departments
Reduce Costs/Avoid Additional Costs	• Despite a thirty per cent increase in order volume, the division's data entry group has held its headcount constant with a decrease in abandoned calls • The percentage of orders input using the e-business solution has risen from zero to thirteen per cent in a year and a half, while orders transmitted via higher-cost, higher-error methods like telephone and older telex-based EDI technology have dropped • As a result, Boeing has eliminated twenty-five per cent of order processing costs
Generate Revenue	• **Increase in spare parts revenue likely to accrue from Boeing's ability to better serve smaller customers who are not EDI-enabled**

The e-business Solution

• Boeing's spare-parts division implemented the PART (Part Analysis and Requirements Tracking) page, an Internet-based interface, which allows customers to:
  – Enter orders directly to Boeing's system, avoiding clerical transcription time and errors, and resulting in fewer incorrect parts delivered
  – Receive immediate acknowledgement that Boeing has received their order, eliminating the need for the customer later to match up and confirm acknowledgement messages with purchase orders
  – Receive immediate response to information queries regarding part price, availability and order status
  – Gain shipment status visibility throughout the delivery process through a direct line to package carriers' web sites

Figure 7 – Boeing's PART E-Business Solution

Despite a thirty per cent increase in order volume, the division's data entry group has held its headcount constant with a decrease in abandoned calls. The percentage of orders input using the e-business solution has risen from zero to thirteen per cent in a year and a half, while orders transmitted via higher-cost, higher-error methods like telephone and older telex-based EDI technology have dropped. As a result, Boeing has eliminated twenty-five per cent of order-processing costs. Finally, an increase in spare-parts revenue is likely to accrue from Boeing's ability to better serve smaller customers who are not EDI-enabled.

Lesson learned. A key challenge was to integrate the wide variety of internal Boeing spare-part systems that were not previously interoperable. Web-based technologies were capable of this integration task and helped to address key business priorities.

CASE STUDY: CHRYSLER'S ON-LINE INTEGRATION

For Chrysler Corporation, a major US manufacturer of vans, sedans, jeeps and trucks, communicating standards and sharing critical software applications with its almost 20,000 suppliers of parts, packaging and technology is a monumental task. Even though Chrysler provides vendors with dial-in access to its mainframe systems so that they can download information and applications, many suppliers with outdated PCs, incompatible hardware, or limited technical knowledge continued to rely on mail, faxes and phone calls to stay informed. Other suppliers were often frustrated by the dozens of application diskettes sent to them by Chrysler's Supplier Communications Group.

Chrysler developed and implemented the Chrysler Corporation Supply Partner Information Network (SPIN), an intranet-based supply chain management and support environment for distributing files over the web. In its first year of operation, SPIN increased productivity over Chrysler's entire 'Extended Enterprise' family of suppliers by twenty per cent and reduced operating costs significantly.

The SPIN solution has enabled Chrysler to distribute applications and communications packages about policy, procurement and inventory methods over the Internet. According to Jeremy Hamilton-Wright, the team leader in Chrysler's IS department, 'SPIN supports everything from developing product to delivering parts and sending payments. SPIN works for all of Chrysler's different types of suppliers: production suppliers, parts suppliers and the suppliers that package parts.'

Over 3500 supplier locations are registered to access the Chrysler SPIN web site. More than 12,000 users have IDs with which they can access information, such as portable document format (PDF) files of Chrysler's EDI Guide, and QS9000 certification policies and procedures. They can also access dynamic database applications, such as real-time materials requirements data, procurement analyses and strategy applications. According to John Kay, 'Being able to get critical production information to our external suppliers as soon as it becomes available internally is a definite competitive advantage for all concerned.' He explains that for the first time Chrysler's Part Quality Supply System now tracks parts notices on-line from engineering to purchasing to the supplier. If any part has a quality problem, or if there is a parts change notice, that information is avilable on-line immediately, saving both the supplier and Chrysler time and money.

It is expected that all 20,000-plus Chrysler suppliers will be SPIN-enabled, especially as the company adds applications to its site, such as business process information and invoicing information. 'Anything that Chrysler previously communicated to suppliers on paper will eventually go up on the SPIN site,' he says.

Business costs and benefits. SCORE achieved moderate success when it was first introduced in 1989. But in the three years that the programme has been on-line, it has yielded substantial dollar savings, an amazing US$2.5 billion since 1993 and US$1.2 billion for the 1996 model year alone, greatly improving margins for Chrysler and suppliers.

Lessons learned. Chrysler learned by experience that the Internet presents an excellent medium for transferring time-sensitive information, applications and other large files to a multi-platform universe. The solution made it easy for Chrysler to extend its enterprise, communicate with suppliers and put as much useful information on-line as possible.

By 2000, users were dialling into SCORE, using full Lotus Notes clients. Concerns about security have made Chrysler reluctant to let suppliers access the system using a web interface. But Russell DuRoss, system administrator at Chrysler, notes that the company is working on creating an extranet that will allow suppliers to access the system securely using a web browser: 'Because the Internet is so standardised, it will be easier for the suppliers to communicate with Chrysler.'

The most critical element of the infrastructure was the security

integration code. This piece of software acts as a gatekeeper between the web server and the Chrysler applications and data. When users access the Chrysler network from a standard web browser, the security code checks the validity of incoming user IDs and passwords. If there's no match the user's log-in request will either be rejected or the user will be asked to log in again.

Implications and Conclusions

B-to-B e-commerce is rapidly changing the commercial environment. New business models are being tried out and announcements of their adoption are accelerating. During 2000 there has been a particular focus on redesigning supply chains because it is here that the more obvious and easier to achieve business efficiencies and cost savings can be achieved. There seem to be three clear implications from our review.

Benefits can be achieved from B-to-B e-commerce. A recent survey of companies in Europe, Asia and the Americas, sponsored by IBM, revealed that over three-quarters of the companies interviewed claimed some success from their B-to-B e-commerce initiatives. The remaining companies stated that it was either too early to tell or they were uncertain.[4]

Benefits can be generated in several areas including:

- **Creating a new distribution channel.** Where traditional channels are high cost or do not provide direct access to customers or fail to capture profitable segments, a new low-cost channel can be implemented that provides real-time access to the full range of products. Establishing a dialogue with end customers will enable rapid enhancement of existing products and development of new products.
- **Improving distribution channel support.** Where the current distribution channel sells competitors' products and services, or where a large number of trading partners interact with the end customer, extranets can be used to publish up-to-date product information and marketing material, while giving access to internal systems that make operations easier than with competitors.
- **Integrating suppliers.** Where there are a large number of

suppliers with frequent interactions and information flows are critical, integrating suppliers with internal procurement, inventory management and development systems can reduce inventory, administrative costs and time to market.

- **Improving customer relationship management.** Where the product or service is highly configurable, requiring significant interaction with customers, implementing electronic customer service can enable customers to self-configure, while reducing workload on call centres and capturing data on customer behaviour.

Executive sponsorship and clear value proposition are critical success factors. We have met these factors in other chapters, especially Chapters 1, 2 and 7. Existing businesses with considerable investments in physical assets and distribution channels find it hard to initiate the change programme necessary to transform into an e-business. Current profitability, organisational inertia and uncertainty of the future combine with the almost certain risk of channel conflict to create an atmosphere of inaction. To overcome this barrier to change, it is necessary to have senior executive sponsorship with a clear strategic plan that can see the company past the short-term upheaval into the new market space.

Uncertainty about the future can be reduced by conducting scenario planning, reviewing initiatives elsewhere in the world in similar sectors and by conducting detailed planning. A key hurdle to overcome is the development of a positive business case to justify expenditure. In many cases traditional business case methodologies do not capture adequately both the opportunities and the threats posed by B-to-B e-commerce.

Integration is yet another area that will demand senior-level focus and near-flawless execution. Integrating business systems with suppliers and customers will only achieve value if internal systems are operating efficiently and provide access to the correct data. Exposing poor internal systems to trading partners will hasten disintermediation or replacement by competitors.

Finally, though – as Chapter 4 indicates – it is not always that obvious, it is important to recognise that established 'bricks and mortar' companies can have significant advantages over new entrants. The challenge for these more traditional companies is to transform into a 'clicks and mortar' company by complementing existing distribution channels and physical presence through web enablement.

Implementing B-to-B e-commerce is a complex journey. Research summarised in the Introduction (see Figure 2 there) indicates that companies go through multiple stages of adoption, starting with awareness, followed by developing a web presence, piloting of specific B-to-B applications, adoption of B-to-B for core systems, improving core processes and, eventually, integration of processes across value network partners. Each stage of adoption poses its own specific challenges and opportunities. Key challenges are concerns about security, difficulties of integration with core systems and developing clear value propositions for industry-changing initiatives.

Different industry sectors are at different levels of e-business adoption. Financial services, telecommunications, IT vendors and the travel sector have been early adopters, while other sectors like (water) utilities and building and construction have been later adopters. Having said that, there have been some exciting developments recently, even with the 'later adopters'. Cases in point include buildpoint.com, reladder.com and cephren.com (all electronic trading exchanges for construction materials and labour); and also a new exchange being assembled by Scottish-Power for the utilities industry (including water utilities). So we find that even in the most traditional of industries there are opportunities and threats being explored and exploited by players attuned to the world of B-to-B e-commerce.

Divergent business objectives and value propositions across a range of B-to-B trading partners make communications especially important to ensure that all stakeholders' needs are addressed. Many trading partners will be disadvantaged by the shift in power. Non-participation by one critical partner could mean the difference between success and failure. In B-to-B the interconnectivity can be a double-edged sword. When it works it can be incredibly powerful. But the connected corporation is also as strong as its weakest link and can fail as spectacularly as it can succeed, making risk and security issues and technical robustness key agenda items not just for B-to-B, but for all forms of e-business.

NOTES

1 Forrester Research, cited in *Wall Street Journal* Special Report 'Selling Points', 7 December 1998.

2 See Sawhney, M. and Kaplan, S., 'Lets Get Vertical', *Business 2.0.*, September 1999, pp.85–9. See also Kaplan, S. and Sawhney, M., 'E-Hubs: The New B2B Marketplaces', *Harvard Business Review*, May–June 2000, pp.97–106.

3 The main book dealing with the theory of virtual communities is Hagel, J. and Singer, M., *Net Worth: Shaping Markets when Customers Make the Rules*, Harvard Business School Press, Boston, 1999.

4 The McKenna Group, 'E-Business Value in Asia Pacific', Research Sponsored by IBM, The McKenna Group, Sydney, 1999.

The CEO and the CIO in the Information Age

David Feeny

'**Y**ou read everywhere that the CEO's commitment is the most important thing. I can vouch for that. In trying to progress our e-business thinking, we had a series of false starts before we got the CEO's buy-in.' This comment, from the e-commerce manager of a financial services group, both echoes the prevailing wisdom and captures the attitude I have consistently found in the companies I have researched.[1] But of course it is only natural to hope for the support of the CEO in any significant business endeavour. Why should that support be particularly critical to e-business initiatives? In my experience there are four persuasive arguments:

- **Creating a positive climate and priority for 'e' initiatives.** During the second half of the 1990s, opinions of executives in 'old economy' companies were understandably divided about the importance of Internet technology. While some enthused, it was easy for others to point to the inability of 'new economy' companies to make profits and to the potential dangers to their own existing profits from e-business initiatives which risked channel conflict and product cannibalisation. Thus, in one multi-product business group, the e-business project was for two years an isolated initiative, which provoked both scepticism and hostility from the heads of the established

product businesses. The situation only changed when the e-business champion and the Group CIO combined to get the Group CEO unequivocally to commit himself and the executive team to a series of events which confronted the e-business opportunity on a group-wide basis.

- **Breaking out of the planning/budgeting cycle.** Large established companies have invariably established over the years a formalised planning cycle, which drives the availability of investment funding for the next twelve to eighteen months. Such cycles are in conflict with the uncertainties and rapid change associated with e-business. Even in a company in the photographic sector – surely an obvious candidate for change in the information age – I found that the CIO had been struggling each year to win business department support for specific investment bids. A series of small and fragmented e-business initiatives resulted. The situation changed dramatically when the CEO experienced a personal conversion to the significance of e-business. His immediate action, unsupported by any business case, was to step outside the cycle and quadruple the funds available.

- **Tackling organisational issues.** There are often many types of organisational issue triggered by e-business, including those associated with implementation of e-business projects. (Chapter 4 explores some of the organisational design and transformation issues.) In one example of a deep-rooted issue, a large insurance group remains stalled in its attempts to progress e-business. It has pursued a number of small initiatives, some of which have achieved excellent acceptance. However, its perceived e-business future is based on propositions which are customer-based rather than product-based and there is no existing organisational mechanism to achieve this. The group is effectively structured as a holding company with highly autonomous product-based businesses – a 'financial control' regime – and at the time of writing the Group CEO remains unwilling to disturb an organisation that is seen to have been effective in delivering the bottom line.

- **Moving from 'e' strategy to business strategy.** I have argued elsewhere in this book (Chapter 2) that in most sectors, and for the foreseeable future, the most effective customer proposition will be one that combines benefits from both 'clicks' and 'bricks'. At 'Bank A', for example, I can choose any combination of account service from within the bank's branch, telephone, and Internet-based offerings. However, at

'Bank B' I must opt for either the traditional offering or an Internet-only service. The contrast results from different approaches to business strategy: in Bank A the CEO requires his management to develop their business strategy with an understanding of how new technology may provide opportunities for enhancement; Bank B's CEO, however, has positioned e-business as something special and poorly understood, to be developed separately from the mainstream strategic thinking of the bank.

Each of these issues is individually significant. It is also easy to see that they are in many ways related. Specifically, the CEO who is motivated to address one of them is likely to understand and to tackle all of them. No doubt this is why my research interviewees – when asked to address the organisation's e-business 'journey' – have consistently distinguished between a phase when the CEO was not involved and one when he/she was a central player.

The Meaning of CEO Leadership

METAPHOR	CHARACTERISTICS
HYPOCRITE	1. Espouses strategic importance of IT. 2. Negates through personal actions.
WAVERER	1. Reluctantly accepts stategic importance of IT. 2. Not ready to get involved.
ATHEIST	1. Convinced IT is of little value. 2. Publicly 'comes out' with this belief.
ZEALOT	1. Convinced IT is stategically important. 2. Believes he is an authority on IT, too.
AGNOSTIC	1. Concedes IT may be strategically important. 2. Has to be convinced over and over.
MONARCH	1. Accepts IT is strategically important. 2. Appoints best possible CIO to handle IT.
BELIEVER	1. Believes IT is an enabler of strategic advantage. 2. Demonstrates belief by his/her own behaviour.

Figure 1 – Seven IT Creeds of the CEO

In a recently published article[2] a colleague and I suggested we could distinguish seven archetypal attitudes of CEOs towards IT (Figure 1). We deliberately used quasi-religious and somewhat disrespectful labels for these attitudes because we found that both CEOs and their reporting executives consistently used such language in their own descriptions. 'Hypocrite', 'Agnostic', 'Atheist', 'Zealot', 'Believer' are all descriptors we have had volunteered to us; CEOs who have become 'Believers' are very consistently described – by themselves and by colleagues – as having undergone a 'conversion' experience. CEO actions in relation to IT generally and e-business specifically are seen to be driven more by belief states than by managerial economics. Thus the reactions to any proposed e-business initiative by each of our CEO types can be anticipated:

- Hypocrite CEOs provide oral support for such initiatives, but their unwillingness to address any of the four issues described above belies their commitment.
- Waverer CEOs seem quite genuine in their support, but their inability to prioritise between the (usually) very many initiatives to which they have given their support denies them the time to address the critical e-business issues.
- Atheist CEOs (a now shrinking community) have generally signalled their attitudes so clearly in advance that any e-business initiatives are likely to be subterranean, off their radar screen.
- Zealot CEOs (a growing species) typically clash with and sideline their own 'dinosaur' IT management, and invest hugely in untried technology to roll out simplistic business ideas with the help of outside vendors.
- The Agnostic CEO's insistence on 'a proper business case' channels e-business energy into projects which provide customer service at lower cost than call centres, or supplier links which replace existing EDI technology.
- Monarch CEOs give their CIOs and e-business initiatives strong moral support, but do not understand that success requires their personal intervention in the sort of issues described above.
- Only Believer CEOs provide the active involvement and decision-making required for real e-business success, and they provide it not because it is about 'IT' or 'e' but because they understand that strategic business advantage is at stake.

So what exactly do Believers believe? I have found it is best captured in the ideas generated by Schein's[3] study of CEO attitudes towards IT. Schein recognised that all forms of IT can

be exploited for multiple purposes and therefore the deployment of IT was framed by the perspective of commissioning executives on what the purpose of IT investment should be. He identified four perspectives or 'visions' from the CEOs surveyed in his study. With some modifications of the original wording, I represent them as follows:

- **The Automation Vision** – in which IT is seen to be about replacing (expensive/unreliable) people through the deployment of (cheap/reliable) technology.
- **The Control Vision** – which sees IT as the means of providing greater visibility of information to senior managers, enhancing their ability to manage/control more closely all aspects of organisational activity.
- **The Empowerment Vision** – in which IT, through its handling of routine/repetitive tasks, provides operating-level staff with the information and time to generate performance improvement.
- **The Transformation Vision** – which focuses on the ability of IT to enable radical change and improvement in some critical aspect of the business.

The first point to note here is that these visions are not technology-specific. For example, ERP packages have been deployed in pursuit of automation, control, empowerment and transformation.[4] Call centre technology has been used further to automate an often poor level of customer service (the notorious 'if this, press n' syndrome); or to transform the nature of service provided – I recently had a stolen lawnmower replaced within six hours of phoning to report the theft, an achievement which has won the general insurance company concerned my lasting loyalty. Coming to the present day and e-business, the most casual survey of web sites will show how some are seeking to offload costs to the customer, others to transform the service provided.

Second, while none of these visions can be labelled 'right' or 'wrong', the first three represent restricted perspectives, which tend to result in limited benefits from IT exploitation. Some of my own earlier research into CEOs and CIOs[5] first highlighted the significance of CEOs subscribing to the transformation vision. Subsequent work has confirmed and strengthened this finding. The transformation vision implies that the CEO understands that IT has multiple potential applications within the organisation, and

that the CEO is intent on focusing its use into that subset of applications which enable radical business improvement. These CEOs do not therefore look to IT to support preconceived business strategies; they approach each strategic issue open to the possibility that technology may enable a new and superior response. They are the Believer CEOs. Unprompted, they describe IT as an agent of business transformation and ensure (Figure 2) that IT is included in 'first-order, not second-order thinking'. In other words they see IT as integral to their strategic thinking rather than as a support for independently formulated strategy.

Third, I have found the visions to be mutually exclusive in the sense that each CEO I have interviewed is quite clear about which of them captures their own perspective. Furthermore, any of these CEOs who have changed allegiance between the visions can pinpoint exactly when that change occurred and specifically what prompted it. In my early research in this field,[6] CEOs who had become Believers/Transformers described one of two conversion experiences: either they had been involved in some leadership role in an IT-enabled business change project earlier in their career; or – usually at the time of assuming CEO responsibility – they had invested significant reflective time in developing a vision for the future of the business, and in the process had realised that technology would play a fundamental and inevitable role in achieving that business vision. In my most recent research, the reported conversion experience has consistently been triggered by personal visits to the leading technology companies – Dell, Cisco, IBM are the most frequently mentioned. In these visits CEOs have both witnessed (rather than been told about) the transforming effect of web technology on the host company's way of doing business and been exposed to the evangelising enthusiasm of Michael Dell, John Chambers, or Lou Gerstner. These peer-to-peer visits seem to represent the most direct route to a new CEO perspective, the equivalent of a Road to Damascus.

Figure 2, also from Earl and Feeny,[7] seeks to capture the consequences of CEO belief that new technology must be included in 'first-order thinking'. Believer CEOs are distinctive both in the day-to-day 'living out' of their beliefs – the behaviours they consistently demonstrate in relation to IT; and in their 'practising' – the actions they take and the interventions they make to ensure that the use of technology is fully integrated into the strategic development of the business. Rather than repeat here the content of the existing article, let me highlight a subset of the points it develops.

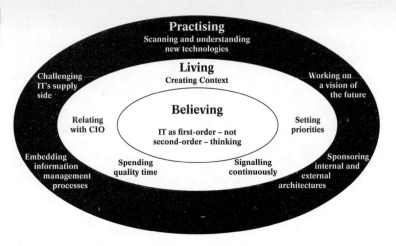

Figure 2 – Profile of the Believer CEO

Three points of particular emphasis in the **living** context of the Believer CEO:

- Unlike the Zealot who declares how technology will be used, the Believer **creates context** by challenging key aspects of business performance. When CEO Ian Robertson mandated that the new Land Rover Freelander be brought to market twice as fast as previous models in the company's history, he created a context in which the development team knew that success could not be achieved by previous ways of working. With Robertson's support and encouragement, the team developed a radically new approach, which was enabled by intensive use of technology. Technology was integral to the chosen way forward, but so were many other changes. By creating the right context, Robertson ensured that IT was recognised as having transforming potential, but only within a holistic design for a new way of working.[8]

- In **setting priorities** the Believer CEO is declaring the strategic priorities of the business (such as 'customer service innovation' or 'faster time to market') and thereby providing the means to focus the use of IT. It has long been the case that there are many possible organisational applications of IT which can provide 'useful' levels of benefit, but a much smaller number that will have 'strategic' impact (see the Introduction of this book). This issue is now exacerbated by the almost limitless application potential of fast-changing web technology. Believer CEOs systematically channel

investment money to IT applications which align with their strategic priorities and deny it to those which do not – even if the latter claim through traditional ROI analysis to deliver satisfactory financial benefits.

- For Believer CEOs strong **relationships with CIOs** are an important part of the 'living' experience. This can be good or bad news for CIOs, as illustrated by the words of an incoming CEO who asked his new executive colleagues why there was no CIO in his management team. 'We have a CIO,' they replied, 'but we are not sure he is good enough to be a part of the top management team.' 'Well bring him into the team,' replied the CEO, 'and if he is not good enough I shall find another one.' In the information age, CIOs need to be integral members of the leadership group. This has implications which will be discussed in the next section.

But first, three references to the **Practising** dimension of Figure 2, highlighting the elements which may be less immediately obvious:

- Believer CEOs **sponsor internal and external architectures** because they understand that these architectures – and the infrastructures which result from their implementation – determine the platform that defines the boundary of what can be achieved through IT. BP Amoco CEO John Browne personally sponsored the investment in a 'common operating environment' across the company because without it his vision of the learning organisation could not be realised.[9] Land Rover CEO Ian Robertson understood that his goal of building Freelanders to customer order depended on acceptance by all key suppliers of a common IT architecture along the supply chain. In the age of e-business, architectures are integral to the capability and cost structure of the business.
- Because Believer CEOs position IT as an element of first-order thinking in the strategic development of the firm, they **challenge the IT supply side**. Unlike Atheist CEOs, who outsource IT in order to reduce costs, Believer CEOs think of outsourcing as accessing the full capability of the external IT services market. If business strategies are enabled by and dependent on IT exploitation, their achievement cannot be constrained by the limted resources of the in-house IT function. In my current research, I have yet to meet an organisation which is pursuing its e-business initiatives without outside help. The issue – on which more later – is to develop the

in-house IT function in a way which enables it successfully to tap into and manage external resources (for more on this issue, see Chapters 9 and 10).

- CEO attention to **embedding information management processes** is critical in the information age because long familiar processes of managing IT finally break down. The alignment of IT investment with business strategy cannot be achieved through an annual strategic planning cycle; approval processes for IT investment which is e-business related founder if traditional financial analysis is used; e-business projects cannot succeed if their IT dimensions are managed using the Systems Development Life Cycle. In each case the confounding factors are uncertainty and speed. Arguably, the old ways of managing IT investment were never appropriate to a strategic context, but now they are manifestly deficient. Successful information management processes in the information age are top priorities for both CEOs and CIOs, and I will provide a description of their essentials in the final section of this chapter, after considering the leadership role of the CIO.

At this stage we have hopefully seen enough to understand why organisations engaged in e-business initiatives emphasise the leadership role of the CEO and are clear about the principal components of that leadership role. A common question at this point is: if the CEO is an IT Believer, and has influenced other members of the top management team to become more 'IT literate', do we still need a CIO? And if we do, is he/she properly a member of the real leadership team? I have certainly encountered organisations in which the CIO has been marginalised or excluded from the e-business initiatives, but is this appropriate? If so, why have the icons among dot.com companies – Amazon and eBay, for example – appointed highly experienced CIOs to their leadership teams? My experience is that while the technology has undergone revolution, the role of the CIO is characterised by evolution – and CIOs remain critical to success in the era of e-business.

The Evolution of the CIO Leadership Role

	Mainframe Era	Distributed Era	Web-based Era
Executive Attitudes	IT for Automation, Cost Displacement Project concerns	IT Governance concerns Polarisation of views – IT as Strategic Resource? IT as Non-Core?	IT/E-Business recognised as Strategic Issue
CIO Roles	• *Operational Manager*	• *Technology Architect* • *Organisational Designer* • *Informed Buyer* • *Strategic Partner*	• *Technology Adviser* • *Business Visionary*

Figure 3 – CIO Role Evolution

In another recent article,[10] a colleague and I have gone to some lengths in tracing the historical evolution of the CIO role; Figure 3 is adapted from that paper. We chose the approach not because of an interest in history per se, but because we believed that the role of today's CIO is best understood through a historical perspective. Over the years and the changes in technology, CIOs have entered new contexts and acquired new roles, but they have not discarded old ones – the role today is the sum of its historical parts.

Taking the highlights of Figure 3 in turn:

- In the era dominated by mainframe technology (roughly 1960–80), the requirement of the CIO was to demonstrate competence as an **operational/functional manager**. IT was being applied in the form of transaction processing systems to improve the operation of the basic processes of the business. As the business became increasingly operationally dependent on those systems, executive management looked to the CIO (or 'IT manager' as the typical label of the day) to manage within budget and provide a robust service. The star practitioners then were those who also managed to deliver new projects to time and budget, to the surprise and delight of the executive team. Twenty years on, the means of delivery have changed with extensive use of external service providers; there are the increased challenges of service delivery across complex networks, with the 24/7 availability commonly required by e-business. But the successful provision of service remains the first responsibility of the CIO, the *sine qua non* for survival.
- When the PC arrived, closely followed by data-networking

capabilities, the distributed era (1980–95) began to introduce much greater complexity to the CIO role. Shorn of the relative technical stability of the mainframe era – the IBM security blanket – CIOs had to become **technology architects**, to devise distributed networks which mapped on to the structure and needs of their host corporation. As technology became more pervasive and distributed, CIOs as **organisational designers** had to transition previously centralised IT functions into complex structures, which were both responsive to business units and protective of corporate coherence. Next, while some resisted the very idea of the emerging potential to outsource IT activity, smarter CIOs proactively developed the role of **informed buyer** – the ability to engage external resources in ways that added value but did not jeopardise the longer-term ability to respond to the potential of new technology.[11] The ultimate test became the CIO's ability to contribute on a wider basis as a member of the top management team, to become convincingly a **strategic partner** in the development of business strategy. As Earl and Feeny[12] recorded, executive teams in the mid-1990s were strongly polarised between those who believed IT was a strategic resource and those who saw IT as a non-core activity. The personal ability of the CIO to build relationships at the executive level, and to facilitate understanding of how business and IT strategies could be effectively integrated, was generally instrumental in the organisation's positioning of the significance of IT. Has this now changed? Does any of these roles no longer require attention? I think the evidence is clearly that all remain essential and indeed more challenging than ever. What I particularly notice is that CIOs who have failed to establish their credentials as strategic partners are commonly bypassed in the organisation's e-business initiatives.

• So does today's era of web technology imply new roles for the CIO, beyond the extra challenge in existing roles? The early evidence suggests that two new roles or emphases are becoming prominent. With technology continuing to develop at an ever faster pace and in quite surprising ways, there is an urgent need for the CIO to act as the trusted **technology adviser** to the management team – someone on whom they can rely to distinguish for them between the fundamental trends and the distracting gimmicks. Second, we see really able CIOs moving beyond the strategic-partner role into one of **business visionary**. This is not, of course, to suggest that the CIO becomes the single or the prime visionary; but we recognise that some CIOs have demonstrably now been accepted into the small 'inner circle' of executives with whom the CEO debates and develops the long-term future of the business.

Looking across this cumulative and daunting agenda for CIO leadership in the information age, what may now be the 'critical success factors' for CIOs? In my current research I have encountered five factors, of which two might be considered 'survival' factors, while three are more associated with 'success'.

1. The first 'survival' factor relates to service delivery, on which depends fulfilment of every e-business proposition. New and old technologies and systems have to be seamlessly integrated; they have to operate securely despite the existence of hackers and viruses; they have to operate robustly for twenty-four hours a day, seven days each week (if you are eBay, or one of several similar examples discussed in this book, your very share price depends upon it). The fact that external service firms carry out much of the operational activity is a mixed blessing: it reduces the size of the technical management challenge, but adds further complexity in the organisational dimension. And the buck still stops at the CIO's desk.

2. The second 'survival' factor is the rebuilding of the IT function on a 'core capabilities' model.[13][14] The development of e-business requires a closer level of engagement with the business than ever before; and an equally unprecedented involvement with a myriad of external providers and partners in order to access rapidly both the quantity and quality of resources required. The traditional IT function was not designed to meet these requirements and cannot be incrementally flexed to address them. The CIO must move to a new model in which predominantly technical skills account for only a small proportion of what becomes anyway a much smaller function. The critical and additional new skills are those associated with business partnership and supplier management.

3. The first 'success' factor is the constant attention by the CIO to the building and sustaining of excellent relationships with all key members of the executive team and particularly the CEO. These relationships determine whether or not the

CIO is 'in the room' when business thinking is developed and decisions are made.

4. The second 'success' factor is achieved when the CIO is seen as a prime source of insight into the implications of new ideas across internal business boundaries. Usually this is the most straightforward of the factors for experienced CIOs to deliver on, since they will have breadth of exposure across the business and (usually) an aptitude for thinking in business systems terms.

5. Finally, the CIO can make a distinctive contribution to the development of business vision by devoting time to external networking across industry boundaries. Most executive colleagues, including the CEO, will be steeped in the wisdom of their own industry sector; the CIO has a particular opportunity to network widely and to inject into the strategic discussion those ideas from other sectors which new technology may now enable as a source of advantage for the host business.

In summary the role of the CIO does not perish with the arrival of e-business, but it does raise the stakes for CIOs. Those who can fulfil only some of the leadership roles described above may well be passed over; other CIOs will find e-business career-enhancing. E-business needs the leadership of both CEOs and CIOs. It also needs particular leadership processes.

Leadership Processes for E-Business

As I commented earlier, the familiar processes of strategic planning, investment evaluation and project management are proving wholly inappropriate to the management of e-business. I have argued elsewhere[15] that quite different processes are conducive to the strategic exploitation of IT. My current research experience is underlining how important it is to adopt those different processes in pursuit of e-business. While it would be foolish to be closely prescriptive as to how to manage an emerging phenomenon, I shall in this section overview what seem to be the most important principles.

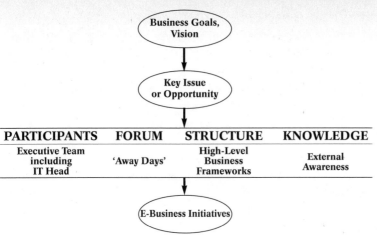

Figure 4 – The Strategic Development Process

For e-business the traditional planning cycle is ineffective because it is not timely, it is not sufficiently challenging and it does not properly allow for debate across established organisational boundaries. In each case where I have encountered Believer CEOs, a workshop approach has been established which contains all the elements of Figure 4:

- If this is the first such event, the declared target has been to develop a new potential vision of the business which recognises the potential of e-business; subsequent events take as their trigger a particular business issue or opportunity which, if successfully addressed, will radically advance progress towards the target business vision.
- The CEO has mandated attendance by the entire executive team. Well-positioned CIOs have tended to be the designers and facilitators of these events.
- The events take the form of 'away days', concentrated time out with no operational issues on the agenda. Initial e-business events have usually lasted two to three days, including 'educational' inputs on e-business, group work assignments and plenary workshop sessions.
- High-level frameworks such as value chain analysis have been used to orchestrate discussion about the potential for dis-intermediation, re-intermediation in an e-business world; scenarios developed on how a new start-up business could most severely damage the incumbent company.
- There has been an emphasis on raising the level of external

awareness through pre-assigned readings, inputs from perceived thought leaders such as consultants, e-business gurus, leading suppliers, 'new economy' business CEOs.

- The required outcome has been the broad specification of one or more e-business initiatives, to be transferred – with funding – to a multi-disciplinary team or teams for further development and implementation.

We can trace through the model the relevance of some of the leadership elements we have discussed. CEO leadership is exercised in commissioning the event, in declaring its scope/focus, in mandating attendance – including, of course, his/her own attendance – in encouraging rather than resisting any challenge to 'sacred cows', in committing to the outcomes. CIO leadership delivers the design and facilitation of the event, the availability through the CIO's external network of the potentially important external knowledge, the holistic thinking, which helps to clarify the likely impact across the business of ideas being discussed.

Strategy professionals point out, quite rightly, that this is not a new model; they may point to its use as one available component within the established planning process. The recognition that this is already the pattern for the creation of 'breakthrough' rather than incremental thinking is helpful. The e-business environment does not require the invention of a new strategic development process, but it does require a transfer of allegiance from the traditional annual process. The new model is now centre-stage, driving the strategic development of the business; the old model probably continues to exist, but it is now positioned as an annual housekeeping exercise, which aggregates and records the consequences of initiatives triggered throughout the year.

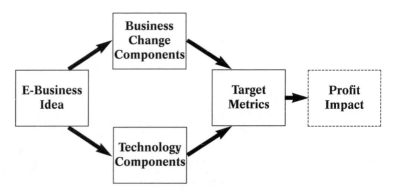

Figure 5 – E-Business Evaluation

Another benefit flows naturally from the strategic development model of Figure 4 – it links to the investment evaluation model of Figure 5. Whereas most organisations still operate investment appraisal processes which demand cost/benefit analyses of proposed IT expenditure, Figure 5 recognises correctly that IT expenditure alone does not lead to business benefits. Only the adoption of new business ideas, which may be enabled by IT, can lead to business benefits; and new business ideas always require business-side changes (and costs!), as well as any technology investment. In the case of e-business initiatives, these business-side costs will include the necessary marketing of the new idea – promotion programmes, incentives for adoption etc.

A second feature of the model, which is particularly important in the e-business context, is the separation of completion criteria – the 'target metrics' – from the hoped-for profit impact. In e-business initiatives we are commonly seeking to introduce a new service, which may have no existing parallel in the business; we need to establish completion criteria – such as 'adoption by first n customers' – so that the initiative can be properly managed. But the profit impact of such innovations over time can only be a matter of judgement. The model invites the CEO to consider all the key elements of the proposed initiative – the quality of the business idea, the full set of costs, the clarity of completion criteria and (probably) a range of estimates of potential profit impact over time – and then to provide the leadership which is the particular responsibility of the CEO by making a judgement to go or not to go with the idea. In the present context of e-business the alternative process of submitting this investment bid, along with many others, to take its chance within the next annual planning/budgeting cycle is manifestly absurd. It is either a promising initiative to be pursued with urgency, or it is nothing.

Delivering new technology-based projects faster and more efficiently has always been desirable. In the e-business context it becomes essential. There may or may not be a first-mover advantage at stake (refer to my other chapter); but even if there is not, the successful organisation will be one which moves quickly along the learning curve of e-business. The third critical leadership process involves implementing dolphins not whales (Figure 6).

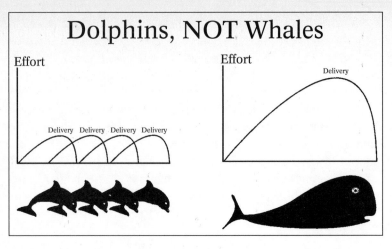

Figure 6 – Implementation of E-Business

We are all familiar with the IT whale, the multi-year mega-million-dollar project which arrives late and over budget, if it arrives at all. What exactly is a dolphin? Many have looked at Figure 6 and comforted themselves that they are pursing dolphins when in fact they are building modularised whales. In other words they have taken a traditional project and have structured it into a number of components – the marketing module, the technical modules, the training module and so on. That is not a dolphin approach, it does not work the same way and it does not produce the same result. The essential characteristics of a dolphin are these:

- A dolphin project is carried out within a mandated and challenging 'time-box'. Instead of asking 'how long will this take?', leadership mandates to the dolphin team the time they have available. In my e-business research I am finding consistently that the answer is 'ninety days' per dolphin. Ninety days is apparently the new cycle time in organisations pursuing e-business initiatives.
- There is one dolphin team per e-business initiative and each team is a multi-disciplinary team, comprising all the necessary business and technical resources, assigned on a full-time basis to work under a single team leader for the duration of the project.
- Each dolphin team has a particular goal, which is to implement a chosen e-business idea to the defined completion criteria (the target metric of Figure 5) within the allocated

time. The team are all measured by that goal; success will make all team members into heroes, failure is not an option.

- Apart from potential architecture constraints, which specify how the result must be able to interface to existing or planned related processes, the team are free to choose whatever method they see fit to achieve the goal. There is no requirement specification. The team are being asked to devise a river crossing, but not to build a particular bridge. They may decide a bridge would be best, or they may choose a ferry, a tunnel, a ford, depending on what they learn about the nature of the river.

- The whole purpose is to force departure from the classic engineering-orientated approach of the systems development life cycle (SDLC), which proceeds sequentially through requirement specification, external design, internal design etc. The SDLC is fine when the requirement detail is well understood, when we are in familiar territory, but it cannot cope with the high degree of uncertainty present in e-business initiatives and other innovative projects. The time-boxed dolphin represents an alternative management model, which encourages rapid and iterative learning by the team and forces them to use the pareto principle (focus on the twenty per cent that will deliver eighty per cent of the value) – to identify the subset of functionality which will deliver the business goal quickly, rather than the total 'wish list' of potential functionality, which takes for ever to achieve.

The dolphin approach represents a paradigm shift, which may appear very threatening to those familiar with the SDLC. But it works and it becomes essential in the e-business context. CEO leadership will commonly be required to support the introduction of the model, given the initial discomfort of the technical community with the nature of the approach and the resistance from business-side managers to the idea that they must make some of their best people available full time to the team. Supporting leadership from the CIO will involve endorsing the approach to technical staff, and ensuring that all the necessary technical skills are promptly available from a combination of internal and external sources. Implementing the dolphin approach completes the transition to leadership approaches and information management processes, which are appropriate to the information age.

Conclusions on Leadership in the Information Age

ORIENTATIONS	STYLE
• Seeks Stretch Goals, Strategic Change • Emphasise Revenues before costs. Growth before margins • Talks to Customers, Builds External Networks • Sees IT as first-order factor of Strategy Making	• Team Leadership • Focused in terms of Issues, Use of Time • Values Expertise • Makes him/herself Accessible • Takes Calculated Risks

Leadership Profile

SKILLS/CAPABILITIES	KNOWLEDGE/LEARNING
• Holistic Thinking • Listening/Hearing • Envisioning Directions • Conceptualising Ideas	• Business and Organisational Dynamics • IT Capability in terms of Concepts, Trends, Indeterminance • Leadership of IT-enabled Projects

Figure 7 – Leadership Characteristics in the Information Age

I have discussed what effective CEO and CIO leaders do in the information age and why their actions are so important. But what is the broader make-up of the effective leader? Let me conclude with Figure 7, a compendium of 'leadership characteristics in the information age'. Figure 7 was generated through analysis of all the characteristics which our 'IT Believer' CEOs[16] seemed to have in common. I then reflected that there was a great deal of overlap with the characteristics of leading CIOs I have encountered in research over the years. I offer it here as a lens for reflection on leadership in the information age.

NOTES

1 Between October 1999 and September 2000 the author researched the 'e-business' responses of large established firms in Europe, USA, Australia and Singapore.

2 Earl, M. J. and Feeny, D.F., 'How to be a CEO for the Information Age', *Sloan Management Review*, Winter 2000.

3 Schein, E. H., 'The role of the CEO in the management of change: the case of information technology', Management in the Nineties working paper 89–075, Sloan School of Management, August 1989.

4 Feeny, D. F. and McMullen, G., 'Is standardised global IS worth the bother?', *Financial Times*, 1 March 1999.

5 Feeny, D. F., Edwards, B. R. and Simpson, K. M., 'Understanding the CEO/CIO relationship', *MIS Quarterly*, 16, 4, December 1992.

6 Feeny, D. F. and Plant, R., 'IT: a vehicle for project success', *Financial Times*, 1 February 1999.

7 Earl, M. J. and Feeny, D. F., op. cit.

8 Feeny, D. F. and Plant, R., op. cit.

9 Prokesh, S. E., 'Unleashing the power of learning: an interview with British Petroleum's John Browne', *Harvard Business Review*, September–October 1997.

10 Ross, J. and Feeny, D. F., 'The evolving role of the CIO', in Zmud R. (ed.), *Framing the Domains of IT Management*, Pinnaflex Educational Resources, Cincinnati, 2000.

11 Lacity, M. C., Willcocks, L. P. and Feeny, D. F., 'The value of selective IT sourcing', *Sloan Management Review*, Spring 1996.

12 Earl, M. J. and Feeny, D. F., 'Is your CIO adding value?', *Sloan Management Review*, Spring 1994.

13 Feeny, D. F. and Willcocks, L. P., 'Core IS capabilities for exploiting information technology', *Sloan Management Review*, Spring 1998.

14 Cross, J., Earl, M. J. and Sampler, J. L., 'Transformation of the IT function in British Petroleum', *MIS Quarterly*, 21, 4 December 1997.

15 Feeny, D. F., 'Information management: lasting ideas within turbulent technology', in Willcocks, L. P., Feeny, D. F. and Islei G. (eds), *Managing IT as a Strategic Resource*, McGraw-Hill, London 1997.

16 Earl, M. J. and Feeny, D. F., 'How to be a CEO for the Information Age', op. cit.

Human Resource Strategies in the New Economy

Marc Thompson

She points to their nametags. Each has a blinking green digital display in the center – some pointless boys' club high-tech trick, she figures. 'Why do you LED your ID numbers like that? And why is your number seven digits and Robbie's only five? . . . They look kind of cool,' she says.

*Ms New Yorker! They're not supposed to **look** cool. It's not an ID number, it's how many shares and exercisable options we own. He flips his tag up and looks down at it, then points to a little line of type. 'The ID number is printed down here.' He glances up. 'You just zapped Robbie in his sore spot. He's only got, what, ninety thousand shares, and I've got a million-one. But I've worked for the company **three** years,' he says. 'Robbie feels he's gotten to the start-up party too late. You know? Like all these kids out here now. They're jealous of how much easy money people our age piled up in the nineties.'*

Kurt Andersen, Turn of the Century[1]

While the above fictional account underlines some of the potential absurdities of the new economy (displaying your share options on your ID), it is also strangely closer to organisational reality in the high-technology sector than we may care to realise. The resentment that Robbie feels for those who reached the silicon Klondyke first may have potentially negative ramifications for work relations and organisational performance in this fictional firm into the future. Because Robbie feels he has missed the stock option boat his allegiance to the firm may be transitory as he looks for better opportunities elsewhere. If he does leave, this may result in an important loss of hard-to-replace knowledge and skills for the growing firm. Indeed, his co-worker recognises the temporary attachment individuals have with firms in the new economy by underlining the fact that he has been with the firm for 'three' years – a veritable lifetime in Internet years. The extract shows, too, the perceived importance of financial incentives in these new firms but it also reveals some familiar old economy concerns – felt fairness and equitable treatment. The unanswered question is whether Robbie is staying with the business because he feels locked in by his share options (which are likely to be exercisable after some years) or whether he is motivated by the challenge of the work and the ability to use his skills and capabilities to their fullest extent. Developing Human Resource (HR) strategies to recruit, retain and motivate the Robbies of this world is becoming a considerable challenge for firms in the new economy.

These issues in turn link to broader questions about appropriate governance and ownership structures. While small high-tech start-ups need to offer stock to attract talent when their cash flow means even paying median-level market salaries is not possible, the challenge to larger more mature businesses operating traditional shareholder models with salaried employees is how to compete for such talent. Why work for some large, boring, bureaucratic company when you can opt for the buzz, excitement and potential stock option riches of the dot.com start-up?

Our interest in this chapter is in exploring the implications for organisations' HR strategies of the emerging 'new' or 'digital' economy. We focus on the employment relationship and its changing nature in the context of these new pressures. Will convergence in information and communication technologies eventually give rise to a new organisational model that will support a specific form of employment relationship characterised

by a particular set of HR strategies? Might we expect to see a more or less common set of employment policies and practices for the e-business firm of the future, much in the way that the bureaucratic model dominated the Fordist economy over the last century? Is there one best way, or are there many different but equally effective ways, to organise and manage the employment relationship?

We start by looking at some of the challenges of e-business for HR thinking and practice. We draw upon research at Templeton College and other leading-edge centres on the character and effectiveness of HR strategies. We suggest that three models for HR in the new economy are emerging, and examine the extent to which they exist in the most advanced high-tech community in the world, Silicon Valley. Finally, we confront the most immediate challenge for most companies – the skills shortage.

★ E-Business: The Challenges to HR Strategies

The rise of the Internet and its accompanying changes in business models and practice have created a formidable set of challenges for both established and establishing organisations. As with most new developments, the cacophony of the hype – what IT can do for your business – drowns out the prosaic issues at the core of managing people for strategic ends. Yet our experience is that much is changing in HR and must continue to change if the opportunities of e-business are to be realised. The current revolution in information and communication technologies is speeding and reinforcing ongoing trends in human resource management. As innovation, knowledge, flexibility and creativity become core organisational capabilities, firms are seeking to introduce HR strategies that support the development of these behaviours and attitudes. Figure 1 shows how HR strategies can influence employee behaviour, which in turn enables greater organisational agility and ultimately higher firm performance.

Figure 1 – The Role of HR Strategies in E-Business

Among the companies that are setting the trends in terms of creating new ways of doing business, there are signs that we may witness convergence of HR practice, with more organisations seeking to introduce or extend high-performance or high-commitment work systems. This is because they hold out the possibility of creating more adaptive and responsive organisations better able to cope with rapid change. Ensuring that these HR strategies do not lead to static cultures that resist change (as IBM's and Digital's did at times in the past) will become one of the biggest challenges facing organisations.

One of the principal changes occurring in the new economy is the rise of the network organisation. In this section we explore the characteristics of this form of organisation, its implications for the way managers and employees think about HR, and the challenges posed by organisations extending their boundaries through forms of consolidation.

THE NETWORK ORGANISATION

The power of information technologies is revolutionising our concept of the firm and this raises a number of challenges for people management in the new economy. Whereas before, firms competed within industries and product markets, and their activity was bounded, today firms can increasingly compete across industry boundaries and offer quite distinctive products through networking with other firms in either their own or entirely different supply chains.

This means that the business leadership skills of the future will be more about identifying networking opportunities and combining organisational competencies in a way that can offer customers higher value. The success of firms like Nike and Visa (very much old-economy firms but with path-breaking business models) is based on this very approach. Similarly, Dell's approach to value creation in the computer industry was based on using the supply chain in a radically different way (see Chapter 10 for further details).[2] Competing in this way means that strategic thinking becomes important not only within the top

team but also across wider tranches of the business. This is because business opportunities can come from the multiplicity of contacts a firm generates through its network structures. This means two things: (a) the development of stronger conceptual skills at senior management level, (b) wider communication of the firm's goals and objectives to employees in order to encourage wider flexibility.

Given that e-business competition is governed by speed, the winners in this new environment will be those firms that can move quickly to combine their talents and assets. This poses real challenges not only for combining and sharing information but also for putting in place an architecture that is agile enough to respond to market opportunities. Firms will need to be able quickly to slot their systems and processes into a new market at the lowest possible cost.

As one commentator recently remarked:

> Dispersed, networked organisations take a great deal of patient management. They only work with a strong sense of common values and rules. If an organisation becomes too decentralised, it will find it difficult to take concerted action when needed (Leadbeater, 1999).[3]

It is here that we find a profound role for HR strategies and systems because they can help create 'common values and rules'. While it is recognised that open systems are important when firms are in networks and need to share information, and develop common database platforms, the development of the network enterprise model also means that firms may find it advantageous to have common HR policies and practices. For example, they may need to create a common skills and competences database from across a range of partner firms in order that the most effective teams can be put together at short notice to take advantage of market opportunities. The skills and attributes of a firm's employees then become a common resource in network structures.

Career paths and employees' motivation are two issues raised by the network enterprise model, which dispose companies towards greater homogeneity in HR strategies. If career paths are to be self-constructed and composed of own-organisation and partner organisation experiences, the switching costs between organisations in networks need to be low for employees in order to increase network problem solving, innovation and performance. One

strategy, therefore, is for network partners to adopt common HR systems, much as many multinational enterprises operate consistent HR systems for their managers across the world. This greater standardisation helps reduce switching costs between different operating environments and facilitates organisational agility.

The other force towards greater similarity among HR systems is manager and employee motivation. If a firm's manager and employees see the firm as a network or a set of relationships, rather than a clearly defined and bounded organisation, they will start to identify not merely with the larger whole but with components of it, such as better employment conditions enjoyed by other members of the network. Thus, if one firm's employees are working on a regular basis with employees from other firms in a network, the inadequacies of certain HR systems will become transparent and this will adversely influence productive working. To counteract this, firms can collaborate on the design of their HR systems. Imitation of the leading company in a network should achieve the same result, but less directly.

ACQUISITIONS, MERGERS AND HR STRATEGIES FOR INTEGRATION

In addition to managing competition through networks, e-business is driving acquisitions and mergers, which also present real HR challenges. The wealth of creative opportunities arising from e-business has resulted in the formation of many companies in highly specialised e-business niches with equally specialised skill bases among their workforce. As the competitive environment heats up, companies are seeking to acquire smaller firms that fit with their developing business models. The war for talent is also pushing ambitious companies to buy firms that have the requisite skill sets when open market recruitment of individuals takes too long. Because teamworking is critical in networks and within firms, organisations often want teams of employees with proven capability to work effectively together so that they can slot them quickly into new business ventures. It is therefore no surprise that in knowledge businesses such as investment banking whole teams are poached from competitors because firms realise that it is the tacit knowledge and work relations of the team that create value rather than any one individual. This trend for progress by acquisition means that the ability quickly to integrate acquired businesses and their people is increasingly a strategic competence. HR processes will be crucial in delivering this organisational capability. The FI Group is a typical example. An IT consultancy, the firm has acquired a number of businesses

in the last couple of years to strengthen its value proposition. Much of the value of its acquisitions lies in the people it acquires with each company. It sees employee share ownership as a distinctive component in its 'employee brand' by which it hopes to retain its new staff, and one that can help facilitate faster integration of its businesses.

Cisco Systems identifies its skills in integrating new businesses as critical in its development. Cisco estimates that it has paid between $500,000 and $2 million per employee in an acquisition – good reason to try to retain them. Here, too, the emphasis has been on stock options. Base pay in Cisco is below the industry standard but *'paltry pay checks, however, are leveraged by bonuses and stock options higher than the industry standard'*.[4]

Thus we see the growth of the network or extended enterprise model and the current trend for acquisition as militating in favour of increasing convergence among HR strategies. In particular, the adoption of a high-commitment HR strategy is seen as facilitating faster integration and organisational agility. However, we are un-likely to see convergence towards a single HR system for all circumstances. Instead, we will see the development of several types, the differences being shaped by technology, organisation strategy, workforce characteristics, work organisation and cul-ture. In other words there may be convergence in some areas but also divergence in others. The key challenge for e-business firms will be determining what strategies should be common to the network and which ones distinctive to individual firms.

In the following section we examine the nature of HR strategies. We then move on to describe some of the different types of model we can expect to find emerging to meet the needs of e-business.

HR Strategies for E-Business

While dot.com start-ups attract the attention of the business press, the reality is that e-business will bring about more change in established organisations as they seek to compete in the new paradigm. Whereas the HR story in the dot.com is about managing the tightrope walk between order and chaos in a fast-growing, fast-moving business environment, the story in established firms is

likely to focus on the need to create 'managed' chaos to release entrepreneurial talent, while at the same time maintaining the integrity of the existing HR system. If ICTs are the 'hard' strategies that firms use to respond to an increasingly competitive environment (through, for example, redesigning organisational structures), HR strategies are the 'soft' strategies in their armoury.

Various choices appear to be open to traditional organisations (see Chapter 4). One option is for firms such as Prudential to set up ring-fenced dot.coms, which have the freedom to develop entirely new HR strategies. This strategy proceeds from the analysis that the brand image of the parent organisation (old, stodgy, bureaucratic) will negatively influence the firm's ability to attract and retain the type of staff it needs to grow the business. In Prudential's Internet bank, Egg, a wholly owned subsidiary, HR strategies are taking on their own distinctive character.

> . . . initially we built on the Prudential banking base and used established policies and processes but it soon became apparent that while the tools we would be using were the same – most good-quality HR practices are well-established responses to statutory or economic conditions – how we applied them (the pace, method and their use) would differ.[5]

The ring-fencing may, of course, have other objectives. In the case of Prudential this is the future full flotation of its subsidiary. Whatever the principal objective, it does create the space for creative thinking in the HR arena.

Another option is to grow e-business organically. The Co-operative Bank, which also set up an Internet arm, Smile, gives employees the same benefits, terms and conditions as the main bank. The HR strategies are common except for recruitment, where there is an emphasis on Internet-related knowledge and skills. The Co-operative Bank sees its existing HR strategy and corporate brand as distinctive in the marketplace and sees no reason to change or dilute it: 'With its partnership approach and ethical stance, the Co-operative Bank already has a cutting-edge approach in HR of which we are very proud.'[6]

These two cases illustrate the different paths established businesses are taking in developing their Internet offering and reveal the importance of organisational brand values in shaping these choices. The cases unfortunately do not help us understand in detail the nature and content of their HR strategies – are they similar but delivered in different organisational contexts as the

Co-operative Bank suggests, or do these organisations have distinctly different HR strategies? This raises questions about the nature of HR strategies and we now turn to consider this in more detail.

In simple terms, the ability of an organisation to develop and utilise its people in a way that furthers the strategic needs of the business is the aim of human resource strategies. Figure 2 is a model outlining how HR strategies influence firm performance. An HR strategy effectively comprises an objective (or objectives) and a plan (usually comprising specific policies and practices) of how to achieve the objectives. Its policies, such as 'rewarding performance', give rise to a number of other choices around specific HR practices. In the case of rewarding performance, for example, the firm may do this at an organisation-wide level, a group level or an individual level. The practices chosen are likely to be determined by reference to specific organisational objectives or a broader set of principles.

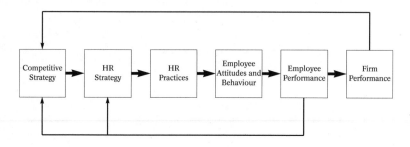

Figure 2 – A Model of HR Strategy and Firm Performance

For example, a firm may wish to encourage greater employee interest in and identity with the performance of the organisation, and may therefore introduce practices such as share ownership schemes or annual profit-related bonuses. Or it may want to encourage greater individual accountability for achieving performance improvements and instead introduce bonuses based on individual contribution.

Consequently, HR strategies are a combination of both an espoused policy objective (i.e. create greater employee commitment to firm performance) and a set of practices to achieve this end. What are these practices?

Jeffrey Pfeffer, in his book *The Human Equation*,[7] argues

that firms, regardless of their operating context, should adopt the following HR strategies:

- people recruited on the basis of their trainability and commitment;
- structured career paths or ladders to provide incentives for individuals to develop skills;
- employment security;
- broad job descriptions enabling high levels of flexibility;
- flatter management structures and the ending of status differentials;
- team structures used to organise work, facilitate problem solving and help information flow;
- attention to job design and the creation of task environments that are challenging, have variety and are intrinsically motivating;
- a performance feedback system and recognition of individual contributions (including pay);
- employees responsible for their own work quality.

But are all of these practices appropriate in all contexts? Will the distribution warehouses and home-delivery firms that may characterise e-tailing in the future want to offer broad job descriptions and jobs designed to enable high variety in work tasks? Will call centres be able (or indeed want) to adopt all these HR practices? Why would a dot.com start-up in its first year pay attention to job design or performance management when it needs to give all its attention to recruitment?

While we cannot provide definitive answers, recent Templeton College research in the UK Aerospace sector has found that a distinctive set of HR practices was associated with much higher value-added per employee.[8] More successful firms (those with strong growth in value-added per employee) tended to use the following bundle of practices: teamworking, sophisticated recruitment practices, broad jobs, responsibility for own work quality and formal appraisal.

The research followed a panel of ninety firms over two years and found that those that used more of these innovative HR practices for a greater proportion of their employees were much faster at adopting other organisational innovations such as lean production techniques. This suggests that the adoption and use of high-performance work practices is helpful in creating a responsive, agile and adaptive organisational system. This in turn

provides the business with important capabilities, enabling it to compete more effectively in a time of product market uncertainty and turbulence.

Furthermore, the aerospace research found that those firms using high-performance practices also enjoyed a productivity premium of some twenty to thirty-four per cent, which suggests that investments in HR strategies are very important in harnessing the full benefits of investment in new technology. As aerospace is a highly advanced high-tech industry, these findings are extremely pertinent for e-business as a whole. In short, it suggests that the 'hard' strategies companies may adopt around ICT investment and new organisational structures can only pay dividends if firms are successful in implementing appropriate 'soft' strategies (i.e. HR policies and practices) to ensure they are utilised effectively.

This section has looked at what we mean by HR strategies, their content and also evidence of their impact. It suggests that firms investing in a more strategic approach to the management of their employees are more likely to create flexible and responsive organisational environments that are much faster at integrating innovations in other systems (such as production) and can deliver higher levels of bottom-line performance. Given the turbulence in markets and the need to respond quickly to new opportunities, the real challenge for e-businesses will be developing agile organisational architecture and capabilities. However, they will also be about designing HR strategies that are fit for a purpose. We turn now to consider what these HR strategies might be.

Three Models of HR for the New Economy

The new economy will be like the old in many ways. Thus while e-business will lead to the greater exploitation of networks, we may also see developments on other more recognisable organisational forms with quite different implications for employment models. For example, call centres could be seen to become a new form of factory where close managerial supervision, narrow repetitive tasks and monetary motivation shape the employment system. Three different types of employment model can be seen to be gaining shape amid the turbulence of e-business.

1. THE STAR MODEL

The first is the 'Star' employment model where the success of the business is dependent on attracting key talent. These are people who are leaders in their field and have the ability to generate large revenue streams through their business and specialist knowledge. These firms will have a high density of professional employees and will be keen to lock them into long-term career trajectories within the business. These firms are likely to achieve supernormal returns and will reward their key employees well. In addition to high base salaries and target-related bonuses, key employees will be given company stock, usually on a deferred basis in order to tie them to the business for a number of years. The employees in this firm are likely to be motivated by challenging work, considerable professional autonomy and share equity. This is reflected in the comments by Howard Charney, the ex-CEO of Grand Junction, an Internet company acquired by Cisco: 'What I really love about this place is the contest of ideas. Because we have people from different companies, there are different approaches to solving problems. That creates an atmosphere of excitement that even the best small company can't duplicate.'[9]

They are also people who have considerable market power and will move if they are unhappy. Keeping these 'stars' engaged in the organisation for a reasonable time will be a key challenge. According to a senior manager at International Data Corporation in Massachusetts, 'You have to provide intangibles like cutting-edge projects to retain IT personnel.'[10] *Fortune* magazine (May 2000) reports that the war for talent is at its height, with firms exerting considerable imagination, energy and resource identifying and stealing key talent. Introduction fees of $1500 are being paid to staff who identify potential recruits and further bonuses of up to $5000 if these people are recruited.

2. THE NEW FACTORIES

These are organisations where stability, predictability and control are important. They are firms in a value chain where work is fairly routinised and employees have limited autonomy or control. The emphasis is on efficiency and cost reduction. An example would be certain types of call centre. The HR strategy at play in these

organisations is likely to be one where considerable attention is given to selection and recruitment in order to identify workers who can give high levels of service. Once given induction training, the emphasis then shifts to productivity, with employees working to tight scripts and routines under regular supervision and with output targets. As a result, employee turnover is likely to be high but the firm may calculate that the cost of changing the employment model is more expensive than the costs of high levels of turnover. There may be an implicit belief that higher turnover is better because of the boredom and stress of the job role.

This has been termed a 'sacrificial HR strategy'.[11] Firms that use this approach achieve efficiency and high levels of service at the same time. At the core of this HR strategy is the 'deliberate, frequent replacement of employees in order to provide enthusiastic, motivated customer service at a low cost to the organisation.[12] Other research in call centres has identified more enriched jobs, with higher levels of autonomy and discretion where career progression is possible and pay levels are attractive.[13] It would appear that within new forms of work organisation created by ICTs there is a process of segmentation, which is leading to quite different HR strategies and work experiences. The challenge for firms is to fit HR strategies to organisational needs.

3. THE PROJECT ORGANISATION

These are firms where technology and the work that they do are at the leading edge. Getting things done requires both task effectiveness and ability to work in multiple teams. People are attracted to these companies because they are surfing the wave of innovation. What keeps them in the organisation is the variety of work assignments and the opportunity to learn as well as develop new skills. That is what attracts engineers to companies like ARM in Cambridge UK and Cisco in the US. Furthermore, companies like Microsoft have 'built a resilient and loyal culture, not only by rewarding workers with stock options but also by treating software developers like kings. Many on the company's Redmond campus are insulated from doing anything but writing code, keeping developers passionately focused and loyal.'[14]

These firms are likely to operate HR systems that are loose (in that there is considerable discretion in how they are implemented) but at the same time tight in that there is recognition that systems are needed to co-ordinate people. There will be an ongoing tension between the need to have control and the recognition that too much control can alienate and prevent

creativity and innovation. The real trick, as Bill Parsons, HR Director at ARM acknowledges, is 'to find some balance between order and chaos.'[15]

What is happening in practice? Dell, one of the iconic firms of the new economy, follows the high-commitment HR strategy approach. Its menu of HR practices include the following:

- sophisticated recruitment and selection practices (including realistic job previews and critical incident interview techniques);
- continual job redesign (known as 'segmentation');
- team-based pay;
- 360-degree feedback;
- profit-sharing and stock options;
- problem-solving groups;
- flat organisational structures;
- continual learning and development.

Dell has grown and developed its HR approach over a number of years as its operating environment has changed and will no doubt continue to review and adjust its HR strategies. It combines elements of the 'Star' in its approach to the CEOs of its acquired businesses but also has aspects of both the 'Project' and the 'New Factory'. Clearly, for a business as large and diverse as Dell, this is probably not surprising and it is likely to be the case that most 'new economy' firms will be hybrids, not fitting exactly one of the types outlined earlier.

Unfortunately there is virtually no empirical evidence that we can draw upon to suggest how widespread these forms or their hybrids are currently. It is salient to note that the OECD in its recent *Economic Outlook*[16] warned against the hype around the idea of a new economy. It argued that only in the US, and in particular California, was there strong prima facie evidence of the development of a new economic model. With this in mind we now turn to review developments in Silicon Valley and what they can tell us about emergent HR strategies in the new economy.

Silicon Valley's Approach to HR

The epicentre of the digital revolution is Silicon Valley in California. This area has the biggest concentration of high-technology firms and it is widely thought that trends discernible here will affect all other firms in one way or another in the future. A recent study of the labour market in this area reveals some quite startling insights into the character of work in the digital economy and into the dominant HR strategies being pursued. In brief, the research concluded that the new labour market dynamics are seeing a 'shift in the locus of work organisation from relatively permanent, stable collections of "jobs", to individualised "flexible" employment'.[17]

The Silicon Valley labour market is characterised by a high level of professional and managerial skills (thirty-four per cent of the Valley workforce compared with just under twenty-four per cent in the US as a whole). However, in tandem with this growth in high-end skills, projections are that low-end occupations such as shop assistants, waiters/waitresses and cleaners will also grow rapidly (mainly to service these high-income professionals). This dynamic is likely to lead to a polarised labour market structure of winners and losers, and potentially to give rise to a range of social problems. The high-commitment HR policies of San Francisco companies like Cisco Systems is acknowledged to be leading to the unravelling of the social fabric:

> Cisco is its own village, and has engendered intense loyalty and happiness through some of the same myth-making techniques used by propagandists. The concept of corporate perks has moved beyond the simple fillip to complete need fulfilment. Human Resources maintains lists of Cisco clubs that go way beyond the corporate softball team. Wal-Mart, offering every routine product and service under one roof, has been blamed for destroying small-town life. Cisco, like many other Silicon Valley companies, out-Wal-Marts Wal-Mart. Former employees have commented on the sterility of life entirely within the Cisco bubble: nearly everyone there shares the same interests, socio-economic status and education. Local communities have lost the involvement of the employees of Cisco and other similarly high-commitment companies. And many of these communities are falling apart.[18]

New forms of work are also growing and in particular the contingent workforce. The proportion of employees working on temporary contracts or through labour-supply intermediaries (such as temping agencies) accounts for 3.5 per cent of the workforce. Self-employment covers 7.8 per cent (although other commentators have placed it as high as twenty per cent) with part-time employment perhaps covering as much as eighteen per cent.

These forms of contingent work are being partly driven by a second important trend. Companies are subcontracting or outsourcing activities, which are not seen as core to their business models. As firms vertically disintegrate, stick to their core competences and outsource all other areas, the jobs that move from the 'core' to the 'periphery' tend to attract less pay and fewer fringe benefits, and are also more insecure and less protected. Taking these trends together, Benner estimates that between forty and eighty per cent of net job growth in Silicon Valley is accounted for by the growth in contingent employment.

This suggests that a key HR strategy is the spot contract for employment. Firms no longer can or want to offer long-term commitments to employees. This means that many firms have created a vacuum for employees. In the words of the HR Director of Double-Click, 'Loyalty is dead because of what employers did to it but employees are still looking for something to be loyal to'.[19]

This scenario of a labour market segmented on both skill and type of employment contract is further complicated by the large demand for young, highly trained workers by the 'new economy' firms. The rapid pace of change in the high-technology industry means that the half-life of skills is in the order of eighteen months and, instead of developing internal processes to encourage continuous learning, many firms seek to recruit these skills directly. This is leading to a dominance of young employees in the core firms and means that professional experience does not attract the same wage premium as in other industries. This narrow focus may undermine firms' strategies continually to innovate, a point recognised by Leadbeater: 'We need to value the diverse, marginal and apparently redundant who are written off by the mainstream – older workers, middle managers, ethnic minorities – because they may be the source of the most imaginative ideas.'[20]

Another feature of the Silicon Valley labour market is rising wage inequality, with production workers in the electronics industry seeing a six per cent decline in their real wages, while the wages of top executives increased by 390 per cent over the same period. This is further tearing at the heart of the social

fabric in the Bay area. Overall, the Silicon labour market has become a much more volatile and uncertain place, with profound implications for employers, employees and labour market institutions.

If the experience of US high-technology firms can be seen as indicative of how businesses in this sector will respond on a global scale, we are looking at a significantly different employment model for the future. It needs to be borne in mind that many US high-technology firms have overseas operations and may seek to replicate organisational and employment models in these businesses. However, we also know that societal and institutional factors can mediate the strategies of international businesses and that those firms with similar technologies and products can organise employment in quite different ways in different countries. Firms' strategic choices over their organisational forms, their HR practices and their employment strategies are in reality constrained and take on different characters across societies. One constraint that is remarkably common for 'new economy' firms in all countries is the shortage of skills.

Skill Shortages and Firm-level Responses

A recent study by BIPR-IFO-Lentic (1998)[21] on the implications of rapid liberalisation and technology diffusion in the telecommunications industry estimates that there will be in the order of 1.3 million new IT-related jobs created in Europe by 2005, leading to a significant IT skills deficit of around 1.7 million jobs. A study by Spectrum Strategy for Andersen Consulting estimates that more than 850,000 Internet-related jobs will be created in the UK by 2003 and that ten per cent of these will be unfilled because of skills shortages.[22] A recent Templeton study[23] calculated the shortfall in IT skills in the UK to be in the order of 220–300,000 people between 2000 and 2003. Projections in the US suggest that IT vacancies could rise to 1.2 million over the same period.

A number of other developments will also serve to increase the demand for IT skills. These demands are likely to fall at both the high end (graduate level) as well as the low end. Related to this second level of demand, the wider diffusion of IT across all

business processes will make it mandatory for workers to have familiarity with IT systems. UPS, the American parcel delivery business, now demands that all drivers not only have a licence to drive but also pass a test that proves they can use the company's IT system. Increasingly, firms seeing themselves as e-businesses are also stipulating that all job applications are completed electronically via the Internet. BT has just moved all graduate recruitment to the Internet. Ford Europe has recently given all its employees home computers as one way of trying to encourage a wider understanding of new technologies and to develop the skills for using them. Along with other leading global businesses, they are moving to source their components through an electronic marketplace.

Employment projections in the US and Europe suggest that in the midst of this wave of Schumpeterian 'creative destruction' there will be net job creation and that the overall balance of jobs will be in the higher-skill category, bringing with them higher wages. This process may go some way to narrowing the rising wage inequality in the USA (in particular) and the decline in real wage growth of industrial workers over the last twenty years. However, as we have seen in the case of the Silicon Valley labour market, technological progress is also forcing greater segmentation and polarisation, with a strong growth in low-paying personal services employment.

The demand for new skills is not without problems and will provide real headaches for employers. Higher-level skills requiring a university-level training take three to five years to develop, but college intakes show that there are likely to be substantial shortfalls in key areas. For example, the UK produces around 10,000 IT graduates annually but currently has around 30,000 vacancies at this level. The 'war for talent' will steadily move up a gear.

These labour market pressures are likely to see a number of short-term and longer-term responses from employers. First, a shortage will force up the price of labour and there will be overheating in some key labour markets (both regionally and occupationally). The effect of this was felt prior to the millennium bug, which also focused attention on legacy IT skills rather than building competencies in new skills.

Second, firms will seek to upgrade the IT competence of those in their internal labour market or try to understand the extent to which IT skills exist within the company but remain untapped. For example, BT is seeking to build a skills and

competencies database of all its employees in order to understand the extent of IT-related skills. This is opening up a much wider pool of potential labour for internal jobs through job posting on their intranet. In addition, BT is also able to target people for training investment and encourage internal developmental job moves. These horizontal and vertical job moves can provide key staff with the diversity and interest which can help retain them in larger firms.

Third, firms may start to target alternative employee groups such as older workers and women returners. There is a wide and convincing body of research that shows that training investment in older employees is likely to pay high returns because they are less likely to leave the firm. Furthermore, a more diverse workforce is seen as important in encouraging innovation and creativity. However, according to one recent review 'it's difficult to find any e-business recruiter who is interested in achieving a balanced or diverse workforce' (*People Management*, June 2000).

Last, as we noted earlier, firms will acquire other organisations for access to their skills base. Both FI Group and Cisco systems use employee share ownership as an important strategic lever in this context.

The dilemma for firms is that their best plans to estimate skills and training needs will always be out of kilter with the rate of development of new skills in the economy. The one thing that is sure is that organisations will require more skills than they anticipate and therefore must put in place processes that give them the ability to grow their skill sets. Failure to do so will mean that they are unable to take advantage of new market opportunities.

This means that the importance of on-the-job learning will increase. For many fast-moving businesses, institutional providers of vocational training cannot respond quickly enough to their specific needs. This vacuum has seen the development of corporate universities plugged into the strategic and operational needs of large businesses. This is evidence that employee learning and education has become a strategic issue for these businesses and has been internalised.

The implication of tighter labour markets and a market failure in skill supply will also mean that firms will need to increase the value of their 'employment brand'. Firms will not only be selling the benefits of joining their organisation but also convincing their own employees that it is a good place to work, 'forward-looking companies are working on the assumption that they have to do a continuous selling job to the employee'.[24] They will need to

understand what key employees want and be prepared to be flexible in their employing models. ARM, the Cambridge chipset designer, recognises the importance of this and has developed a new flexible benefits package to aid employee retention. This includes perks such as an extra week's holiday for a five per cent reduction in pay, a fully paid four-week sabbatical after four years with the company and a sympathetic policy towards job sharing, part-time or term-time working and other flexible forms of employment.[25]

A persistent theme in this chapter is the way in which e-business will accelerate existing trends in human resource management and organisational change. We have suggested that the high-performance work model is one potential route that firms may take because it is geared to creating a more flexible and adaptive organisational system, which can respond effectively to today's turbulent marketplace. However, we have also seen the potential downsides of the Silicon Valley model, which can lead to greater polarisation in the labour market and the ongoing destruction of the area's social fabric. This is one of the unintended consequences of the high-commitment HR strategies pursued by companies like Cisco and Microsoft.

Conclusions

This chapter has reviewed the emerging issues and challenges in HR confronting both firms and policy makers in the move to the 'new economy'. While there are pressures whose logic will lead to some convergence towards a new and common employment model, we anticipate that the next decade will be characterised as much by heterogeneity as homogeneity in firms' HR systems. Silicon Valley is probably the most advanced example of what may be to come, but it is unclear whether its model can be or should be transferred to other countries with differing societal and institutional characteristics.

The dynamics at play within the Silicon Valley labour market point to a much more unstable employment system, with increasing evidence of labour market segmentation and polarisation. The European social model is unlikely to tolerate the high levels of polarisation and risk implied by the US market-based high-tech model.

For firms moving to e-business we suggested that there will be three broad employment models – the Star, the New Factory and the Project – each with its own distinctive characteristics. We also drew attention to the importance of ICTs for creating new organisational forms and in particular underlined the significance of the *networked enterprise* for HR strategies. With competition based on creating value from players in supply chains within and between industries, HR strategies will have to develop people with the capability to work across changing multiple boundaries.

The need for agile and adaptive organisations in the 'new economy' suggests that high-performance work systems may become more widely diffused. In the short to medium term the pressing challenge for firms will be their ability to respond to skill shortages. Such pressures will force greater attention on firms' 'employment brand' and the consistency between how they treat their customers and how they treat their employees. Firms seeking to recruit and retain scarce skills in competitive markets will increasingly need to ensure consistency in their HR strategies. This is all the more important for well-established firms that may find it difficult to create the energy and fun (and potential high rewards) of a dot.com start-up.

For social scientists and novelists alike the future of the Robbies of this world is a story we will watch with interest.

NOTES

1 Andersen, Kurt, *Turn of the Century*, Headline, 1999.
2 Dell, Michael, *Direct from Dell: Strategies that Revolutionised an Industry*, HarperCollins, 1999.
3 Leadbeater, Charles, *Living on Thin Air*, Penguin, London, 1999.
4 Bunnell, David, *Making the Cisco Connection: The Story Behind the Real Internet Superpower*, John Wiley & Sons, New York, 2000.
5 'Joining the Dots: HR in the e-Economy', *People Management*, 22 June 2000.
6 Ibid.
7 Pfeffer, Jeffrey, *The Human Equation*, HBS Press, 1999.
8 Thompson, M., *The UK Aerospace People Management Audit 2000*, Society of British Aerospace Companies and Department of Trade and Industry, London, 2000.
9 Bunnell, op.cit.
10 'Skill shortages spurs outsourcing', *Computerworld*, Framingham, USA, March 2000.

11 Wallace, C., Eagleson, G. and Waldersee, R., 'The sacrificial HR strategy in Call Centers', *International Journal of Service Industry Management*, Vol.11, No.2, MCB University Press, 2000.

12 Ibid.

13 Hutchinson, S., Purcell, J. and Kinnie, N., 'Evolving High Commitment Management and the Experience of the RAC Call Centre', *Human Resource Management Journal*, Vol.10, No.1, 2000.

14 Skapinker, Michael, 'Begging for Workers', *Financial Times*, 18 June 2000.

15 'Don't worry Bill', *Human Resources*, Haymarket, London, 2000.

16 *Economic Outlook*, OECD, 2000.

17 Benner, C., 'Silicon Valley Labor Markets: Overview of Structure, Dynamics and Outcomes for Workers', Task Force Working Paper No.7, The Task Force on Working Partnerships, USA, 1999.

18 Bunnell, op. cit., p.100.

19 Grimes, Christopher, 'Software giant strives to stem exodus of staff', *Financial Times*, 13 June 2000.

20 Leadbeater, op. cit., p.240.

21 BIPE-IFO-Lentic, 'The impact of liberalisation in the EU telecommunications industry', European Commission, 1998.

22 Grande, Carlos, 'Internet "to create 850,000 jobs in 3 years"', *Financial Times*, 13 June 2000.

23 Willcocks, L., 'The impact of IR35 on IT Skills in the UK', Oxford working paper, 2000.

24 Grimes, Christopher, op. cit.

25 'Don't worry Bill', op. cit.

Managing the Infrastructure Challenge

Christopher Sauer

The image of e-business is inextricably tied to the glamour of web sites. Yet web sites are merely the shopfronts, trade counters or auction rooms of far more complex commercial operations. Moving beyond the façade, e-business is principally about taking advantage of web technology to develop and extend electronic integration. Forrester Research has found that electronic marketplace companies, which today do no more than match customers and suppliers, all expect to be providing integrated credit, payment and fulfilment services within two years.[1]

E-business integration can be internal to the firm (linking separate functions), external to the firm (linking suppliers, customers and trading partners), or both. In order to achieve such integration, the organisation requires an appropriate underlying infrastructure and the capability to exploit it. Ensuring it has this is the infrastructure management challenge.

So what do we mean by infrastructure? In this chapter we focus on the firm level where typically infrastructure has referred to tangible assets, which serve as fixed prerequisites for conducting the company's business. For our purposes the firm infrastructure consists of the combination of tangible assets such as branches, telephone systems, manufacturing plant, call centres and distribution centres, and intangible, IT-based assets including data resources such as databases and data warehouses, and systems such as enterprise resource planning (ERP) systems that are necessary for the firm to conduct its business. It is more than just IT, but IT is the key to achieving end-to-end integration.

Tim Gregory, head of IT at Lloyd's, has described 2000 as 'the year when infrastructure moves out of the IT department and into the area of business-critical support for the e-business revolution'.[2] Jeanne Ross of MIT and her colleagues have described IT infrastructure as one of the three strategic levers for transforming an organisation into an e-business.[3] E-business constitutes both an opportunity and a threat. It is the opportunity to leverage IT-enabled integration across traditional boundaries and the threat that others may be better positioned to achieve this. The boundaries may be internal organisational boundaries such as those between business functions or product groups. But they are increasingly between separate organisations such as suppliers and their customers, or suppliers and intermediaries. E-business presents a management challenge, therefore, in that it requires infrastructure that may not be shared at present.

Infrastructure management is currently not an advanced art. It is rarely high on senior management's agenda. Infrastructure is simply assumed to be available. With e-business, infrastructure will continue to be taken for granted, but now it will cross more boundaries and be more challenging to design, install and operate. This chapter demonstrates the need for and importance of explicitly managing infrastructure, and provides ways of thinking about it that can help define the infrastructure a company needs.

The approach proposed in this chapter is distinctive in three respects:

- It is e-business model driven.
- It defines infrastructure in high-level, non-technological terms.
- Its objective is to create infrastructure *capability*.

We start by exploring why infrastructure is so important for e-business and then develop the infrastructure perspective – a view of what infrastructure involves. We then describe an approach to designing and delivering infrastructure for e-business, and conclude by outlining the management challenge for now and the emerging future. In summary, this chapter helps e-business executives to address the nitty-gritty question of what it will take, apart from new ideas, to do business using web technology.

The Challenge of E-Business

As earlier chapters have shown, e-business radically challenges existing business models. As dot.coms set the competitive pace, established firms have to review their existing ways of doing business. They often do not have the infrastructure to compete successfully against the new business models. The Australian department store chain, David Jones, launched a web site that was highly attractive to visitors but inefficient to operate because it was not linked into a well-designed order fulfilment process. The product range on its site was rapidly reduced to a single line – food hampers – that was already available by mail order.[4] Other companies have suffered from too much success in attracting customers. They have generated more business at peaks than their IT infrastructure has been able to cope with. At Christmas 1999 several high-profile e-tailers, including Toys'R'Us and Wal-Mart, experienced operational hiccups.[5] On-line brokerages such as E*Trade and Ameritrade have also experienced capacity problems. In February 1999 E*Trade experienced three days of computer outages. Over a matter of days its share price dropped thirty-five per cent.[6] This kind of incident has served to highlight the importance of the IT infrastructure. The fact that the financial markets have been seen to punish these companies so severely has underlined this lesson.

What makes e-business such a challenge is as much the intensity of its demands as its novelty. Its characteristics include:

- high uncertainty about future business needs;
- reducing time-to-market;
- dependence on rapidly developing technologies;
- operation in parallel with non-e-business channels;
- increased reach and range;
- greater personalisation;
- risk to market share from increased customer mobility;
- increasing transparency of internal business processes;
- more and closer inter-organisational relationships;
- exposure to intruders;
- exposure of customers to cyber-theft.

Business process change has always been bedevilled by uncertainty about future needs. Because competition is moving so

fast and because new competitors are emerging from unexpected quarters, e-business intensifies uncertainty. Likewise time-to-market has been a continuing issue for many years, but the speed at which e-business operations like Amazon and Egg have built a brand and market share has heightened its importance for all players. Dependence on rapidly developing technologies also continues an earlier theme but this too assumes greater importance as competitive advantage increasingly depends on being a leader at exploiting technology.

For established companies their e-business usually becomes another channel operating alongside existing channels. New channels are not themselves an unprecedented innovation for a company to cope with. What is different about Internet channels is that typically the intensity of the competition creates extraordinary pressure to respond, regardless of the impacts on more traditional channels. This can create demand for change in the established channels. Barnes and Noble's store customers believed that their established stores should be able to deliver at least as good a service as their more recent Internet channel. They expressed dissatisfaction when they found that the stores did not have access to the same book order system and therefore in-store ordering did not match the barnesandnoble.com channel.

While some familiar problems are accentuated, e-business also gives rise to novel characteristics. Increased market reach is classic. It has become a cliché that any company establishing an Internet site thereby becomes a global corporation. Yet without the accompanying infrastructure to support global distribution any immediate gain may be short-lived. This point was made by the head of e-business initiatives at ElectroComponents, a multinational, business-to-business distribution group, who noted that by servicing some 140 countries prior to establishing its e-business site the company knew how to handle the export/import formalities when e-orders started to come in from far-flung parts. A domestic competitor, the company noted, might have been able to attract the same order but not service it and therefore would not secure repeat business. By contrast to organisational reach, increased product range is less a novelty of e-business, merely so much simpler to do, as a single site can act as a portal for an indefinitely extensive set of products. This is apparent both in pure portal sites such as Yahoo! and in the rapid extension of direct sales by companies such as Amazon, which has moved from books into music, electronics, games and beauty products in rapid succession.

Another new characteristic is mass personalisation – that is, the products available may not vary, but the way they are sold is individualised on the basis of electronically stored customer information. At the same time, one of the unexpected discoveries of Internet-based business is that customers are highly mobile. A single unsatisfactory experience is sufficient to lose that customer. This has become particularly true about order fulfilment. Dell satisfies its customers by consistently delivering ahead of the lead-time quoted at the point of order. Another novelty to have emerged is transparency of internal processes. As companies vie to offer better service, they delve deeper into their own organisation for information that will help the client. This often involves exposing stock levels, lead-times and distribution information, as with couriers such as DHL and UPS who allow clients to track the progress of their packages.

A characteristic that connects with several others is the strength and number of inter-organisational relationships. Both reduced time to market and increased reach and range are more likely to require partnerships with other providers. Such partnerships are typically quickly arranged and require a degree of intimacy that previously would have taken years of trust to develop. In a novel development in construction, the Sydney-based architecture practice, Flower and Samios, has sought to link itself with design consultants such as structural engineers and quantity surveyors, and with building contractors through a shared database of design and construction. Previously, arm's-length relationships become more intimate as all participants share the same information. The boundaries between their roles change as opportunities emerge for each participant to add value at any time.

E-business also creates significant new risks. Web sites expose corporations to both desired customers and undesired intruders. The more integrated a web front-end is with back-office systems, the more potentially exposed the company's systems are. The increased commercial traffic with customers submitting payment details, particularly credit cards, creates another form of risk – cyber-theft.

The reason e-business poses a special challenge for infrastructure is not that it suddenly makes infrastructure important – infrastructure has always been important, for example in the branch networks that have been crucial for retail banks, supermarkets, fast-food outlets and so many other businesses. Rather, e-business makes integration through IT the very basis of the business. Infrastructure, as the basis for integration, defines a company's competitive options.

The Infrastructure Perspective

Modern organisations have been highly dependent on technology infrastructure but their conscious awareness of it has been limited. Many IT directors make a point of never talking about infrastructure to their business peers because the latter, they say, are not interested. At best, infrastructure has been treated as a necessary evil, discussed briefly and grudgingly approved when a new mainframe has been required or 10,000 desktop computers have needed an upgrade. At worst, IT directors have silently bundled infrastructure costs into their applications projects. The reasons for such subterfuges and lack of interest are various. Core business executives have traditionally either seen infrastructure investments such as distribution centres as part of a specific capital project with a clearly defined business payback or they have seen them as 'no-brainers' like the telephone system. In other words, infrastructure has not been a major continuing issue for management. It is therefore worth spelling out what it means explicitly to take the infrastructure perspective.

The infrastructure perspective amounts to viewing infrastructure as a capability in relation to tangible and non-tangible assets that serve certain organisational purposes and which are appropriately defined in non-technical terms. We start by talking about IT infrastructure because it is at the heart of e-business infrastructure issues and because, over recent years, it has become increasingly important within the IT function. But, we argue, infrastructure is more than IT. Further, it is more than just physical assets but needs to be thought of in terms of capability. We then address the need to understand the different dimensions of infrastructure capability in terms of the purposes it serves. Finally, we analyse how to define infrastructure characteristics for e-business in a generic, non-technical form.

For the IT unit, infrastructure was initially a technical preserve. Once the mainframe computer had been purchased, further decisions were straightforward. Infrastructure design was largely incremental, a matter of extending the existing technology

platform with products from the same supplier to achieve improved capacity or performance. The IT unit was probably a cost centre. Infrastructure investment was therefore seen as necessary expenditure to be assigned to its budget.

Over the last two decades that world has gradually changed, moving infrastructure more into view. The increased dependence of business processes on IT has made robust infrastructure more important. The advent of client-server and networked computing has meant that a wider range of technologies had to be linked. The arrival of viable enterprise software has spurred intra-organisational integration requiring common or linked IT platforms. A trend for closer supply chain links across organisations has led to more inter-organisational systems. A wider range of IT costing and charging mechanisms has emerged, permitting alternative allocation of costs.

More recently, evidence has been collected to demonstrate the business value of infrastructure.[7] So, contrary to earlier beliefs that IT infrastructure expenditure was better not discussed because it was a sunk cost, it now appears that businesses that have invested more in infrastructure have gained commercial benefits over those who invested less.

We have already defined infrastructure as consisting of more than just IT including the combination of all tangible and intangible assets that are necessary for the firm to conduct its business. Like it or not, companies now find that to create an Internet presence is to make a statement that is interpreted by public and business community alike as an intent to deliver a seamless, integrated and effective service. Amazon and Dell, among others, have set the standard. Stories of assistants in on-line grocery operations pushing trolleys up aisles picking orders in competition with in-store shoppers reflect a lack of appropriate order fulfilment infrastructure. Many distributors and logistics operations such as Entertainment UK, a substantial player in the leisure goods supply business with twenty-five per cent of the UK CD market, are taking the opportunity to upgrade their distribution centres so as to be able to handle the twin demands of bulk supply to stores and personal delivery to individuals.[8]

E-business is a way of conducting business on a continuing basis. Infrastructure may provide the platform, but its continuing success requires infrastructure capabilty. This is the capability to exploit the mix of assets that constitutes the infrastructure itself. In relation to IT infrastructure, for example, this would include the relevant technicians who keep systems serviced and updated

with the latest releases of essential software. In relation to a shared distribution centre it would include the staff and operational systems. The extent to which the centre could cope with changing demand would be a function not only of its physical characteristics such as size and layout, but also its people and systems. Companies accustomed to despatching large consignments to retail outlets are already finding that some distribution systems can be a constraint on their ability to provide delivery to personal customers of their Internet channel. The extent to which infrastructure can deliver its full potential depends upon the organisation's capability to exploit it.

Infrastructure and infrastructure capability are not simple, but have characteristics that serve different purposes and fulfil different roles. The first and most obvious characteristic of infrastructure is that it is the platform on which today's business operates. In talking of a platform, we are talking of assets whose potential application is wider than their current use. An assembly line that can be readily reconfigured for different products is infrastructure, as is a computer that can be used either for weather forecasting or a web site. The second characteristic is related, inasmuch as it constitutes a platform on which a changed business could operate in the future. As a perspective on infrastructure management, the first implies a narrow focus on today's operations, whereas the second implies concern for tomorrow.

The third characteristic is developmental rather than operational. It emphasises the environment and tools that enable business development. This is clearest in the case of IT infrastructure, where software and programming tools are essential parts of ensuring today's operations run successfully, but also enable programmers to build new systems so that the business can run better in the future.

The fourth characteristic of infrastructure is that it implies sharing. Many different business units might use the same logistics centre so that the facility, its operational systems, staff and management are shared. In IT, it is a set of shared facilities needed by many different applications. From the point of view of management, attention to this facet often implies concern for access and cost allocation. The shared asset is probably not seen as part of the competitive core.

More recently, though, a fifth characteristic has started to emerge. This turns our attention to shared systems that *are* core. It features in the context of Enterprise Resource Planning (ERP) systems that provide core business functionality. This reflects two

divergent management mindsets. One sees IT as a commodity and ERP as a simple, single supplier solution to a burdensome problem. The other sees ERP as enabling internal, end-to-end integration through sharing information across business units and functional boundaries.[9] On this latter view ERP is infrastructure because ERP is the platform on which new competitive initiatives will be taken. In shifting the level of the platform to core business applications, this facet of the infrastructure perspective reminds us that infrastructure is not a single hard-and-fast thing, but a set of ideas for helping to manage a complex business.

Dow Corning provides an illustration.[10] It has opted for a global implementation of an ERP system, in its case SAP. This has provided it with replacement core systems but, more important, it offers a shared platform on which to develop its processes in three successive stages. The first is to be global supply chain integration, followed by re-engineering of core operations processes comprising customer focus, product delivery, financial management and personnel management, and completed by re-engineering of decision-making processes including opportunity development, portfolio management, people development, and direction and planning. In this case the SAP infrastructure has provided the company with a platform for the present and the future, a toolset with which to develop it for the future, full sharing across the business at the core of the company's operations.

How, then, should we define an e-business infrastructure capability? We have seen that e-business can be distinctively challenging in a number of ways. Table 1 demonstrates relevant infrastructure implications.

These implications suggest four broad categories of infrastructure capability:

- Responsiveness
- Leverage
- Operational performance
- Risk management

Uncertainty implies the need to be able to respond flexibly to the unexpected. The potential increase in volume of business from increased reach and range requires the capacity to scale up quickly. Shorter time-to-market for Internet channel products and services implies increased build speed for web site development and associated services. The rapid development of Internet technologies requires an infrastructure that can be

extended quickly to accommodate new technology. New relationships require high connectivity. Flexible response, the capacity to scale, increased build speed, platform extensibility and connectivity are all characteristics of responsive infrastructure. This will be one critical area for business-to-business Internet exchanges as they move from customer–supplier matching into value-adding services of credit management and logistics over the next two years.

E-Business Characteristics	Infrastructure Implications
High uncertainty about future business needs	Flexibility
Reducing time-to-market	Increased IT build speed, increased adaptability and responsiveness
Increased risk to market share from increased customer mobility	High build quality, operational robustness, customer friendliness, integration with business processes
Increased reach and range	Scalability
Exposure to intruders	Security
Exposure of customers to cyber-theft	Payment security
Increasing transparency of internal business processes	Backwards integration of applications
More and closer inter-organisational relationships	Connectivity
Dependence on rapidly developing technologies	Extensibility
May operate alongside non-e-business channels	Operation, maintenance and development of non-e-business infrastructure

Table 1 – Infrastructural Implications of E-Business

The second infrastructure category is leverage – the ability to exploit available resources to compete differently. Increased internal transparency implies backward integration into existing infrastructure. Greater personalisation implies access to existing data resources such as customer databases. Inter-organisational relationships can be turned to advantage if it is easy to connect with partners. Backward integration, access to data resources and connectivity are characteristics of leverage from infrastructure. Safeway is an example of a company that has invested heavily in leverage in relation to information on its ABC card-holding customers. It has both extensive databases of customer behaviour over five years, sophisticated analytical capabilities

and links into customer-facing processes such as promotions.

The third category is operational performance. Increased customer mobility implies the need for quality e-business systems, robust operations, and increasingly 24/7 availability. The existence of parallel channels implies a degree of operational consistency across them. Inter-organisational relationships require connective infrastructure for ease of operation. Quality, robustness, availability, consistency and connectivity are all operational characteristics of an e-business infrastructure. Amazon has been the pacesetter in this respect, with initiatives such as Abbey National's Cahoot and Halifax's on-line trading service examples of infrastructures that have initially not been able to provide the necessary levels of operational performance.

The fourth category for infrastructure capability is risk management. Exposure to intruders implies the need for site security and for firewalls to prevent break-ins penetrating beyond the public web site. Exposure of customers to cyber-theft implies the need for payment security systems. Risk to market share and stock price from customer mobility implies the need for operational robustness to ensure continuous service. Site security, payment security, operational robustness are all risk management characteristics of e-business infrastructure.

Companies do not need to be equally capable in all aspects of infrastructure. Partly in response to the changing infrastructure needs of e-business and partly as a result of the development of the marketplace, the IT industry, in particular, now offers new products and services. In addition to the traditional suppliers of hardware, software and networking, and IT facilities management, ERP suppliers offer e-business facilities bolted on to their core systems, application service providers offer an alternative to buying and managing application software. Specialist companies provide web server hosting and associated services. Others offer web site design or security products. The effect is to make infrastructure capability available through contracting with suppliers rather than having to be entirely home-grown.

The infrastructure perspective provides us with a clearer and more explicit understanding of what is required to deliver e-business. Its advantage is that in an era when Internet stock valuations are heavily predicated on potential, it is important to understand both one's own ability to deliver on potential and one's competitors' ability likewise.

Approach to Managing Infrastructure for E-Business

Figure 1 summarises the approach proposed in this chapter. An effective e-business requires an effective infrastructure. The e-business model therefore defines the infrastructure requirements. Once the requirements are known, decisions are needed which factor in practical considerations such as cost and existing infrastructure, and then trade off competing requirements. Thus infrastructure management issues meet infrastructure technology issues.

These decisions must also pay attention to the sourcing or supply issue (see also Chapter 10). The objective is to achieve an infrastructure capability. It is a capability in two senses. It includes all the necessary knowledge and experience to deliver against the current business model. And it has a degree of self-developmental potential to permit evolution of the infrastructure in response to evolution of the e-business model.

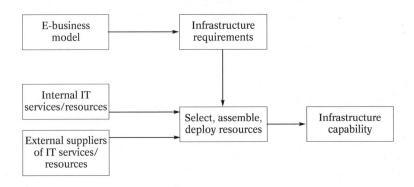

Figure 1 – The Path to Infrastructure Capability

What is required of any given infrastructure is a set of per-formance characteristics together with developmental potential. However, there is variability in how this is provided. Infra-structure capability may be derived from the configuration of existing, newly bought-in and externally sourced resources. The whole may consist of components owned or managed by different parties. Thus Thames Water outsources its operations and maintenance to a business partner in IT services, contracts a

specialist firm to build web applications and itself owns the physical infrastructure on which its sites run. There is also variability in the levels of management control applied. Because of this variability in provision and control, it is more useful to define infrastructure in terms of non-technical characteristics such as adaptability, scalability, integration, security, build speed and the like.

Of course, these characteristics vary in the ease with which they can be measured and translated into a form that will help in assembling an appropriate infrastructure capability. Scalability can be assessed relatively straightforwardly by considering the implications of increases in volume and pressure of business. The volume that can be handled may be influenced by factors such as web server capacity, connection bandwidth, storage capacity and others. The key is to define the weakest link in the system and ask what it would take to upgrade it. Then, supposing it has been upgraded, look for the next weakest link. The point at which a weak link requires a discontinuous change in the technology defines the limit of the infrastructure's scalability.

Adaptability is less easily assessed systematically. Adaptability is needed because of uncertainty as to business requirements. It typically requires an informed judgement as to likely business directions. It also needs to take account of the available capability. Thus, even though the technology platform may be available to accommodate a shift in business direction, the expertise needed to realise it may be lacking. And while mostly such expertise can be bought in the marketplace, the speed at which e-business development takes place means that a delay of two or more months caused by search, negotiation, contracting and subsequent familiarisation may have serious competitive implications and constitute a failure of adaptability.

The process of selecting, assembling and deploying resources to achieve an infrastructure capability draws on the requirements of the e-business model and upon the sourcing of IT services and resources. In the next section we explore the definition of infrastructure requirements based on the e-business model. In the following section we explore delivery issues.

Infrastructure Requirements of E-Business Models

Figure 2 defines our approach to identifying a company's answer to the question, 'What will it take to do business using web technology?' It presents a prismatic model. Different elements of the total business model directed through the prism of e-business yield different infrastructure requirements. The elements of the business model that we use are:

- intended financial contribution of the e-business channel;
- type of commerce it involves;
- structure of the business;
- organisational reach of the technology;
- stage of e-business maturity.

Analysis of these elements generates a spectrum of infrastructure requirements under the categories of responsiveness, leverage, operational performance and risk management. This multi-faceted approach is necessary to capture the full extent of the implications for infrastructure capability. The rapid rate of change in the e-business environment means that any single element of the business model may become obsolete overnight. By using different facets we increase the probability that no significant implication will be overlooked.

The first and most important element of the business model to be examined is the intended financial contribution of the e-business channel. While entrepreneurs conjure up many exotic business models, there are six fundamental sources of bottom-line improvement:

- increased volume of sales;
- reduced cost;
- increased range of products and services;
- enhanced revenue from improved product quality;
- enhanced exploitation of a niche;
- first-mover advantage.

Innovative companies seek to leverage several within the same business model.

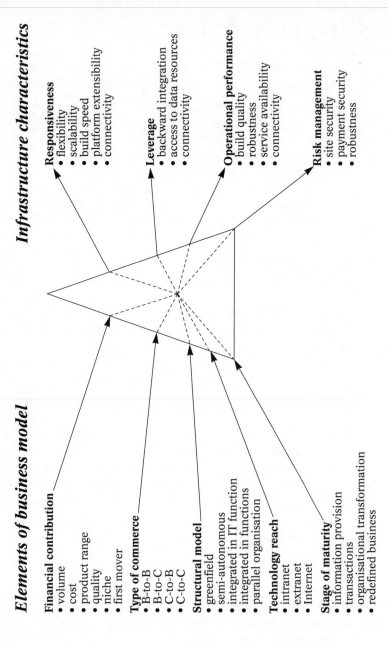

Figure 2 – Prism Model for Identifying E-Business Infrastructure Characteristics

If the intent is to pursue a volume strategy, then operational performance, particularly capacity and connectivity, are crucial. So, too, is recruitment and retention of customers, which is very sensitive to quality of service. Site unavailability and poor order fulfilment result in permanently lost customers. This has been particularly true of a number of the leading business-to-consumer operations such as Charles Schwab (see Introduction to this book) and Egg, the British on-line bank.

Cost reduction can be pursued in a number of ways. Leverage of existing capability and connectivity are important. If the target is internal efficiencies, then process redesign may be required rather than extended IT infrastructure. If the target is cheaper prices through aggregated purchases, then little more may be required than membership of an industry Net exchange and the appropriate connectivity. If cheaper transaction costs are sought, then improved purchasing technology and processes may be demanded. These can require close linking with external supplier organisations through the Internet or extranets. If the goal is more effective purchasing, then the whole purchasing organisation, its constituent jobs, its systems and its management processes may require redesign. However, solutions do vary. British Telecom has focused on purchasing transaction cost reduction. It expects that these can be reduced from £50 to £5 per transaction by the use of BT MarketSite, a common site for its supplier catalogues. MarketSite links into CommerceOne's BuySite to enable BT to purchase direct from the suppliers whose catalogues are included on MarketSite. In this case integration, and hence efficiency, is achieved because MarketSite is powered by CommerceOne software and therefore links well with BuySite.

Offering increased product range in Internet time often requires acquisitions or alliances. This suggests complex leverage. Connectivity will be important for leveraging partnerships. To provide a consistent offering may require backward integration into multiple back-office systems with consequent variability in performance.

Enhanced revenue from improved quality requires continuing innovation. One popular direction is towards greater customisation. This requires leverage of data resources, for example, in quickly identifying an individual and slotting that person into a particular profile of history, preferences and entitlements. Airlines exploit this aspect of their infrastructures to provide web-based services around their customer loyalty programmes. For them the crucial infrastructure requirements are access to data resources

and backward integration into processes such as reservations.

Exploitation of a niche via the Internet can result from extended reach. For example, US-based suppliers of anglers' products, which are cheap to freight relative to their purchase price, found that establishing Internet sites brought them increased sales from overseas markets. In such cases the crucial infrastructure may be operational performance in the form of distribution as markets requiring service multiply. Another company using the Internet to exploit a niche is the Sydney-based Advanced Environmental Concepts. A company of engineering design consultants, they prepare design briefs, which they supply in the form of an Internet address to their consultant partners who may be in London or San Francisco. They use the Internet as a common infrastructure to overcome the fact that their partners may be with them only for the duration of a single project and therefore do not want to invest in the expensive and specialised analytical software they use.

Many companies have seen first-mover advantage as the principal incentive to engage in e-business (see also Chapter 2). This is essentially an acknowledgement that it is extremely difficult to secure a sustainable advantage on the Net. The implication is that speed and maximisation of potential business is essential. Attempts to retain first-mover advantage beyond a single major initiative require continuing innovation and continued speed to market with new Internet-based products and services. Build speed becomes the crucial infrastructural characteristic.

A second element of the business model from which infrastructure requirements can be elicited is the type of commerce it involves. For example, a B-to-B channel may not require Internet payment facilities. But it may need to link into a buy-side model (the customer has an extract of the supplier's product catalogue integrated into its own purchasing system) and a market-based model (the customer buys through an Internet exchange such as GlobalNetXchange). Because such arrangements may be distinctive to small sets of major business partners, connectivity among them is critical. It is for this reason that Eastman Chemical took a web technology route for its e-procurement initiative. B-to-C channels for mass market products are more prone to hit capacity problems but even B-to-B can be affected, particularly where there is heavy advertising. B-to-C, C-to-B and C-to-C models typically have to be flexible and platform extensible in being more able to accommodate a diverse range of customer infrastructure, whereas B-to-B models may need to be carefully tuned for operational performance, say to facilitate access by favoured clients.

The alternative designs by which organisations are structuring their e-business initiatives (see Chapter 4) represent a third element of the business model that must be analysed. As Moore and Ruddle note, each structural model has different implications. The ability to act according to Internet culture, and to recruit and retain staff, may be highest in the greenfield model, permitting the establishment of organisational and human resource infrastructure, but it does not help to make the parent firm's existing organisational infrastructure more e-business capable. IT infrastructure may require only upgrade at the margins where e-business is integrated into the parent firm, whereas it may need to be heavily replicated by a greenfield model. But as many firms have already outsourced their IT infrastructure, the more substantial challenge posed by variant models of organisation relates to issues of control, culture and competences. Thus, BP Amoco has engaged in a major e-business-orientated cultural change programme in order to provide a basis for the establishment of appropriate capability throughout the organisation.

The organisational reach of the technology is the fourth element of the business model. It can be most simply classified into intranets, extranets and Internet sites. IBM has used intranets for much of its human resource operations. With the objective of stripping out cost, it has invested in complementary technologies and people in the form of call centres of highly trained personnel staff to handle non-standard queries so as to create an effective process at lower cost. To achieve the required quality and availability of service, the company has had to invest in a more extensive infrastructure than that immediately needed to support web technology.

Extranets can add business value by enabling re-engineering of inter-organisational processes without incurring the costs of a proprietary technology like EDI. Crucial issues are connectivity, operational performance and potentially leverage, depending on the service to be provided.

Open Internet sites introduce many infrastructural issues. Operational performance is important because demand is unpredictable. Risk management is important because of the openness of the site and the openness of the connection between supplier and customer.

The final element for analysis is the stage of e-business

maturity. The model described in the Introduction identifies four stages, which translate into levels of penetration of e-business. In the first, the creation of a web presence, companies offer only a façade to the world. This may range in information richness from a simple set of information about other channels by which to reach the company to the rich and varied content of a news provider such as the *Guardian* newspaper or CNN. The purpose of such a site may vary. Many established companies have created their first site as a technological experiment and vehicle for learning. For the most part, the infrastructural requirements are undemanding, a rudimentary web presence needing very little storage or processing, site design, some straightforward programming, a web server and line capacity. Because most such sites are not expected to have direct impact on the bottom line, infrastructural shortcomings such as lack of capacity and poor site design can be given low priority. As new sites have ceased to be news, so even the potential embarrassment of insufficient capacity on site launch has diminished. Sites such as newspapers that generate advertising revenue per visitor or per click are an exception. For them, operational performance characteristics are most important. The other exception is sites attempting to develop a platform incrementally. An example is Remo, an Australian general store that in early 2000 set about reinventing itself as an Internet retailer by creating a fun site intended to become a platform for delivering revenue-generating services. For such sites responsiveness, leverage and operational performance are important.

Second-stage companies open up an Internet channel for business transactions. Usually this means being open to take orders and/or receive payments and/or distribute products and services. It may also involve establishment of complementary services such as Internet channel help desks. The infrastructure requirements immediately become more complex and more important to get right. Capacity needs to be such that no more than a tiny number of attempts to visit and place an order fail. Storage is required to capture data. Security such as SSL (Secure Socket Layer) is required to take payments with minimum risk. Operational robustness becomes important as site unavailability can cause loss of revenue, customers and company value.

The third and fourth stages involve greater integration of the Internet channel into business processes. This can mean providing greater transparency, for example, by providing backward access into the company's databases to show stock availability

and production schedules to customers. Or it can mean feeding transaction-specific information in the other direction into the customer's purchasing system. The former requires firewall security and integration tools such as middleware, purpose-built translation programs or interface mechanisms. The infrastructure effect is increased complexity.

The prism allows us to define the ideal set of requirements for a company's e-business. We analyse each element of the business model in turn to identify the particular infrastructure capability requirements. These then need to be evaluated in terms of internal inconsistency. These are likely to be tensions between requirements such as IT build speed and quality, and operational robustness. They need to be resolved by reference to the business imperatives that implied them in the first place. It makes no sense for an infrastructure designer to favour build speed if the result will be operational breakdowns with consequential damage to revenue flows and market value. Some have suggested that major problems such as those experienced by Egg and Cahoot in their first days of trading were the result of too much speed and not enough emphasis on robustness. On the other hand, too much attention to operational robustness may extend time-to-market with loss of first-mover advantage. Such trade-offs have potentially significant business implications and require informed business decision-making.

Over time, the relative weighting of these criteria may change. It will be necessary to reapply the analysis on a regular basis to identify changing requirements. Today technology evolves so fast that even with intelligent foresight processes most firms do not attempt to plan infrastructure more than one stage (twelve to eighteen months) ahead. For this reason, the infrastructure analysis will bear review every six months.

Definition of infrastructure requirements sets the scene for the organisation to deliver the new infrastructure.

Delivering New Infrastructure

The infrastructure task for a company moving to e-business is to deliver technology capabilities that enable the most immediate e-business initiatives, while making the best possible provision for future possibilities. This is challenging for three reasons. First, as

we have noted, some of the infrastructure requirements of e-business are inconsistent. While it would be ideal if tensions were resolved at the stage of defining requirements, in practice they may be left to the delivery stage for resolution. The second challenge is that in order to meet business's reducing time-to-market, and in order to use new technologies satisfactorily, most IT units have recognised that they must make some use of external suppliers because it takes too long to up-skill existing staff. Third, the IT services marketplace is itself rapidly transforming, creating a wide range of new sourcing options.

Having defined the requirements, Figure 3 provides a map for delivering on them. For a start-up, the requirements are what needs to be delivered. For established firms there will be existing infrastructure capability. So it is then necessary to determine what gap there is between requirements and existing capability in terms of responsiveness, leverage, operational performance and risk management.

In a neat and tidy world, the next step would be to supply whatever was needed to fill the gap. However, infrastructure choices, as we have already noted, are not distinct from the means by which they are delivered. In today's business environment, for example, many firms have chosen to outsource their logistics to a specialist. The advantages go beyond the mere provision of a specialist service. Such arrangements give the customer access to advanced expertise, advanced technology, scalability, risk management and the like. Or again, in selecting an IT supplier, says Exodus, as your web server host, you are positioning yourself not merely to take advantage of the particular services for which you contract but also for the potentiality implicit in the supplier's specific capabilities. In the case of Exodus this would mean that in addition to operational services including security and robustness, you would be positioning your company to take advantage of the supplier's ability to scale up should demand increase rapidly. While this enlarges the range of available possibilities, it also thereby creates more complex choices. In effect, the task of delivering the infrastructure required for e-business becomes a matter of assembling, organising and deploying the right mix of human and technology resources.

The next chapter addresses the sourcing issue in detail. For the present purpose, two points are important to make. First, there is a consensus that companies cannot tool up fast enough to compete in Internet time without using some external suppliers. Second, many companies who have already substantially

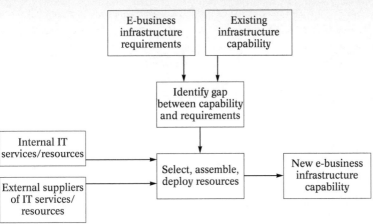

Figure 3 – E-Business Infrastructure Gap Analysis

outsourced their IT are finding that their existing suppliers are not well positioned to provide the new capabilities required by e-business. It therefore becomes necessary to identify and build relationships with new suppliers. This can be time-consuming as demand is so strong and supply so short that some well-regarded suppliers are simply not returning calls from potential clients. Third, the multiplication of suppliers can create new and additional complexity. One utility company outsources its IT operations and maintenance to a major supplier but obtains its e-business systems development from a smaller, more nimble company. It finds that the larger company requires a longer lead-time to take new systems into operation than it takes the smaller company to build them. Time to market is thus constrained not by IT build speed but prior supplier constraints. The sum of these points is that in practice selecting, assembling and deploying the resources for a new e-business infrastructure capability is a more challenging task than Figure 3 might suggest in principle.

Conclusion: Management Challenges for Today and Tomorrow

In this chapter we have recognised that e-business poses new challenges for managers. In this concluding section we argue that in the future it will be more important to design and manage infrastructure than it will be traditional organisational structures. For the time being, we are in a transitional phase in which managers are seeking to establish the necessary e-business infra-structures within a relatively unchanged management framework. Rather than seeing a given structure as the means by which a strategy can be enacted, senior executives will be exploring what a given infrastructure will enable them to manage. The infra-structure perspective and infrastructure capability will become much closer to centre-stage.

Of the many management challenges that face companies in leveraging their infrastructure, the organisational design issue is set to become central. Traditionally, organisational structure has been a management device for facilitating specialisation by fo-cusing attention and resources. Its flip-side has been the problem it creates for managing integration across structural boundaries. Information technology changes this trade-off by facilitating communication and co-ordination regardless of organisational structure and permits greater integration without loss of specialisation.

However, organisations can only overcome the problem of structural boundaries with information technology if they meet two conditions. First, it must have the appropriate IT infra-structure, that is, quite literally, IT must be configured to go beyond structural boundaries. Second, management must be effective over the scope of the infrastructure. Cross-functional infrastructure subject to functional fiefdoms is unlikely to lead to substantial and effective integration across boundaries. To build firm-wide infrastructure with IT as its backbone needs corporate-level authority and leadership. To obtain the business benefits the infrastructure enables requires major change to existing structures. To see this, consider an organisation that builds a relatively low-level IT infrastructure. Its platform involves a common desktop

and e-mail. Across the organisation people are able to communicate and share files freely. There is potential for integration. But there is no motivation for them to go beyond superficial sharing. Each unit within the structure will continue to develop its own IT and its own business processes in whatever way is most appropriate to its strategy. Alternatively, consider an organisation that adopts a relatively high-level IT infrastructure such as an ERP system to be used throughout the corporation. It directly enables tighter integration of business processes. But while the existing intra-organisational boundaries are retained, there is little incentive for units to realise the benefits of integration. So whether they build weak or strong infrastructure, it proves inadequate simply to establish a corporate level IT unit with infrastructure responsibility. Either way, the existing structure constrains the extent to which the infrastructure is leveraged.

As yet, chief executives and boards have not started to design their management structures in terms of the infrastructures they want. Instead, many are creating hybrid arrangements. Some have created distinct e-businesses, some retain them within their existing structure and appoint a general manager for e-business, for e-procurement or for supply chain management. Whatever the precise job title, the objective is similar – to span intra-organisational boundaries. There are several reasons for pursuing the hybrid approach. These include risk management, conservatism, and valuing of established knowledge and capabilities. Of these, the last is particularly important. Darryl Mattocks, Group Chairman of Travelstore.com, while himself very much the new breed entrepreneur, remarks that his ideal senior executive team has grey hair and deep industry experience. Too rapid a transition to a radically new structure risks loss of established knowledge and capabilities before mastery of the e-business alternative has been achieved. In effect, the hybrid role is intended to secure an incremental transition.

The above analysis puts infrastructure firmly on the management map. It suggests that for companies to compete differently through e-business their strategy needs to be complemented by an appropriate infrastructure. Instead of asking what structure permits the strategy to be effectively managed, senior executives should ask what is a manageable unit of infrastructure and organise around that. Thus as the distribution infrastructure for physical goods and information goods may be so different that a company that sells both may decide this is a sensible division according to which to manage. While some have established

e-business units on the principle that the demands of e-business are quite different, few have yet truly analysed the infrastructure demands of their strategy and organised accordingly. But this is what will be required for mature e-business. This is not just a challenge to management practice, it is a radical challenge to a deeply entrenched orthodoxy of organisation design. But it is tomorrow's challenge.

Today's challenge is that of managing infrastructure in transition. Most e-business is currently somewhere in the second stage of the model presented in the Introduction. It is an add-on to the existing business rather than a truly integrated alternative model. Thus infrastructure either has to be managed within the confines of existing organisational boundaries by the existing management structures or managed across those boundaries by special linking roles, groups and processes. As with all such necessarily fudged arrangements, the outcome is an infrastructural camel. As increasingly boundaries are broken down, so deficiencies in infrastructure will be revealed and new investments made. This may be sub-optimal but it is not an unreasonable price to pay for avoiding the risk associated with a massive-scale infrastructure project and associated organisational and management change.

NOTES

1 Lief, V., 'Net Marketplaces Grow Up', Forrester Research Report, December 1999.

2 Gregory, T., 'Stay One Step Ahead of Business in the Year of Technology i nfrastructure', *Computer Weekly*, 27 January 2000, p.32.

3 Ross, J., Beath, C., Sambamurthy, V. and Jepson, M., 'Strategic Levers to Enable E-Business Transformation', CISR Working Paper 310, MIT, Boston, May 2000.

4 Sauer, C. and Burton, S., 'Is There a Place for Department Stores on the Internet: Lessons from an Abandoned Pilot', *Journal of Information Technology*, 14, 4, 1999, pp.387–98.

5 'Shopping Around the Web, A Survey of E-Commerce', *The Economist*, 26 February 2000.

6 Leah, S., 'Will e*Trade move beyond e*Tragedy?', *Business Week*, New York, 22 February 1999.

7 Weill, P. and Broadbent, M., *Leveraging the New Infrastructure*, Harvard Business School Press, Boston, 1998.

8 See also Chapter 5, where Reynolds gives details of predicted growth in distribution centre investment.

9 Davenport, T., *Mission Critical: Realizing the Promise of Enterprise Systems*, Harvard Business School Press, Boston, 2000.

10 See Ross. J., 'Dow Corning Corporation: Business Processes and Information Technology', *Journal of Information Technology*, 14, 3, 1999, pp.253–66.

Sourcing Internet Development

Robert Plant and Leslie P. Willcocks

To be successful, strategy must be implemented effectively. This is as true for e-business as any other form of strategy. What is different about e-business is speed of competition and the scarcity of expertise. Both have led companies to consider sourcing externally. In the specific area of IT the motive has been to implement e-business projects swiftly, using externally available expertise rather than bear the costs of delay while developing new expertise internally. More generally, though, companies have recognised that strategic outsourcing of non-core activities such as logistics can be appropriately contracted to a specialist provider. In the world of e-business, where supply chain integration is becoming more common, such sourcing decisions are becoming a core activity of strategic management.

In this chapter we offer the reader clear guidance on when to adopt different e-business sourcing approaches. Our advice is based upon the research we conducted for the study described in Chapter 1. We start where most companies start – with the e-business project. We start by examining internal and external development approaches and how organisations need to staff e-business projects. We then move on to examine how companies undertake strategic sourcing with business allies to compete more effectively on what has been called a 'co-opetition' or 'core

capabilities' basis. We summarise our findings in two decision-making matrices for strategic e-sourcing.

Towards Internet Implementation Capability

To make a mark in e-business it is essential to have access to Internet implementation capability (see Chapter 9). This normally means using some external sources of specific capabilities. Usually any specific sourcing choice involves trade-offs. The result is a variety of different sourcing mixes. In what follows we identify those practices and trade-offs that have proved most effective in business terms.

Figure 1 shows where sourcing fits into the larger picture. The desired outcome of e-business is added value, whether it be to paying customers or internal customers in other units. To achieve this there must be corporate ownership and leadership of e-business initiatives, a strong infrastructure (Chapter 9) and integration of e-business activity with other core business processes. To deliver the e-business activity systems, development is required and this may come internally, externally or from a combination of both sources.

Our research confirms much of what has been said in earlier chapters about the importance of leadership (Chapter 7), process integration (Chapter 4) and infrastructure (Chapter 9). The fourth component of the successful Internet implementation capability is sourcing of capabilities and skills.

The sourcing routes organisations took consisted of one or a mix of four possible options:

- internal development – corporations created their Internet systems within the boundary of their organisation;
- external development – corporations largely outsourced to third-party management their systems and web site development;
- selective sourcing – corporations combined partial out-sourcing with some in-house development;
- insourcing (or partnering) – corporations selectively sourced, contracting external skills to work under in-house management, alongside in-house resources.

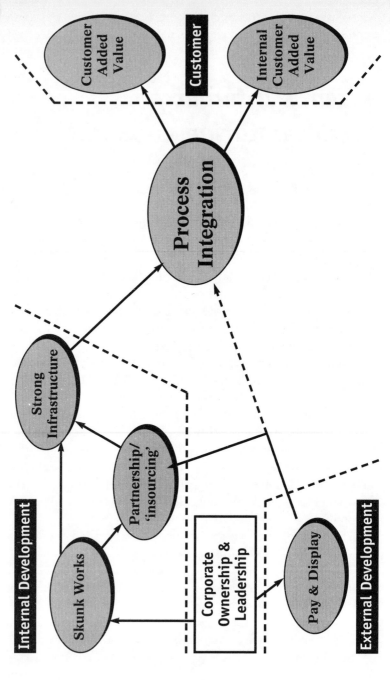

Figure 1 – Sourcing Internet Development: Overview © Copyright Leslie Willcocks 2000 (Source: Robert Plant-working paper)

As we shall see, this last approach has proved particularly effective among several of the leaders who required fast implementation together with high internal learning and skills building.

Sourcing E-Development: Four Routes

The central dilemma for most organisations considering their sourcing options for e-business development is the trade-off between speed to market and organisational learning. The fastest route to securing Internet presence and capability – outsourcing – may well undermine the organisational need to build up internal understanding. The concern to develop internal knowledge is driven by anxiety that Internet-based business processes will be fundamental in the future. In this section we describe how some leading organisations dealt with this dilemma.

Figure 2 provides a framework for selecting appropriate sourcing options based on the twin drivers of speed and learning. In addition to these four options, companies may choose to mix their sourcing, either selectively sourcing or changing their sourcing options over time (see Alamo example below).

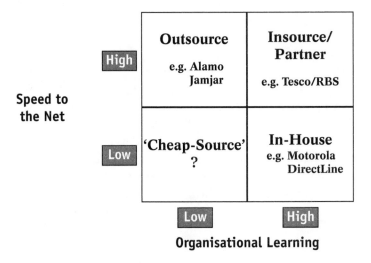

Figure 2 – Internet Development Sourcing Options

THE IN-HOUSE DEVELOPMENT PATH

In our research, companies going successfully down this route included UPS, Motorola, Direct Line, Citicorp, MeritaNordbanken and Dow Jones. The primary determinant of internal development was a credible project champion, usually an executive officer or CIO, who oversaw the 'Internet development group'. Success via this route was assisted by high-level project sponsors who created space, facilitated the necessary budget and resources to get off the ground, and protected the project at all times. Typically a project champion provided and sustained the vision and the motivation to the project, and the political influence needed to move it forward. Such projects were often dubbed 'skunk works' by their developers.

A clear example of the skunk works internal development route can be found at stockbroker Charles Schwab. Upon seeing a browser-based demonstration of the company's traditional trading system, the co-CEOs created, protected and nurtured a new stand-alone Internet development group in order to acquire, learn and adapt the technology to their needs. Ultimately re-creating the company based upon Internet technologies, Charles Schwab was by 2000 the largest on-line brokerage company in the world (see also Introduction).[1]

Early movers used the skunk works teams to focus initially on organisational learning, gathering experience with the new medium, assessing the costs of development, the nature of the technology and its platform. This tied in with the organisation's ability to determine which technologies were worth pursuing early on and which were not. Many of the skunk works projects were funded from R&D budgets, initially at low cost. A power utility executive also took this approach in 1995: 'We knew that we had to have a vanity page, the static stuff was out there but we knew that we needed to understand from an IT perspective "how do you make it more active?".'

The second step on the internal development route was to build a strong infrastructure. Seen as the key to technological and organisational flexibility by many CIOs and executives, the IT infrastructure was critical to the successful transition of the Internet presence from the static to the dynamic. The correct infrastructure can be defined as one facilitating the implementation of value-added services through different organisational business drivers, so delivering a positive return on investment.

The executives and CIOs involved in our study indicate that

in order to be successful, the infrastructure has to be designed to accommodate the major issues facing each company in its marketplace, in essence creating a market space dimension of the organisation. The creation of a strong yet flexible infrastructure was a precursor to the third element of the development, that of process integration. This was the point at which companies had to leverage the organisational learning and experience acquired through the internal development route into customer added value (see Figure 1).

Motorola provides an interesting case of effective internal development. They moved from skunk works experimental activities through process integration to highly market-focused value-adding e-business. They then institutionalised their organisational learning through the creation of a specialist group. Their journey started in 1994 when a senior manager with a marketing background was searching for a communications vehicle to underpin the Motorola On-line Channel Access concept to bring on board its supply chain partners. Emerging web-based technologies provided opportunities that eventually resulted in an e-business development plan, as it became recognised across Motorola that the technologies had large-scale implications. By late 1994 twenty-four activities related to web-based technologies had been grouped into four chronological phases; creating awareness through a technology presence; then co-ordinating the brand and how the company was represented on the web; providing a service to customers and channel partners, while achieving cost and labour reductions; finally moving to revenue generation and one-to-one marketing.

An initial web presence was established in 1995, followed by nine months spent integrating back-end systems. Through 1996–9 the number of e-business initiatives and groups grew across ten business units. By 1999 an Architecture and Process group had been established consisting of a director and eight technical developers responsible for back-end systems and web presentation. Their role was to deal with the business units, keep web content fresh and meet corporate guidelines. This centralised pool formed an organisational resource pool and also oversaw co-ordination and planning for all e-business development initiatives.

THE CHEAP-SOURCING PATH

An organisation that is not pressured in its 'market space' to be at the leading edge of Internet presence would be advised to

apply a 'cheap-sourcing' principle to its Internet development. This is often the case with organisations that occupy niche market positions, for example, Tiffany & Company, the jewellers – their site does not require a direct sales model, and does not need to change with the frequency of a retail site. It can be managed at relatively low cost. The primary driver for such organisations is the promotion of the organisation's brand; a direct sales channel would dilute the overall corporate marketing position rather than reinforce it. However, due to the need for a sophisticated branding image to be maintained, the company may wish to outsource the site's graphic design work, marketing and site development to specialists. It may not be in the long-term plan of the organisation ever to have a direct sales channel and therefore the need to internalise that learning is minimised.

THE OUTSOURCING PATH

Many organisations find themselves in the position of needing to develop a Net presence rapidly, yet do not see any immediate economic advantage in extending their internal IT capability. In this situation the most advantageous policy is to outsource the development. Here Internet use is developed by bringing in external consultants and service providers to inject the expertise otherwise gained through skunk works projects. Such external providers offer services in a variety of forms including Internet agencies, technical and application service providers, direct marketing agencies and relationship marketers. However, ownership responsibility for the development should still belong with the contracting organisation, and issues such as infrastructure and leadership still necessitate internal attention and action. Actual web development learning will be passed to the outsourcer, however, though internal learning on contract management and allied skills will still take place. Some internal technology learning will also occur where the Net technologies and the existing infrastructure interface.

An organisation in this situation was Lego. In March 1999 it was trying to establish its World Shop for its new children's game products. Competitively, speed was of the essence. As a result Lego outsourced its site and e-business development to IBM, though it hired a separate independent consultancy to do web site design work. Compare also Jamjar, an on-line motoring information and car sale service, set up in May 2000 by UK-based insurer Direct Line. According to its IT Director: 'It's a major development, and we went for external hosting, because it's a

huge system, with huge volumes, running twenty-four hours a day, seven days a week.' The Jamjar application was developed by Quidnunc and hosted by SiteHost, a Computacenter e-business outsourcing service. In turn, SiteHost uses the data centre facilities of web host Exodus, where it has its own service operations centre.

THE PARTNERING AND INSOURCING PATH

Should the rate of change in an industry be rapid and the resources of the organisation become stretched too far, then competitive edge can be lost. This is counter-productive from an organisational learning perspective and requires 'partnering' to become the primary development practice. Thus in several corporations infrastructure building, balancing and development were performed by an internal group. Graphical Internet site design or other specialised tasks were externally sourced and business process consultants were engaged to integrate the new channels created through the Internet with existing processes in the most effective way possible. A successful example of this approach is provided by American Express: 'It goes to our basic philosophy, which is we do not have to build everything. The question is, how do we get our products and services integrated into Internet interactive commerce? And you do it through people who are already working on it' (Amex senior executive).

MIXED DEVELOPMENT PATHS

We found organisations adopting different sourcing options at different times, or for different purposes, in their moves to the Internet. As we saw above, insurer Direct Line took the out-sourcing route for its Jamjar on-line business. Direct Line was set up in the late 1980s to sell motor insurance direct via the phone. The business expanded into other types of insurance during the 1990s. In the late 1990s it also set up Directline.com to sell insurance services via the Net. However, this was developed in-house for less than £50,000. According to its IT director: 'Directline.com is very much at the heart of our insurance business. It's totally and tightly integrated with our core systems. We couldn't have done it so quickly had it been outsourced.' Interestingly here, not only was the application seen as core business, but also, because internal expertise and business-specific knowledge were higher than that available on the market, the necessary speed could actually be achieved by in-house sourcing.

Another mixed approach was adopted by Tesco, the UK's leading food retailer. In 1998 Tesco piloted its on-line shopping business, Tesco Direct (subsequently Tesco.com), with 20,000 grocery products and six trial sites. By March 2000 Tesco.com was part of multi-channel strategy, with some hundred stores involved and looking to gain more than half its on-line revenues from non-grocery items. In 1999 it made losses of £11.2 million on sales of £125 million but was looking to treble its half-million customers in one year and to break even in 2002. It had spent £21 million on developing its Internet offering in-house and by mid-2000 was looking to invest another £35 million. However, in early 2000 Tesco also entered a less familiar, but faster-moving market – on-line banking – in which it planned to leverage the power of its brand. The Tesco Personal Finance service was developed in three months through utilising technology developed by its partner, the Royal Bank of Scotland (RBS), only needing to modify the software to allow customers to transfer money to and from their accounts at other banks. Both partners invested in a series of Compaq 3000 servers, running internally developed software, allowing Tesco customers to link in with the RBS IBM9672 mainframe, which holds account details. Here the need for speed and the availability of a complementary partner in an unfamiliar business became the key determinants of the sourcing decision.

An example that brings together much of this discussion is the development route pictured in Figure 3. The path taken between 1995 and 2000 by Alamo, the US-based car hire company can be described in these terms.

Alamo outsourced its early Internet development. It ran into a number of problems. The web site was too stand-alone and not linked back into the technology infrastructure. It suffered a number of technical hitches and required continuous redevelopment. It also experienced some supplier commitment issues:

> The one issue I had was ownership. An internal group, if I call them and say our web site is down, they feel it like I feel it; it is hitting profitability. A contractor does not have the same level of business commitment . . . and if they are not enamoured with this particular arrangement they might not give you quite as good service. Whereas with an internal service you would have clearly defined roles and responsibilities . . . (Alamo marketing executive).

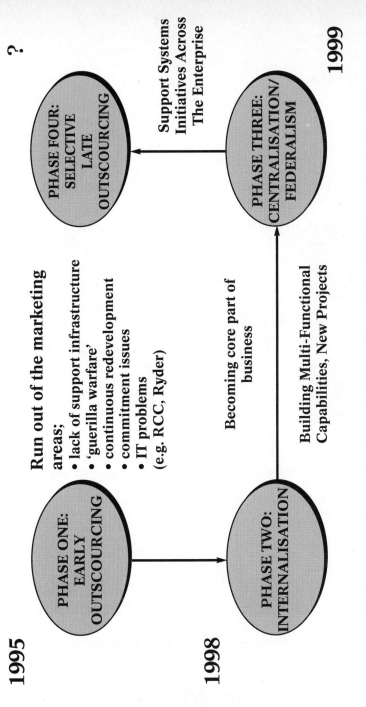

Figure 3 – A Four-Phase Mixed Sourcing Path
(adapted from a Forrester Research framework)

Outsource	Insource/Partner
Advantages • Taps into existing expertise • Variety of external services offered • Quickly get up to speed **Disadvantages** • Does not immediately facilitate internalisation of learning • Builds vendor expertise, not yours • Vendors may not be skilled in organisational processes • Organisation may lack basic infrastructure • Requires in-house skills to manage the supplier • Cost (includes vendor profit margin) • Ensuring technological alignment with strategic alignment • Co-ordination of content owners?	**Advantages** • Taps into existing expertise • Wider variety of external services on offer • Quickly get up to speed • Share/build expertise with vendor • Facilitate internalisation of learning • Organisation can focus upon other e.g. infrastructure, issues **Disadvantages** • Requires in-house skills to staff and manage the project – availability? • Requires business managers' commitment to achieve business and technology alignment • Contract management costs to co-ordinate project
'Cheap-Source' **Advantages** • Low investment • Low internal effort and resources • Gains from a 'follower' Internet strategy **Disadvantages** • Little internal learning, or from market • Functional only in relation to a specific type of business strategy • Does 'followership' pay with Internet applications?	**Internal Development** **Advantages** • Internalise organisational learning • Understanding of organisation's processes and integration issues • Understanding of internal IT infrastructure **Disadvantages** • Opportunity cost of mistakes • First-mover expense • Scarce IT skills resources may inhibit development • Will the business side commit necessary resources?

Figure 4 – E-Development Sourcing Options: Advantages and Disadvantages

By 1998 Alamo began internalising Internet development, realising that web-based technologies were becoming a core part of the business. A series of web projects were launched and in 1999 a central group was developed to provide enterprise-wide service, support and control of business units' Internet initiatives.

This pattern – of early outsourcing to gain the advantages of speed to the Net, followed by internalisation due to the rising business importance of the Internet and the need for internal learning and capability – was frequently repeated in other organisations we studied, for example at Ryder Systems and P&O. The pattern also seemed to reflect those organisations' own increased learning about the advantages and disadvantages of different sourcing options. This learning also sharpened their ability to make more selective and precise sourcing decisions during phases two and three of Figure 3, and also undertake selective late outsourcing of development and web operations in a fourth phase, on criteria we shall look at in the next section. Figure 4 provides a summary of the issues that leading organisations tended to take into account when attempting to achieve trade-offs and mitigate risks in the choice and management of their sourcing options.

E-Sourcing: From Projects and Technology to Strategic Partnering

So far this chapter has focused on sourcing technical development for e-business projects. But e-business sourcing is not solely about balancing learning and early use of new technology. It is also about making best use of the mix of internal and external suppliers throughout organisation's business processes. This involves understanding who has what core competences. In this section we examine the possibilities for external sourcing throughout the customer resource life cycle, in supply chains and through value networks. The examples of Cisco and Dell are used to illustrate effective sourcing practice. We start by looking at the notions of core competence and co-opetition, and see how they have been applied to business, information technology sourcing and more recently to the e-business world.

During the 1990s a very strong literature developed, focusing on core competence business strategies. Commentators such as Pralahad and Hamel, and Quinn argued that an organisation can only be effective at relatively few core activities and should

concentrate on developing these to world class. Anything else should be eliminated, minimised or outsourced.[2] Here core competence refers to a distinctive, not easily replicable assembly of skills, techniques, ways of organising, technologies and know-how that enable an organisation to acquire, deploy and leverage positioning and resources, including relationships, in pursuit of business advantage.

Debates about a specific firm's core competence are invariably bedevilled by two issues, which both apply to e-business. The first is that it is frequently not easy to distinguish between a core and a non-core competence. For example, what is the scope of a core competence and for how long can it remain a competitively differentiating factor? Federal Express and UPS would recognise some of their core competence as lying in parcel logistics, but how do they differentiate themselves from each other, and what implications does the Internet have for redefining core and non-core in these firms? Second, and related, core competences, built over time as ways of dealing with problems and achieving stakeholder value, can create rigidities and resistances to value shifts in the competitive arena. This can be especially damaging in the fast-moving Internet-based business environment, where survival belongs to the fast and focused.

EXTERNAL SOURCING AROUND THE CUSTOMER RESOURCE LIFE CYCLE

In an earlier chapter David Feeny presented an E-Vision Opportunity Model (see Chapter 2, Figure 7). He stressed the importance of gaining repurchase decisions by managing the customer's total experience in such ways that the customer would regularly prefer the organisation's products/services. If the customer resource life cycle of an on-line business is broken down into eight major activity areas, it is clear that the technical means and businesses exist for each area to be sourced adequately by an external service provider.[3]

1. *Attracting customers* – Services like Link Exchange and Befree can provide fully developed customer affiliate programmes. DoubleClick can offer targeted advertising. These and many other companies basically provide technologies and services that attract and deliver targeted audiences to your e-business.
2. *Informing customers* – Organisations like OnDisplay.com and Cardonet.com act as content mediators, serving up-to-date, relevant content to a web site. Consider one of our

researched organisations, W. W. Grainger, in the maintenance, repair and operations business. It offers hard goods supplies to US businesses. Traditionally this has been done by printing 2.6 million catalogues and operating over 500 physical stores. In 1998 it partnered with OnDisplay, which then proceeded to utilise the information from 2000-plus supplier databases to develop on-line interactive catalogues for Grainger's three web sites. Grainger's on-line sales exceeded $150 million in 2000.

3. *Customising (self) service* – Companies like Firepond.com, Selectica.com and Calico.com build configuration software that is such a strong feature of the Dell site offering build-to-order computers, and the Cisco Systems and Cabletron Systems sites selling routers and networking gear. Calico provides Cabletron with a configuration workbench that prompts a customer as a salesperson would. It shows product features, analyses the customer's needs, budget and time constraints, identifies compatible components, suggests options and generates price quotes. It also generates an order that is automatically passed to Cabletron's fulfilment systems that in turn update stock, shipping and accounting databases.

4. *Transacting* – There are many companies, notably Ariba, Commerce One, Oracle, Moai Technologies, that offer market-making platforms. Ariba offers shared commerce services in B-to-B marketplaces. Its key customers include (as at 2000) Federal Express, Cisco Systems, Charles Schwab and Chevron. CommerceOne offers web-based B-to-B procurement and platforms for creating vertical trading communities. Customers include British Telecom and Booz Allen and Hamilton. Moai Technologies provide B-to-B exchanges and auction platforms. One of its customers is GoCargo.com which provides real-time pricing in its on-line auction business. GoCargo.com provides a market for the buying and selling of maritime container space.

5. *Securing payment* – As we saw in the Introduction to this book, many organisations and customers have concerns over the security of payments over the web. These concerns have encouraged the development of companies to look after the payment and financing functions of on-line transactions. Thus eCredit.com provides real-time credit underwriting engines, while Paylinx offers systems that support credit and debit card transactions.

6. *Customer support* – Many organisations new to e-business may well feel unable to provide the necessary level of information, problem resolution, advice and order tracking for their customers. As a result external service providers have developed offerings for, for example, call centre facilities, live on-line services and the checking of order status.

7. *E-fulfilment* – This represents a major potential area for new and fast-growing e-businesses to outsource. By 2000, in B-to-B, many businesses were outsourcing supply chain management systems that facilitate order fulfilment, and supply and demand forecasting. Examples of companies providing such services include Celarix, Manugistics and i2. In addition many e-fulfilment companies had developed for the business-to-consumer market. As one example, Entertainment UK in the Kingfisher Group developed for its own use an internal warehousing and e-fulfilment capability for items such as CDs and videos. In 2000 they also set up as an e-fulfilment business for the end customers of other supplier companies such as radio channels making special offers to listeners.

8. *Adaptive customer profiling* – We met the notion of competing by understanding the customer best in the context of Lufthansa's web site and InfoFlyway service discussed in Chapter 1. Rather than developing the necessary software and internal capability, companies can now hire collaborative filtering and data mining services from providers such as Verbind.com, Datasage.com, and E-piphany.com. Verbind, for example, provides American Express, Reel.com and Furniture.com with its LifeTime product. This analyses up to one year's on-line transaction data, establishes each customer's buying pattern, and enables e-mail and interactive messaging to customers and one-to-one marketing.

At one level these would appear to be exciting and highly functional developments. However, outsourcing extensively throughout the customer resource life cycle does raise a number of issues. Handing over control of activities creates exposure to risk. What level of exposure is judicious and how can the risks be mitigated? Does increased dependence on suppliers mean that deeper relationships are required? In answering these questions one conclusion is clear – extensive fee-for-service outsourcing and the treatment of every activity as a commodity to be outsourced are never appropriate.

A particularly profound problem occurs with a firm's ownership of the relationship with its end customers. If this relationship is compromised through outsourcing, then so is a potential source of competitive advantage (see Chapter 2). Consider one company (A) we studied. In 2000 it employed an e-fulfilment firm (B) to deliver goods but insisted that these be delivered to A's warehouse and not to the end customer. At no time did B know who the end customer was; it was only given enough information to deliver goods in the right quantity and at the right time to A. These goods were then relabelled by A and delivered to the end customer. In this scenario, conditioned by previous experiences, A's behaviour was designed to protect its customer database and customer relationships.

DEVELOPMENTS IN THE SUPPLY CHAIN

Graham Costello, in Chapter 6, looked in detail at B-to-B commerce. Let us look specifically, however, at the sourcing issues that arise from extensive use of third parties in the e-supply chain. As was made clear in the Introduction to this book, by 2000 most firms were investing over ten times more in this area than in their B-to-C initiatives. By that date 'bricks and mortar' companies moving to the web still had plenty of scope for radical improvements, further enabled by newer applications and external suppliers entering the arena. Many among our study organisations were to be found still developing supply chain management, enterprise resource planning and customer relationship management systems, often with external assistance. All had built electronic links with their suppliers and with their retail outlets, and were at different points down the road of making these web-enabled. Rather fewer were doing this in a more sophisticated fashion, for example, using auctions and exchanges in order to deal directly and more efficiently with suppliers and also with customers.

As indicated above, some had also moved to handing over much of the e-fulfilment to external parties, while companies like Sun and Cisco Systems had handed over most of their manufacturing and delivery to other parties. In all this, few had developed the suite of highly integrated synchronised production scheduling, collaborative product design and development, logistics and demand planning systems that enabled value networks to develop such as those at Dell and Cisco Systems (see

below). Given this variety, let us focus attention and look at the implications of external sourcing/partnering for just one e-application that gained popularity during 2000 – that of web-enabled exchanges in the supply chain.

In November 1999, Ford and General Motors announced separate Internet-based trading exchanges for their supply chains. Ford would partner with Oracle on Auto-Xchange, and General Motors with Commerce One on TradeXchange. By February 2000 a superior model had emerged. A single exchange would establish a global standard and also be much more efficient. Ford, General Motors and Daimler-Chrysler agreed to collaborate on a single automotive-parts exchange run through the Internet. The technology partners would be Commerce One and Oracle. The exchange was expected to deal with over US$300 billion in transactions annually and achieve significant cost reductions for the car companies. Ford claimed, for example, a $10 million saving on a $75 million purchase on its first full use of AutoXchange. Other car makers, like Toyota, Renault and Honda, also considered joining the exchange. At the same time Ford was updating its customer-orientated web sites for new and second-hand cars, announcing a joint venture with software developer Trilogy. These developments are shown in Figure 5.

Subsequently a number of such exchanges were announced across industries. These included an Intercontinental exchange for trading of wholesale energy and metals; Sears and Carrefour announcing they would serve the retail sector with Global-NetXchange; Ariba and Cargill working on Novopoint, an industry exchange for food manufacturers and suppliers; and fourteen energy and petrochemical companies joining with Commerce One to manage the purchasing of $100 billion of goods and save an estimated five to thirty per cent in costs. However, although these developments sound attractive, they hide a number of complexities.

Focusing on just the Ford/GM/DC example, the substantial cost savings for the car manufacturers also imply downward pressure on supplier prices and some switch of bargaining power from suppliers to the manufacturers. The auto exchange will also charge up to 0.5 per cent commission on transactions. This amount will go to the manufacturers and technology developers running the exchange. So how neutral will this joint venture be? Will other car manufacturers using the exchange feel excluded from influence and access to certain benefits? Clearly, the

exchange represents considerable migration of value and power in the supply chain. Not surprisingly, therefore, by April 2000 Volkswagen had announced its own marketplace for procurement, forming a strategic partnership with IBM, i2 Technologies and Ariba. In the face of such proliferation of markets, six of the largest automotive-parts suppliers announced that they would work together on joint technology solutions because of the problem of 'repetitive costs'.

The trading exchange also raised competitive edge concerns among some potential participants. In March 2000, Toyota suggested that it would restrict its participation to trading only in basic commodity items and office supplies. The company had several concerns about the exchange, centring on quality assurance and security on an open network. For Taadaki Jagawa, vice-president of procurement: 'The other companies are our rivals and we are competing on parts. We do not share information about our components,' including information about the price of core parts. Moreover: 'Our parts are not purchased through a bidding process. We buy them by building a relationship with suppliers over time.' Essentially Toyota saw its suppliers more as partners and believed the close relationships with them gave a competitive edge in quality assurance but also in lead-time on new car development. The spot pricing encouraged by a more transparent market could erode such relationships.

Further developments in e-business on the customer side could also threaten the role of dealers in the distribution chain – a notoriously sensitive area, analogous with web-enabled disintermediation in the travel agency and insurance broking industries. Meanwhile, in the supply chain there may well be a number of more technical problems. One is non-repudiation – where an on-line company must be able to guarantee to a supplier that it can legally prove a purchaser's identity and activities in a court of law. A second is establishing standards for information exchange. XML on its own is as broad as data itself. Moreover, technology suppliers are still much more enthusiastic about it than the majority of users, who typically will have different starting points on data protocols. All the issues considered in this section make clear that external sourcing and partnering in remodelled supply and distribution chains can be a lot more complicated than it first seems.

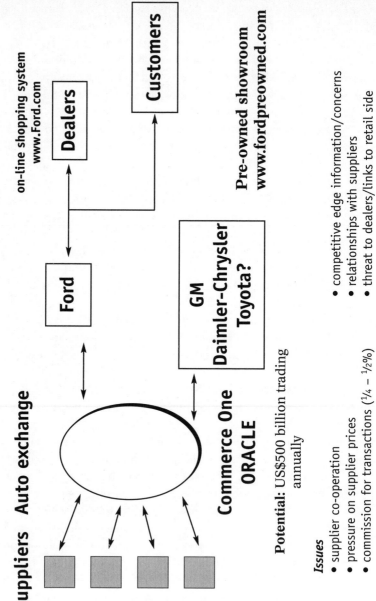

Figure 5 – Ford: Remodelling Supply and Delivery
© *Copyright Leslie Willcocks 2000*

TOWARDS VIRTUAL INTEGRATION

As organisations move to e-business we see, too, new forms of organising, such as the 'M' form and syndication,[4] but also a resurgence of more familiar ideas. Thus concepts such as 'co-opetition' and the virtual organisation have considerable salience in the e-business world, and imply considerable use of external allies and service providers.[5] Co-opetition is about collaborating to compete, by allying with firms with complementary capabilities to mutual competitive advantage. In a schema that translates immediately into the e-world, Nalebuff and Brandenburger posit a value network consisting of the company, its customers, suppliers, competitors and complementors. A player is your complementor if customers value your product/service more when they also have the other player's offering than when they have your product/service alone. Organisations have multiple roles in a value network. For example, on any given day AT&T might find Motorola to be a supplier, customer, competitor or complementor.

A related concept is that of the virtual organisation. As Child and Faulkner point out, few companies are excellent at all functions. Therefore greater value can be created if each concentrates on only the functions it does best and relies on co-operating partners to carry out the other functions. In the value network this requires co-operative attitudes, clear understanding of central objectives, electronic (increasingly web-enabled) co-ordination and communication, and flexible modules, cultures and workforces.

In our research Cisco Systems and Dell provided clear examples of virtual integration. Consider Cisco. Its strategy has been threefold: do what it's best at, make acquisitions (over fifty-five since 1993) and secure alliances. By mid-2000 it had outsourced most of its production to thirty-seven factories. Suppliers made most components, and carried out fifty-five per cent of sub-assembly work and fifty-five per cent of final assembly. All factories were linked via the Net and an intranet was used for most internal work at Cisco. The internal pages received 28 million hits a month. Use of the web was saving Cisco an estimated US$500–800 million a year. Eighty-four per cent of sales were through the web site, which allowed customised configuring and checking by customers. Eighty-five per cent of customer queries were handled on-line.

All this has enabled a high degree of virtuality. According to one respondent: 'We can go from quote to cash without ever

touching a physical asset or piece of paper. You've heard of JIT manufacturing, well this is not-at-all manufacturing.' However, Cisco has been careful to control and dominate the value network. Thus it has maintained three factories itself to understand and give flexibility to its manufacturing base. Cisco designs production methods and uses the Internet to monitor operations closely. It also controls research and development. So for new production methods, for example: 'The source code is developed here and maintained here. So the innovation is all at Cisco.'

Dell has explicitly described its strategy as that of virtual integration. In 2000 it made more than US$40 million a day (over fifty per cent of total sales) via the Internet. Its success is invariably put down to its customer focus. However, an underlying vital component has been sourcing strategy and management. According to CEO Michael Dell: 'I don't think we could have created a $12 billion business in thirteen years if we had tried to be vertically integrated.' With fewer physical assets and people it has fewer things to manage and fewer barriers to change. Through IT-enabled co-ordination and control of its value network of suppliers and partners, Dell can operate with a 20,000 rather than an 80,000 workforce. In the supply arena it has focused on making long-term deals and commitments with as few leading suppliers as possible. Datalinks measure and feed back supplier performance in real time. Close ties with suppliers ('their engineers are part of our design and implementation teams') mean that Dell buys in innovation from its suppliers. Information technologies allow speed and information sharing, and much more intense forms of collaboration. It also means that suppliers can be notified precisely of Dell's daily product requirements. This has allowed Dell to focus on inventory velocity and keeping inventory levels very low.

Dell has also sought strong partnering relationships with key customers. Seen as complementors, customers are often involved in research and development, where Dell's focus is on relevant, easy-to-use technology, improvements in the customer buying process, keeping costs down and superior quality in manufacturing. Dell also offers service centres in large organisations to be close to the customer. Thus Boeing has 100,000 Dell PCs and thirty dedicated Dell staff on the premises.

For present purposes, what is interesting are the criteria these companies are using to make sourcing decisions. Clearly Cisco has adopted practices that leverage complementors and suppliers, while enabling Cisco to dominate the value network it has created. At Dell the criteria would seem to be fivefold:

1. Dell focuses its attention on all activities that create value for the customer. This includes R&D involving 1500 people and a budget of $250 million, that focuses on customer-facing activity and the identification of 'relevant' technology. It tends to outsource as much as possible all other activities that need to get done.

2. Dell carefully defines its core capability as a solutions provider and technology navigator. It uses partners/suppliers as much as possible to deal with such matters as products, components, technology development, assembly.

3. A key core task is co-ordination as against 'doing' tasks such as manufacturing and delivery.

4. A key core capability is control of the value network through financial and informational means to ensure requisite speed, cost and quality. What does Dell control? Basically the company appoints and monitors reliable, responsive, leading-edge suppliers of technology and quality.

5. Dell takes responsibility for seeking and improving all arrangements that give it speed and focus in the marketplace, and in its organisational arrangements.

In Conclusion: Towards Efficient E-Sourcing Decisions

In this final section, to assist e-sourcing decisions, we bring together the thinking and learning of the chapter into two summary matrices. Our research has made clear that, whether at the IT, project or strategic-alliance level, fortunately, we can apply to e-business sourcing many of the principles learned in other contexts in the 1980s and 1990s. Cisco and Dell are not so far removed from what has been called the original virtual organisation, clothing manufacturer/retailer Benetton. Moreover, many of the practices observed in IT sourcing over the last decade can apply directly to the e-world.[6] Let us bring all these principles together.

E-business sourcing must start with the business imperative. In Figure 6 we identify two dimensions of business activities. The first is in terms of its contribution to competitive positioning. In IT, mainframes and payroll applications are frequently perceived as commodities, while British Airways' yield management system gives the company a competitive edge in ticket pricing and is regarded as a differentiator. The second is in terms of the underpinning it provides to business operations. As a broad example one web site might be critical, as is the case for Amazon (no web site, no business), or it could be merely useful, as with the Tiffany example cited earlier. These two dimensions create four quadrants.

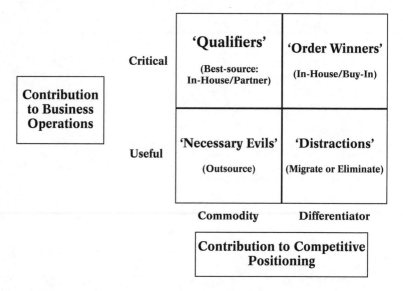

Figure 6 – Strategic E-Sourcing (A) by Business Activity

Let us use the Dell example to illustrate the thinking here. 'Order Winners' are those business activities that critically and advantageously dfferentiate a firm from its competitors. The five Dell items listed in the previous section fall here. The strong message is to carry out these core activities in-house, buying in resources to work under internal control where expertise is lacking and a build-up of internal learning is required. 'Qualifiers' are business activities that must be carried out as a necessary minimum entry requirement to compete in a specific sector. For airlines, aircraft maintenance systems are vital but do

not differentiate the airlines from each other. Often critical differentiators can become commodities and move to this quadrant. Thus, were Dell's excellent customer service ever to become an industry standard, it would be redefined as a 'Qualifier'. As at 2000, assembly, manufacturing and delivery are being defined by Dell as 'Qualifiers'. These should be best sourced and can be done by third parties, where they meet the right cost and competence criteria (see below).

'Necessary Evils' are tasks that have to be done but are not core activity and gain no strategic purchase from their fulfilment. Dell has tended to cut down on administration, inventory and payroll tasks, for example, and would seek to outsource as much of these sorts of activities as possible. 'Distractions' are failed or failing attempts to differentiate the organisation from its competitors. The goal here must be to eliminate the activity or migrate it to another quadrant. Thus in 1989 Dell opened retail outlets, but soon discovered this development was not going to be successful and fell back on its direct business model. A more profound mistake is not to notice until too late the value shifts in a specific competitive arena, for example, IBM against Microsoft and Intel in the late 1980s–early 1990s PC market. When Levi Strauss moved to the web in the late 1990s it did so in a way that was precisely a 'Distraction' (see Chapter 1). Up to 2000, Dell had made few mistakes in this area. In fact, its low-cost web-based distribution strategy had given it a critical competitive edge. Perhaps this resulted from its CEO's explicit recognition that 'looking for value shifts is probably the most important dimension of leadership'.

It is not enough, however, to identify a potential use of service providers or business allies. What is available on the market also requires detailed analysis. If the market is not cheap, capable or mature enough, then the organisation will need to seek a largely in-house solution. A second matrix is needed to capture fully the major elements for consideration.

In Figure 7 we plot the cost-efficiencies and the capabilities the market can offer against carrying out tasks internally. Where the market can carry out a task cheaper and better, outsourcing is the obvious decision but only for 'Qualifiers' and 'Necessary Evils'. An example is Federal Express providing customer delivery for Dell. Where the market offers an inferior cost and capability, in-house sourcing will be the better alternative (assuming that 'Distractions' are best not sourced at all). Where the market offers a better cost deal this should be taken, but only

for non-key activities ('Necessary Evils'). Where the market offers superior capability but at a premium price above what the in-house cost might be there may still be good reasons for insourcing or close partnering with the third party, not least to leverage and learn from their expertise, and apply it to 'Qualifying' and 'Order Winning' tasks.

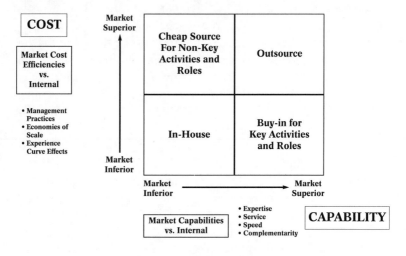

Figure 7 – Strategic E-Sourcing (B) by Market Comparison

Thus Figures 6 and 7 help to summarise the main criteria that can be used for making e-sourcing and, in fact, many other business sourcing decisions. Use of the matrices requires decisions in trade-offs in order to establish the least risky ways external parties can be leveraged to organisational advantage. But as this chapter has sought to illustrate, making the right sourcing decisions does not guarantee their successful implementation. As in the cases of Dell and Cisco, internal capabilities must be developed to manage the risks, relationships and performance issues inherent in the extensive use of external service providers and business allies.

NOTES

1 See Pottruck, D. and Pearce, T., *Clicks and Mortar: Passion-Driven Growth in an Internet-Driven World*, Jossey Bass, San Francisco, 2000.

2 The main popular texts on core capabilities and strategic sourcing are Quinn, J., 'The Intelligent Enterprise: A New Paradigm', *Academy of Management Executive*, 6, 4, 1992, pp.44–63; Pralahad, C. and Hamel, G., 'The Core Competence of

the Corporation', *Harvard Business Review*, 68, 3, 1990, pp.79–91; Hamel, G. and Pralahad, C., *Competing for the Future*, Harvard Business Press, Boston, 1994.

3 For further examples see Davis, J. (ed.), 'How IT Works', *Business 2.0*, February 2000, pp.112-40.

4 Moore, J., 'The New Corporate Form', in Tapscott, D., Lowy, A. and Ticoll, D. (eds), *Blueprint for the Digital Economy*, McGraw Hill, New York, 1998; Werbach, K., 'Syndication: The Emerging Model for Business in the Internet Era', *Harvard Business Review*, May–June 2000, pp.84–96.

5 The concepts are well described in two books. These are: Nalebuff, B. and Brandenburger, A., *Co-opetition*, HarperCollins Business, London, 1996; see also Child, J. and Faulkner, D., *Strategies of Co-operation. Managing Alliances, Networks and Joint Ventures*, Oxford University Press, Oxford, 1998.

6 See, for example, Lacity, M., Willcocks, D. and Feeny, D., 'The Value of Selective IT Sourcing' in Willcocks, L., Feeny, D. and Islei, G. (eds), *Managing IT as a Strategic Resource*, McGraw Hill, Maidenhead, 1997. The IT sourcing options and developments are discussed in more detail in Lacity, M. and Willcocks, L., *Global IT Outsourcing: In Search for Business Advantage*, Wiley, Chichester, 2000.

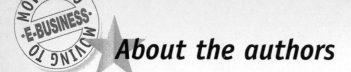

About the authors

Kunal Basu is a Fellow in Strategic Marketing at Templeton College. Previously, he was an Associate Professor of Marketing at McGill University, Canada. He has published extensively on Brand Loyalty, and Marketing Communications, and is currently researching issues in Global Branding.

Graham Costello is Principal of the eBusiness practice of IBM Global Services Australia. He was previously Director of Information Management Strategic Planning for the Australian Army Land Command. He holds degrees from the University of New England and the University of Technology, Sydney, and a doctorate from Oxford University. He also teaches on executive programmes on e-business at the Australian Graduate School of Management. Current research interests include the establishment of electronic communities by interest groups as well as the commercial exploitation of the Internet to establish virtual corporations.

David Feeny is Director of the Oxford Institute of Information Management. His work on key issues in the exploitation of IT – the creation and sustaining of business advantage, the roles of CEOs and CIOs, the management of T as a strategic resource – has become well known around the world and been published in leading journals including Harvard Business Review, Sloan Management Review, McKinsey Quarterly. David is current researching e-business strategies in prominent corporations around the world, working with colleagues at MIT, Australian Graduate School of Management, Melbourne Business School, and the Nanyang Technological University of Singapore.

Karl Moore is a Fellow in Strategy at Templeton College. He is also a visiting professor at Erasmus University and as of September 2000 will be a professor at McGill University. Dr. Moore is widely published with an international reputation in the study of global multinationals with a focus on organising for global advantage. His current research is focusing on how do global firms organise for e-commerce.

Robert Plant is Associate Professor at The School of Business Administration, University of Miami, Coral Gables, Florida, Research Associate in Information Management in the Oxford Institute of Information Management at Templeton College and

Visiting Professor at Universidad Gabriela Mistral, Santiago de Chile. He has published over seventy papers and articles on electronic commerce, mass customization, artificial intelligence and software engineering, in journals such as Communications of ACM, Information & Management, and Journal of Management Information Systems.

Jonathan Reynolds is Director of the Oxford Institute of Retail Management and Fellow in Retail Marketing at Templeton College. He first joined the College to work with UK food retailer Tesco on the application of new information technology, following time spent at the University of Edinburgh, with Coca-Cola, and at the University of Newcastle-upon-Tyne. A geographer, urban planner and retailer by turn, he has published and spoken widely on retailing and technology issues and retail and services marketing. As a faculty member of Oxford University's Saïd Business School, he teaches eCommerce on Oxford's MBA programme. He has recently completed a period of sabbatical leave as Visiting Professor at the Amos Tuck Business School at Dartmouth College.

Specialising in strategic and organisational change, Keith Ruddle graduated in Engineering and Management from Cambridge in 1971. In 1975 he achieved an MBA with distinction from Harvard Business School. He worked with British Aerospace and BP and then spent 19 years with Andersen Consulting, the last 12 as a partner. His work included a number of change programmes for multinational clients including SmithKline Beecham and Ford of Europe. Now teacher and coach on Templeton's executive leadership programmes, he helped design and teach a leadership programme for the UK Shadow Cabinet prior to the last election.

Christopher Sauer is Research Fellow in Information Management at the Oxford Institute of Information Management at Templeton College. Until 1999 he was Senior Research Fellow in the Fujitsu Centre at the Australian Graduate School of Management in Sydney. He is internationally known for his work on IT-enabled transformation and the management of IT project risk, and, with Leslie Willcocks, is currently researching issues in the management of IT infrastructure for e-business. He has taught on executive programmes in the UK, Australia and Finland.

Marc Thompson is currently a Research Fellow at Templeton College, University of Oxford which he joined after having been a Principal Research Fellow at the Institute for Employment

Studies, Sussex University. He has an established track record of research in human resource and employment policy issues going back over 10 years. His current research interests focus on Strategic HRM and in particular the impact of HR strategies on firm performance in the UK Aerospace industry funded by the Department of Trade and Industry. He is also looking at innovation in high technology sectors and the part played by human resource systems. Marc has spoken widely about his work at international conferences and has taught on executive programmes in Europe and Australia.

Leslie Willcocks is Fellow and University Reader in Information Management at Templeton College, University of Oxford, Visiting Professor at Erasmus Universiteit, Rotterdam, Professorial Associate of the University of Melbourne, and Distinguished Visitor at AGSM, Sydney. He is also Co-editor of the Journal of Information Technology. He has an international reputation for his work on outsourcing, information management, evaluation and e-business issues and is the author of 16 previous books and over 130 papers on these subjects. He is, with Chris Sauer, currently researching issues in the management of IT infrastructure for e-business. He is a frequent keynote speaker at academic and practitioner conferences around the world and is regularly retained as adviser by major corporations and government task forces.

Marshall Young's career has spanned operations research consultancy and business development for large and small companies. He has consulted internationally, and worked in both North America and Asia. He has also led a management buyout of a specialist, multi-media publishing company that was subsequently sold to Simon and Schuster in the US. His special interests include knowledge media management and the benefits of interactive electronic media for senior executives.

Index